101 840 660 3

Understanding the Counselling

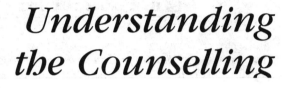

ONE WEEK LOAN

D0767749

PROFESSIONAL SKILLS
FOR COUNSELLORS

The *Professional Skills for Counsellors* series, edited by Colin Feltham, covers the practical, technical and professional skills and knowledge which trainee and practising counsellors need to improve their competence in key areas of therapeutic practice.

Titles in the series include:

Contracts in Counselling
Charlotte Sills (ed.)

Counselling Difficult Clients
Kingsley Norton and Gill McGauley

Learning and Writing in Counselling
Mhairi MacMillan and Dot Clark

Counselling and Psychotherapy in Private Practice
Roger Thistle

Referral and Termination Issues for Counsellors
Anne Leigh

The Management of Counselling and Psychotherapy Agencies
Colin Lago and Duncan Kitchin

Group Counselling
Keith Tudor

Practitioner Research in Counselling
John McLeod

Understanding the Counselling Relationship

edited by Colin Feltham

SAGE Publications
London ● Thousand Oaks ● New Delhi

Introduction, chapter 1 and editorial selection © Colin
Feltham 1999
Chapter 2 © Jeremy Holmes 1999
Chapter 3 © Paul Wilkins 1999
Chapter 4 © Maurice Friedman 1999
Chapter 5 © Keith Tudor 1999
Chapter 6 © Diana Sanders and Frank Wills 1999
Chapter 7 © Stephen Palmer 1999
Chapter 8 © Rowan Bayne 1999
Chapter 9 © Janice Russell 1999
Chapter 10 © Roxane Agnew-Davies 1999

First published 1999
Reprinted 2006

SAGE Publications Ltd.
1 Oliver's Yard, 55 City Road
London EC1Y 1SP

SAGE Publications Inc
2455 Teller Road
Thousand Oaks, California 91320

SAGE Publications India Pvt Ltd.
B-42 Panchsheel Enclave
Post Box 4109
New Delhi 110 017

British Library Cataloguing in Publication data

A catalogue record for this book is available
from the British Library.
ISBN-10 0-7619-5784-7
ISBN-10 0-7619-5785-5 (pbk)
ISBN-13 978-0-7619-5784-3 (hbk)
ISBN-13 978-0-7619-5785-0 (pbk)
Library of Congress catalog card record available

Typeset by Photoprint, Torquay, Devon
Printed and bound by Athenaeum Press Ltd., Gateshead, Tyne & Wear.

For Ann and Sue

Contents

Notes on Contributors

Roxane Agnew-Davies, PhD, is a Clinical Psychologist who worked for 10 years in hospital and community settings for Leicester Health Authority. During that time her PhD thesis, on the conceptual and methodological issues within the field of psychotherapeutic relationships, was awarded by the University of Sheffield. She is currently in private practice, specializing in experiential psychotherapy.

Rowan Bayne, PhD, teaches on the Postgraduate Diploma in Therapeutic Counselling (Integrative) at the University of East London. Before that he worked as an occupational psychologist in the Civil Service Department, with a special interest in selection interviewing. And before that he was a PhD student at Aberdeen University, studying Jourard's theory of authenticity and self-disclosure. He likes writing and editing and has published widely. His main research interest for several years has been psychological type theory and the Myers–Briggs Type Indicator, and particularly its applications in counselling and education.

Colin Feltham, PhD, is Senior Lecturer in Counselling at Sheffield Hallam University, a Fellow of the British Association for Counselling, and a UKRC Registered Independent Counsellor. His 14 books include *What Is Counselling?* (Sage, 1995), *Time-Limited Counselling* (Sage, 1997), and *Controversies in Psychotherapy and Counselling* (Sage, 1999). He edits two book series for Sage, *Professional Skills for Counsellors* and *Perspectives on Psychotherapy*. He is Associate Editor of the *British Journal of Guidance and Counselling*. His professional and research interests are increasingly in critiques of the therapies, and their development into a broader discipline of mental, spiritual and social health.

Maurice Friedman, PhD, is Professor Emeritus of Religious Studies, Philosophy and Comparative Literature at San Diego State University, where he taught from 1973 to 1991, and is Co-Director of the Institute for Dialogical Psychotherapy in San Diego. He has taught at many universities since 1946. His many publications include *Martin Buber: The Life of Dialogue* (University of Chicago Press, Routledge and Kegan Paul, 1955); *The Worlds of Existentialism: A Critical Reader* (1st edition. New York: Random House, 1964; 2nd edition. University of Chicago Press, 1973; 3rd edition. Atlantic Highlands, NJ: Humanities Press International, 1991); *Martin Buber's Life and Work* (3 volumes) (New York: E.P. Dutton, 1982, 1983, 1984 respectively), for which he was awarded the Jewish National Book Award in 1985; *Religion and Psychology: A Dialogical Approach* (Paragon, 1992); and *Dialogue and the Human Image: Beyond Humanistic Psychology* (Sage, 1992).

Jeremy Holmes, MD, is a Consultant Psychotherapist in North Devon. He is currently Chair of the Psychotherapy Faculty of the Royal College of Psychiatrists. Author of eight books, including *John Bowlby and Attachment Theory* (Routledge, 1993), *Introduction to Psychoanalysis* (with A. Bateman, Routledge, 1995), *Attachment, Intimacy, Autonomy: Using Attachment Theory in Adult Psychotherapy* (Jason Aronson, 1996) and *Healing Stories: Narrative in Psychotherapy and Psychiatry* (with G. Roberts, Oxford, 1998), and over 80 articles and chapters in the field of psychotherapy, his interests include attachment theory, researching severe personality disorder, and the integration of psychotherapy within general psychiatry.

Stephen Palmer, PhD, is Director of the Centre for Stress Management and the Centre for Multimodal Therapy, London. He is an Honorary Senior Visiting Clinical and Research Fellow at City University, a Chartered Psychologist and UKCP Registered Psychotherapist. As well as maintaining a clinical practice, he teaches counselling, therapy and stress management worldwide. His publications include *Counselling for Stress Problems* (with Windy Dryden, Sage, 1995); *Dealing with People Problems at Work* (with Tim Burton, McGraw-Hill, 1996); *Client Assessment* (with Gladeana McMahon, Sage, 1997) and *Handbook of Counselling* (with Gladeana McMahon, Routledge, 1997).

Janice Russell, PhD, is a freelance consultant in counselling, counselling training and research. Her interests are in exploring counselling as a sociological object, and in writing. She is the co-author of an irreverent but practical book on counselling, *Challenging Blank Minds and Sticky Moments in Counselling* (1998), with Graham Dexter. She has also recently published her first novel, *Keeping Abreast* (1998), a sensitive and witty account of a woman's journey through breast cancer. Both books are available from Insight Press, York.

Diana Sanders, PhD, is a Chartered Counselling Psychologist working in Oxfordshire Mental Healthcare NHS Trust and a BABCP Accredited Cognitive Psychotherapist in primary care. She is a cognitive therapy trainer and supervisor, with a particular interest in developing cognitive therapy training for counsellors and counselling psychologists. She has a background in research, particularly in health psychology and psychosomatic problems, and in psychological treatments for premenstrual syndrome, cardiac problems and irritable bowel syndrome. She is the author of *Counselling for Psychosomatic Problems* (Sage, 1996), and co-author of *Cognitive Therapy: Transforming the Image* (Sage, 1997).

Keith Tudor is a trained social worker, a BAC accredited counsellor and UKCP Registered Psychotherapist in private practice. He is a Director of Temenos, an organization in Sheffield offering training in counselling and psychotherapy. He is the author of *Mental Health Promotion* (Routledge, 1996), *Group Counselling* (Sage, 1999) and many journal articles and chapters on mental health and on aspects of transactional analysis, person-centred therapy, and the politics of therapy.

Paul Wilkins is a Senior Lecturer in the Centre for Human Communication at Manchester Metropolitan University. He is also a person-centred therapist, supervisor and a UKCP Registered Psychodrama Psychotherapist. He is involved in the development of the World Association for Person Centred Counselling and Psychotherapy and is a member of the editorial board of *Person Centred Practice*. His publications include *Personal and Professional Development for Counsellors* (Sage, 1997). He also edits a book series for Sage, *Creative Therapies in Practice*.

Frank Wills is Deputy Head of the Department of Health and Social Care at the University of Wales College, Newport. He trained as both a social worker and a counsellor, and is a BAC Accredited Counsellor and a UKCP Registered Cognitive Psychotherapist. His current research interests include counsellor attitudes and counselling training. Previous publications include, with Diana Sanders, *Cognitive Therapy: Transforming the Image* (Sage, 1997) and 'Cognitive therapy: a down-to-earth and accessible therapy' in Sills (ed.), *Contracts in Counselling* (Sage, 1997).

Introduction

Colin Feltham

Every counsellor and therapist knows the range of thoughts, feelings and other sensations involved when a new client makes first contact. Early impressions are formed by both counsellor and client, some of them fantasy-based, some robustly realistic. These impressions are modified throughout the counselling process, often to good effect, but sometimes not. The counselling and psychotherapy relationship in all its manifestations and subtleties, partly resembles and partly differs sharply from other kinds of interpersonal relationships. Some things in this area seem fairly certain, however, for example that (a) the relationship is considered by many to be a (perhaps *the*) crucial element in all successful therapy; (b) conversely, problems in relationships between therapists and clients may account for a large part of therapeutic failure or equivocal results, and (c) any practitioner wanting to examine and enhance his or her practice is well advised to consider which relational variables have most bearing on their practice. A fourth consideration is the possibility – a claim made by many – that the therapeutic or counselling relationship could become the key to theoretical integration across all therapies.

This book is written with such considerations in mind. However, it is necessary from the outset to refer briefly to the title, and to the meaning of the 'counselling relationship'. You will find various instances throughout the book of problems with the concept of *the* counselling relationship (as if it could be straightforwardly defined and studied), since counselling is conducted at many levels and generates many nuances, mediated as it is by subjective human beings with all their individual and cultural differences, by perceptions, theories and contexts of all kinds.

Secondly, my own bias is towards treating counselling and psychotherapy as synonymous, and therefore the *therapeutic relationship* as synonymous with the *counselling relationship*. Not all readers will share this bias, but the writers have largely used the term counselling to refer to both activities. Thirdly, for practical-editorial reasons I have kept the focus largely on traditional one-to-one therapeutic relationships and have not dwelt on group and family therapies, creative therapies, brief therapies and so on.

The book has the following structure and rationale. Chapter 1 sets the scene by discussing meanings, historical and contextual background, concepts of energy fields, interpersonal dynamics, recent and diverse views on the therapeutic relationship, comparisons with other helping activities and questions of integration. It also throws up some of the objections to the assumption that the relationship is so central.

The next six chapters present the views of practitioners representing distinctive and different theoretical and clinical orientations, in order to demonstrate the contrasts between them and their strengths in terms of relational understanding, theory and skills. I have invited writers who represent a cross-section of approaches, not all of them obviously placing the relationship at the centre of therapy, but all offering prismatically stimulating views.

Jeremy Holmes provides an overview of the relationship in psychodynamic understanding, with a necessary emphasis on subtle, unconscious communications. Paul Wilkins summarizes the person-centred approach and its well known, distinctive core conditions. Maurice Friedman presents an account of dialogical psychotherapy, a form of existential therapy originating from the work of Martin Buber. These three have in common an explicit concentration on the relationship between therapist and client.

The next three chapters represent something of a turn towards the more technical approaches. Transactional analysis, although stemming from Freudian origins and having an intricate theory of interpersonal relationships, also generates many distinctive clinical and theoretical features of its own such as contracting, and (in Keith Tudor's view) a questioning of the taboo against dual relationships. Diana Sanders and Frank Wills demonstrate the collaborative nature of cognitive therapy and the increasing interest taken by many of its practitioners in relational factors traditionally associated with psychodynamic and person-centred practice.

Stephen Palmer in his chapter on multimodal therapy suggests both that that approach has distinctive ideas about 'relationships of choice' and also that relationship in and of itself is frequently *not* sufficient for therapeutic change.

The final section of the book raises a number of trans-theoretical considerations. Rowan Bayne's account of psychological type theory suggests that counsellors and therapists may enhance their practice, intuitively or otherwise, by attending to the predominant personality characteristics of client and therapist. Janice Russell injects a critical, sociologically informed element into the subject by asking readers to reconsider the significance of intimacy, personal relationships and assumptions of the universal desirability of counselling-orientated human relations. In the final chapter Roxane Agnew-Davies summarizes much of the empirical research into the counselling/therapeutic relationship and its many facets.

1 *Contextualizing the Therapeutic Relationship*

Colin Feltham

The very topicality of the therapeutic relationship in counselling and psychotherapy may cause it to be either taken for granted or over-inflated. In this chapter I aim for some definitional purchase on the term, I then look at certain historical, cultural and trans-theoretical issues, at maps and schemas of the relationship, and finally at critiques of the assumption that the therapeutic relationship is the central factor that it is claimed to be.

Meaning and Aims

The term therapeutic relationship can literally refer to any relationship, professional or otherwise, longstanding or fleeting, in which some form of therapy, help or healing, takes place. Unfortunately the term is often but perhaps inevitably used loosely or ambiguously. Sandler et al. (1992), for example, note the problems of conceptual confusion that are involved, and Keith Tudor explores definitional problems in his chapter in this book. While I do not intend to become ensnarled unnecessarily in fine semantic distinctions, it is as well to attempt briefly to clarify use of the term here.

This book dwells mainly on the specifically relational therapeutic aspects of largely professional encounters in the fields of counselling, counselling psychology, clinical psychology and psychotherapy. These professionally defined encounters usually contain some mixture of intentional use of prior training, theory and techniques, but also utilize elements of relational or interpersonal skill and artistry, placebo factors, and a host of indeterminate therapist and client factors of fortuitous rapport, matching, mis-matching, timing, and so on.

For practical-editorial reasons the concentration is on individual therapy. Clearly the complexity of relationships in couple, family and group therapies is great. Differential considerations in the special nature of the relationship in the therapy of disparate groups – children, tortured refugees, drug addicts, those diag-nosed as having a personality disorder, and so on – as well as the modalities of brief therapy, arts therapies, etc., are similarly not possible to go into separately here.

Our aim in this book is to focus on what transpires between therapist and client consciously and unconsciously, by design and by default, positively and negatively; on the attempt to understand what the components of therapeutic relationships are and how we may better learn from, integrate, utilize or perhaps when necessary surrender to or abandon some of these components.

Some Evolutionary, Historical and Thematic Highlights

Of course there have been healing relationships long before the advent of our modern clinical conceptualizations. Centuries of myth, religion and philosophy testify to the human experience of suffering in many guises and the search for remedies of many kinds. Many of these remedies would appear to have involved faith or placebo factors, longing for relief and expectation of finding it – and therefore finding what we expect to find – in relation to designated healers. Ehrenwald (1976) reminds us that even reluctant healers such as English monarchs were sometimes known to effect cures by their 'royal touch'. It is well noted by certain psychotherapy researchers that the most common trans-cultural healing factors are probably faith in sanctioned healers, designated settings, and so on (Frank, 1973; Kiev, 1964). Along-side this power of the mind to effect healing by expectancy and benign self-deceit, there has perhaps always existed the question of a possible *actual* power, residing in divine representatives (for example Jesus and his miracles), in gifted individuals or in special interpersonal encounters or holy places (Benson, 1996).

We have to consider that for evolutionary reasons humans take a long time to develop from vulnerable and dependent infant to relatively robust and autonomous adult. The implications of this probably are that we are peculiarly prone to emotional suffering and its endurance, and also that we seem peculiarly sensitized to the nuances of mood, threat and warmth in the presence of others. Our lives are lived both in small groups (families, friends and colleagues), from which we derive comfort and suffer hurt, and in larger communities and societies from which we derive sustenance, support and meaning, but which are also a source of alienation, oppression, shame and fear. Presumably we have deeply internalized an awareness of the constant co-existent dualism of love and hate, kindness and brutality, truth and lies, and have evolved adaptive strategies which both protect us and make us sick (Campbell, 1975; Langs, 1996; Stevens and Price, 1996).

The significance of this is that clients seek out therapists for the safety, understanding and healing they represent but any and every encounter combines degrees of benign, civilized interaction and primitive, ambiguous interaction: all is not what it seems. Some healers abuse, and probably all healers fail their clients some of the time. Every human encounter in therapy may be, among other things, partly a polite parlour interaction and professional relationship and partly a mutually primitive, unconscious weighing of trust, attraction and threat. Smith (1998) puts succinctly the argument of evolutionary psychoanalysis that our encounters take place at two levels, one of which is always unconsciously sensitized to pervasive interpersonal deceit. However, as elsewhere, in the emerging field of evolutionary psychotherapy there is relatively little consensus. Campbell (1975) argues that emotional expression has been stunted by the conditions of survival and that the full expression and restoration of feelings is the main task of therapy, whereas Langs (1996) infers from evolutionary science that unconscious communication within a tightly held therapeutic frame is probably the most significant part of therapeutic practice.

Religion

We cannot ignore the influence of centuries of religion and religious practice in daily life and ritual. Although we live in an increasingly secular and multicultural time, almost certainly there is within us some transgenerational and perhaps collectively unconscious knowledge of powerful past community-binding structures and relationships. Here I simply want to highlight the idea of a personal relationship with God; relationship with community, especially via a priest; and the pervasive sense of a call to love. I mention these ironically, since it is probably largely in their loss that we know them. In other words, secular humanism leaves many without a God to turn to; fragmented and mobile, competitive societies leave many without stable supportive communities and community figures, such as priests, who previously supplied many valued facilities including the confessional; and the breakdown of the concept of selfless duty, altruism, or love (Agape) also leaves a large hole in the social and interpersonal fabric. Nevertheless certain Christian counsellors, such as Howard Clinebell and Paul Tournier, have built systems of counselling that are explicitly, religiously, relationship-based (Hurding, 1985).

Religions, like psychotherapies, differ in their understanding of how human beings do and should stand in relation to each other. In some eastern religions, for example, the reality and distinctiveness of selves, and ultimate separateness of persons is considered illusory. However in most western therapies there are by contrast many reservations about the dangers of confluence, symbiosis and over-identification. Some of these problems are identified by Brazier (1993).

Love

Associated with all this is the breakdown of the stable close relationships of marriage and friendship. It is well noted by sociologists that psychotherapy has probably implicitly occupied the void left by the crumbling of these social structures (Halmos, 1965). There has also been a detectable shift from valuing kindness and altruism (words and qualities rich in associations) to a stress on assertiveness and autonomy. While many therapists are wary, particularly in our current professionalizing context, of invoking and being associated with the concept of love, some have explicitly acknowledged this.

> When one brings together the various aspects of the facilitative conditions – empathy, warmth, respect, concern, valuing and prizing, openness, honesty, genuineness, transparency, intimacy, self-disclosure, confrontation – it becomes apparent that they constitute love in the highest sense or *agape*. . . . We already have, in essence, the answer –

the answer that has been reached through thousands of years of human experience and recognized by the great philosophers of various times and cultures. (Patterson, 1974: 89–90)

If God is dead and love in all its varieties (Fromm, 1975; Lewis, 1963) has been subjected to reductionistic philosophical analysis and psychoanalytic doubt, it is understandable that individuals look for meaning, guidance and affection in therapy. And while even Freud could accord love the distinction of being, along with work, one of the indices of mental health, and he could suggest that psychoanalysis is a 'cure through love', it is not at all clear what love is now thought to be. Erotic and/or committed love, also known sometimes by the cliché of the 'deep and meaningful relationship' is perhaps the main form of 'pure relationship' understood by sociologists to exist only for the ends of the participants themselves (Giddens, 1991). According to Giddens, emphasis on pure relationship naturally generates a demand for therapy in order to better understand, define and improve oneself. Unfortunately, the dyadic intensity of most therapy then creates its own problems and, perhaps in too many instances, can lead to dependent, exploitative, abusive and sometimes dehumanizingly ritualistic therapeutic relationships (Heyward, 1993; Rutter, 1989; Wilmer, 1992; Janice Russell in Chapter 9).

Concepts of Energy Fields

Franz Anton Mesmer (1734–1815), while often written off as a charlatan, has at least something to teach us about therapeutic relationship. Mesmer turned his attention from theology to medicine and, initially influenced by the late eighteenth-century Austrian astronomer, Father Maximilian Hell, came to specialize in treatment by magnetism. Beginning with actual magnets (also used by some other physicians), Mesmer achieved some apparently dramatic cures. However, he came to believe that 'animal magnetism' (a kind of fluid) was located in his own body. Ellenberger (1970: 62) suggests that this is analogous to the 'Polynesian concept of "mana", a universal, impersonal energy that can be stored in persons, objects or places'. Mesmer used many electrical metaphors to explain how his therapeutic magnetism worked, but also referred to the importance of a 'general agent' and of inducing crises in sufferers. According to Ellenberger, Mesmer probably did embody high levels of charm and authority and immense belief in himself as a discoverer.

Mesmer was preceded and followed by others (Gassner, Puysegur, Lafontaine, Braid) using similar methods, and magnetism historically shades into hypnosis and its methods. A commonly noted phenomenon was *rapport* and the 'powerful interpersonal attraction issuing from the rapport' (Ellenberger, 1970: 77). The Mesmerist Kluger acknowledged the significance of rapport but spoke of it as a magnetic circle, which Ellenberger (ibid.) refers to as 'a closed world of two individuals, which had to be protected from noise, light, and outward interference'. Another Mesmerist, Hufeland, compared the magnetizer and magnetized to a pregnant woman and her foetus, and the magnetizing process to the stages of pregnancy. Such writing stems from the early nineteenth century. Much later, Winnicottian notions of the maternal reverie and its recurrence in the psychoanalytic dyad, have obvious similarities.

Concepts and practices associated with energy fields are not confined to Mesmer or to his historical niche. Jungians such as Schwartz-Salant (1998) and Stein (1995) argue for the significance of the interactive field between therapist and client, based on alchemical principles stemming from around 200 BCE. The interactive field is also known as a 'third area' or 'analytic third', as the atmosphere between the participants in therapy, or as a palpable mingling of souls (Moore, 1994). It is closely associated with the Greek *pneuma* or 'subtle body'. The Indian *prana* and Chinese *chi* also underpin explanations of psychic energy (Tart, 1975). Metaphorical (or not) references to interpersonal chemistry, magnetism, electricity, vibrations, energy, attunement, etc., are quite common. West (1997) discusses contemporary spiritual healing in somewhat similar terms, although alluding also to a presence which is sometimes felt to be distinctly *other* (for example auras, the presence of healing energies, God and grace).

Grossinger (1982) finds evidence throughout history and prehistory of conceptions of a universal energy. Paracelsus in the sixteenth century referred to a 'quintessence' or nature, force or virtue. This is often conceived in terms of a feminine principle, Grossinger suggesting for example that women are more natural healers than men (see for example, Friedman, 1992; Josselson, 1996; Sayers, 1991). More recently, the physicist David Bohm's (1980) concept of an implicate order has been taken up by Ullman (1991), who argues that interconnectedness, or unbroken ontological wholeness, manifests itself especially in dreams. It may follow from this that illusion-dissolving, healing encounter is supremely available both in therapeutic relationships and in other forms of serious dialogue, as suggested by Martin Buber (1965; 1970); Bohm (1996); de Maré et al. (1991); and Maurice Friedman in Chapter 4.

From Mind to Mind

Another nineteenth-century physician, Carl Gustav Carus (1789–1869) is worth noting for his conception of layers of consciousness. Within his schema, he argued for the operation of interpersonal relationships at these levels: from the conscious of one person to the conscious of the other; from conscious to unconscious; from unconscious to conscious; and from unconscious to unconscious. Again, these ideas were later developed by twentieth-century psychoanalysts. Ellenberger (1970) and later Howe (1993) note the important contribution of certain philosophers, such as Max Scheler, who probed for answers to the question of how we know other minds. Do we know them directly, by inference, or identification? Or because we share pre-existing traits? Hypotheses were put forward by many philosophers, while hypnotism, spiritism and other methods of mind cure were being touted, around the time that Freud, originally interested in hypnotism and other methods, developed his own conception of the unconscious and finally settled on resistance and transference as foci for his work.

Dyadically intense and lengthy therapy as ushered in by Freud and his followers was a particularly powerful movement which perhaps remained virtually unchallenged until after Freud's death in 1939. The growth in analytic group therapy and other forms of therapy and human relations work in groups was particularly marked from the 1940s. Sensitivity training groups, encounter groups and other experimental group formats relied not only on extension of theories from Freud, other therapists and social scientists, but also on willingness to experiment, and hope for radical and widely applicable social changes. Learning from others, one's peers and experts, became paramount. Coincidentally, some of the great mutual aid and voluntary movements such as Alcoholics Anonymous and Relate emanated from the 1930s.

One question to ask ourselves at this point perhaps is whether there has been scientific and philosophical progress in understanding the human mind and the relationship between human minds (and in our context, between the minds of therapist and client) from superstition to knowledge, or whether there are simply ever-changing cycles of experiments, metaphors and methods which are all constrained and created by their own time and culture. Ideas of levels of consciousness and of interpersonal relationship persist, and include the conscious, the unconscious and the transpersonal (Clarkson, 1995). Also, across the centuries the focus for understanding and implementing varieties of spiritual and psychological therapy has clearly shifted from divine intervention to charisma and therapeutic giftedness, to learnable technique and specially cultivated interpersonal conditions. And while many philosophers have dwelled on communication between minds as problematic, others such as Macmurray (1961) have taken human relationship as a logical norm, and have found philosophers of the mind–body split and philosophies representing humans as isolates and alienated beings problematic.

The Early Development of Relationships

Knowledge of early human development and its implications has grown and informed understanding in the clinical (particularly psychoanalytic) domain (Brazelton and Cramer, 1991; Klein, 1987; Stern, 1985). A great deal of therapeutic work now rests on foundations of understanding laid down by Winnicott and Bowlby, among others, on the place and importance of early attachments, continuities, separations and losses, the long-term effects of the most significant early interpersonal experiences, and their unconscious recurrence in therapeutic relationships (the domain of the object relations therapies). Many therapies act essentially as corrective counterparts to early damage and neglect, imposed conditions of worth, developmental lacunae, or faulty early learning, variously providing holding and containment, protection, permission, mirroring and other aspects of reparenting, in the psychoanalytic and related traditions; or identification and correction of anachronistic personal schemas, scripts or unhelpful problemsolving strategies. These phenomena are addressed variously by Jeremy Holmes, Paul Wilkins, Keith Tudor, Diana Sanders and Frank Wills, and Stephen Palmer in this book.

Interestingly, while psychoanalytic writers have addressed these ideas in abundance, it has been mainly left, after Otto Rank, to humanistic theorists to develop the idea that intra-uterine, birth and immediately postnatal experience may first raise inklings of self and other, of safety and threat, of wholeness and separateness. Thorne's (1991) clinical experience suggests that even without intentions towards any kind of rebirthing experience, the intensity of the core conditions may allow for some clients spontaneously to enter preverbal, 'primal' states.

Recent Therapeutic Developments

The assumption of the centrality of unconscious factors in psychotherapy was probably most seriously challenged from about the 1950s with the growth of both the humanistic and the cognitive-behavioural therapies. Perhaps each of these forces underlined the importance of conscious, egalitarian relations between clients and therapists. Certainly those therapists who broke away from their analytic moorings, wanting to include more explicitly the socio-political, cultural and interpersonal domains – such as Karen Horney, Harry Stack Sullivan and Erich Fromm – helped the development of interpersonal psychotherapy and, more generally, the existentialist–humanistic tradition.

Fritz Perls, Jacob Moreno, Wilhelm Reich, Carl Rogers and others led the exodus from cerebral and hierarchical psychoanalysis towards greater trust in feelings, the body and power-sharing. Perls is believed to be among the first to have changed from the traditional use of the analytic couch to chairs facilitating face-to-face contact and a shift from transference relations to genuine contact, confrontation and dialogue. Eric Berne, George Kelly, Albert Ellis and Aaron Beck in different ways shifted the therapeutic focus towards belief in reason, collaboration, conscious choice, and confrontation of irrationality.

Rogers's (1957) well known declaration of the necessity and sufficiency of the core conditions (primarily acceptance, empathy and congruence) has had enormous impact from that time and is fully explicated in Paul Wilkins's chapter in this book. Rather than attempt to summarize Rogers's legacy here, it seems pertinent to remind ourselves of the epigraph used by Rogers (1951: v) in the beginning of *Client–Centered Therapy*:

> We mark with light in the memory the few interviews we have had, in the dreary years of routine and sin, with souls that made our souls wiser; that spoke what we thought; that told us what we knew; that gave us leave to be what we inly were. (Emerson, Divinity School Address, 1838)

Some of Rogers's critics however have judged such sentiments to be romantic and self-serving rather than other-affirming. And again, after Rogers's initial strong impact a breakaway tradition soon established itself in the work of people such as Carkhuff, Egan and others. Hence:

> Good human relations are not enough! Even when the core, facilitative, and action-oriented dimensions are present in a helping relationship, the helpee may be unable to surmount certain difficult problems or to achieve certain goals. (Carkhuff, 1969: 116)

Many publications appeared in the 1970s and 1980s which took on the task of analysing the components of successful therapeutic processes and acting as practice manuals. One such is Hammond et al. (1977). This looks at problems of counsellor passivity, dominance, inappropriate self-disclosure, interrogation, distancing patterns, taboos against crying, fostering social interaction (for example chit-chat), skirting uncomfortable issues, false reassurances, use of crude language, moralizing, patronizing, arguing, dogmatism and pressure tactics. These are addressed by guidance on perceptiveness about feelings, enhancing reciprocity, using additive responses, relational empathy, respect, and attention to here-and-now feelings, among others. Curtis (1981) advocates explicit awareness of the importance of and skills involved in greetings, attention-giving, demonstration of expertise, active posture, appropriate protectiveness, Socratic guidance, enthusiasm and self-confidence.

Gerard Egan (1994) has been particularly critical of the notion that good human relations and persistent exploration are enough, emphasizing instead that skill, and an active, methodical, pragmatic approach is essential. But his use of the term 'client-centred' continues to cause confusion.

Interestingly, in the development of cognitive-behavioural therapy, which has its roots in social learning theory, there is now said to be a danger of a drift back towards the psychoanalytic, and perhaps towards the person-centred too. Just as others have considered person-centred therapy too slow and goalless, now some are finding the goal-oriented approaches insufficiently rooted in a strong relationship with the client. This latter observation has been addressed by Schaap et al. (1993) and by Diana Sanders and Frank Wills in Chapter 6.

Existentialist writers, from Binswanger to Laing, have often demonstrated exceptional awareness of the therapeutic relationship and sensitivity to its nuances. Rollo May (1992) in a revised edition of his original text from the 1930s, considers transference and also goes on to commend empathy. Additionally, May makes many fascinating social-psychological speculations. For example, he ruminates on the common tendency to deceive in everyday encounters and how counselling erodes this tendency:

> I give up the deceit by the means, curiously enough, of a *hypothesis of mental telepathy*, assuming that the other can read my mind and that there is therefore no point in keeping anything from that person. (May, 1992: 70; emphasis in original)

May goes on to speculate about the general and temporary influence of personality, and the influence of ideas, in a way that anticipates those social psychologists who later explicitly studied and applied concepts of social influence in counselling and therapy.

Bugental (1987) shows both existential commitment to 'life-changing psychotherapy' – in the humanistic tradition – and also concern for the technicalities of interpersonal skill required in therapy. He attempts to guide readers through attainment of greater depth of engagement, shifting responsibility to clients, deepening conversational level, use of 'interpersonal press' (although Bugental employs musical analogies to describe this, it resembles the social influence processes of later cognitive-behavioural therapists), and so on. Bugental nevertheless stresses the centrality of presence – above technique and rapport – as *the* healing factor.

Irvin Yalom (1991: 91–2) argues, as others have, that trainee therapists may be as effective as seasoned professionals on the basis of their curiosity and enthusiasm. He goes on in the same passage to state:

> It's the relationship that heals, the relationship that heals, the relationship that heals – my professional rosary. I say that often to students. And say other things as well, about the way to relate to a patient – positive unconditional regard, nonjudgmental acceptance, authentic engagement, empathic understanding.

Also in the existential tradition, Goldberg (1977) wrote one of the most lucid cases for egalitarian, adult-to-adult, consciously and explicitly contracted therapy to be found in the literature. This thread of adult responsibility is strong in transactional analysis (see Keith Tudor's chapter) and wholly and challengingly explicit in Sills (1997). However, existentialists like other groups are not homogeneous, as made clear by Maurice Friedman (Chapter 4).

Aspects of the Psychoanalytic Legacy

The psychoanalyst Greenson (1967) outlined one of the earliest schemas for understanding the multilayered nature of the relationship in psychoanalysis. Acknowledging the contribution of Zetzel (1956) and her use of the term 'therapeutic alliance', Greenson went on to discuss and compare transference relations, the working alliance, the real relationship and corrective emotional experience. He also alluded to primitive antecedents of transference, manifesting in severe regression, which required 'management' rather than the offering of interpretation and facilitation of insight.

The working alliance is the 'relatively nonneurotic, rational rapport which the patient has with his analyst' (Greenson, 1967: 192). Greenson points out that the real relationship can refer both to being reality-oriented and also to relationship which is 'genuine, authentic, and true' (p. 217). Sandler et al. (1992) discuss problems of meaning in use of the terms working alliance, treatment alliance, therapeutic alliance, therapeutic contract and realistic bond. They also draw attention to Freud's uses of the terms rapport, collaboration and pact; and to the problems of misalliance and pseudo-alliance. Horvath and Greenberg (1994) have in recent years developed and empirically researched the working alliance in much greater depth.

Samuels (1985: 186) usefully warns against idealization and misunderstanding of the treatment alliance:

> It does not mean only the patient's conscious wish to get better and certainly it does not infer only a positive, harmonious relationship between analyst and patient. In fact, the essence of the treatment alliance may well be that the patient goes on working even when he hates the analyst and consciously wishes to leave the analysis.

Many discriminations between nuances of relating have been identified and taken up by various analysts since. Indeed the field of object relations, itself departing from Freudian instinct theory, is now characterized by several, sometimes incompatible views on the relationship between self and others (Cashdan, 1988). Langs (1976), the communicative psychotherapist, has spoken of the bipersonal field entailing both cordiality (a necessary minimum atmosphere of human warmth) and frustration (of normal social expectations). Langs (1976) has further developed his views on the bipersonal field as an environment charged with adaptive but essentially unconscious communications. Karasu (1992: 107–19) embraces the views of Zetzel and Greenson, and stresses the necessity for 'controlled flexibility' rather than 'uncontrolled fluidity' for the therapist who needs constantly and skilfully to modulate his or her responses in line with clients' subtly shifting and developing psychological states. Robertiello and Schoenewolf (1987) provide fascinating examples of therapists' clinical errors arising from countertransference and counterresistance. More recent writers such as Benjamin (1998) have brought critical theory to bear on the themes of gender and intersubjectivity in psychoanalysis. Jeremy Holmes in Chapter 2 explores some of the rich and varied terrain of the psychoanalytic views of the relationship.

Bordin (1979) developed Zetzel's and Greenson's notion of therapeutic alliance by breaking it down into bonds, goals and tasks. Bonds concern interpersonal attitudes of client and therapist, well described in person-centred literature, but they are elaborated by Bordin, and later by Dryden (1989). We should also consider how the therapist may need to adapt consciously to different clients' relational styles and how clients are likely to bring certain attitudes of trust, safety, faith, fantasy, reluctance, and so on, to the relationship. Bordin suggested that clearly shared goals presage successful outcomes (and conversely that divergent goals are likely to undermine success). Goals may differ due to failure to make explicit contracts, having unconsciously different and/or vague or unrealistic goals, losing sight of original goals and inability to detect and act on such problems in the relationship. Tasks are the means employed to bring about change towards goals, and include all therapeutic techniques but also requirements of the client, such as dream recall, free association, observation of boundaries, homework, etc. Again, things may go awry where different understandings of tasks exist and are left unaddressed, when tasks are inappropriate or ineffective and when these problems are not resolved.

This trend towards mapping the therapeutic relationship finds quite comprehensive expression in Clarkson's (1995) five relationships framework. This consists of (a) the working alliance; (b) the transferential/countertransferential relationship; (c) the reparative/developmentally needed relationship; (d) the person-to-person relationship, and (e) the transpersonal relationship. These correspond roughly with (respectively) the scientific/academic tradition; the Freudian/Kleinian psychoanalytic tradition; the innate healing forces of life (Physis); the existential/humanistic tradition; and the religious and spiritual traditions. While they may be found predominantly in certain therapeutic approaches, they also overlap and interlink.

Clarkson's fifth relational element – the transpersonal – is probably the least discussed in psychoanalytic literature, possibly because of Freud's well known negative views on religion, although it has found a partial home in Jungian analysis. Yet Symington (1994: 130–1) believes that 'the spiritual struggle takes place *within* the relationship'. Furthermore, Symington argues that 'the greatest spiritual encounters occur in the emotional confrontation with the analyst, . . . a momentous fact that has not been registered either by theologians or by psychoanalysts'.

As we have seen, Clarkson's schema has much in common with, although extending, Greenson's (1967) schema, and also adds to Gelso's and Carter's (1985). However, I suspect that we should also add (a) a hierarchical form of 'top-down' relationship (therapist as scientifically informed expert, client as recipient/beneficiary, or object of benign manipulation – for example, Schaap et al., 1993); and (b) a 'bottom-up' relationship (client as informed, critical consumer and main player – for example, Rusk, 1991). Were we to attempt to construct an even more exhaustive schema, I believe *difference* would also need to be added as a crucial relational variable. The interactions of gender, age, race, class, religion, culture, sexuality, and physical, temperamental and other influential differences between therapist and client presumably deeply affect the therapeutic process for better or for worse.

Maroda (1991: 100–4) supplies a valuable cautionary note when she argues that all such schemas may *hamper* us in actual work with clients, and that only immediate empathy and respect grasps what is simultaneously real, transferential, and so on, in the relationship.

Parallel Movements

It is worth briefly setting developments in counselling and psychotherapy alongside those in social work, medicine and psychology.

Social Work

In 1957 the first edition of Biestek's (1961) social work text
The Casework Relationship appeared. In it, Biestek, a Jesuit,
traces significant references to the centrality of the relationship in
casework from texts from 1929 onwards. Although some psychoanalytic terminology is evident, there is no reference to Carl
Rogers or other contemporary therapists. Biestek defines the
casework relationship and his text ranges across the topics of
acceptance, non-judgementalism, controlled emotional involvement, permissive atmosphere, understanding and response, concern, interest and professionalism. By the end of the twentieth
century we have witnessed original social work values being
eroded and shifted from direct, healing relationship to the ironically impersonal management of high caseloads. Nevertheless,
reminders of the significance of the relationship in social work
and other caring professions, as in therapy, are readily available in
Howe (1993) and Morgan (1995).

Medicine and Healing

Zeldin (1994) has pointed to the importance even to ancient
Egyptians of the doctor–patient relationship, and folk psychology
has attested to the importance of the bedside manner in medicine. Duck (1986), from a social psychology perspective, summarizes some of the empirical research on the physician–patient
relationship. Citing Szasz and Hollander (1956), he discusses the
dimensions of activity–passivity (active doctor – passive patient);
guidance–cooperation (expert advice given to willing recipient);
and mutual participation (shared power and interdependence).
Duck stresses that psychological interpersonal factors play a
significant part alongside actual physical treatment, and suggests
that fear of (and other negative emotions experienced in relation
to) the doctor can be damaging to health. The recommendations
of Benson (1996) and certain trends towards medical humanities
also stress the health-promoting effects of sensitive doctor–patient
communication. The work of Dossey (1994) and West (1997) also

indicates hopeful trends of holistic-health convergence based on relational factors.

Social Psychology

Dorn (1984), following Strong (1968), outlined a systematic social influence model of counselling, based on findings from social psychology. According to such thinkers, the three main dimensions of counsellor influence are perceived expertness, trustworthiness and attractiveness. Dorn added a consideration of the counsellor's social power and of dyadic interaction and client variables. Essentially, this view, based on empirical research, holds that clients are frequently positively impressed and influenced by signs of expertness and credibility (for example, formal office, diplomas, professional language and status, etc.) but that this can be in conflict with perceived attractiveness. Attractiveness includes cooperativeness, physical appearance, liking, similarity and warmth. While these qualities can sometimes act additively, the complexity of the variables listed above means that consciously contrived social influence in counselling is no easy matter. Awareness of how one is likely to be perceived by clients is, however, an important aspect in counsellor effectiveness (Dryden and Feltham, 1994; Howard et al., 1987; Lazarus, 1993). Agreement that clients commonly are deeply influenced by the setting of therapy, the therapist's status and the expectations created thereby, is probably quite widespread (Frank, 1973).

Psychologists have been influential in a number of ways in the development of counselling and psychotherapy. The study of non-verbal and paraverbal behaviours, for example, has yielded some quite striking findings. According to Mehrabian (1971), the impact of actual words used in social encounters contributes a mere 7 per cent to liking–dislike, while a figure of 38 per cent is associated with voice cues and 55 per cent with facial cues. This weighting may reflect certain facets of early childhood development and/or the necessary human alertness to interpersonal deception (see Robinson, 1996; Smith, 1999). Among others, Egan (1990) has based attending and listening skills aspects of his own model partly on the lessons from Mehrabian's research. Awareness of discrepancies between verbal and non-verbal behaviour is a significant aspect of the training of counsellors (it is apparent, for example, in the notions of congruence and incongruence).

Awareness of studies of the phenomena of shared worldviews, relationship formation, communication, conflict and attribution, self-disclosure, and sexuality, is also important but often neglected (Hendrick, 1995). Understanding how clients seek help, how they react to and comply with or sabotage therapy, and why they sometimes drop out of therapy, are also subjects of obvious interest.

Almost certainly such psychological evidence has generally made more impact on cognitive-behavioural than on psychodynamic or humanistic practitioners. However, intuition or emotional intelligence regarding the non-verbal domain no doubt plays a greater role in these latter approaches, and these practitioners are likely to opt for case study and other qualitative research methods rather than for objectivist research paradigms. Buber too spoke of the necessity of 'the bursting of psychologism'. Roxane Agnew-Davies in Chapter 10 gives a robust overview of research on therapeutic relationship factors, which originates from the scientific psychology tradition.

Understanding Conversation

Not all, but probably most therapy is conversationally constructed and reflects the role of language and communication in early human development (Howe, 1993). Conversation is now studied from a variety of perspectives, by therapists, social psychologists, sociologists and sociolinguistics scholars, anthropologists, philosophers and others. Hobson's (1985) conversational model of psychotherapy focuses on the importance of 'a shared language of feeling' in the service of personal problem-solving, involving awareness of in-session 'aloneness–togetherness', negotiation, the here and now, hypothesizing, use of metaphors, and mutual asymmetry. Various writers have spoken of therapy as play, as a dance, judo, or game of hide and seek. Mair (1989) has attempted to build on such metaphors towards a conversational psychology.

Relational communication in therapy and its association with drop-out rates has included a focus on question-and-answer patterns, speech turns, topic initiation, controlling manoeuvres, and so on (Beyebach and Carranza, 1997). Patterns, misunderstandings and conflicts in friendship conversations and in female–male conversational styles have been the subject of much sociolinguistic analysis. The detailed conversational analysis by Silverman (1997) of HIV counselling suggests among other things that what we actually say and do probably departs from theory, intention and non-directive, egalitarian assumptions quite often. Finally, the practice of interpersonal process recall (Kagan, 1980), which is quite well known to many therapists as a method of professional development, includes but goes beyond the understanding of conversation only, working with recall of subtle, affective and unconscious factors.

Integration

We may consider that there are several current trends suggestive of a convergence on the centrality of the therapeutic relationship.

Common Factors

We may be cautiously optimistic that the therapeutic relationship will serve as an integrative focus for the field of the psychological therapies and all its many schools (Bordin, 1979; Clarkson, 1995; Dryden, 1989). While no consensus exists on a precise definition of common factors, there is reasonable agreement on the importance of the following: social and emotional support, an emotionally charged relationship with a helping person, warmth, a healing setting, a plausible rationale for treatment, a plausible interactive ritual, positive expectancy or hope on the part of client and therapist, encouragement, acceptance, active interest, the chance to talk, emotional expression, to be understood (Arkowitz, 1992; Frank, 1973; Howe, 1993). To some extent these factors are now honoured in the views and practices of a variety of integrative practitioners (Clarkson, 1995; Kahn, 1991; Lomas, 1987).

The Client's Perspective

Evidence has been accumulating for a number of years now that clients' views on their therapies and therapists are sometimes at serious variance with those of practitioners. Therapists have traditionally often placed emphasis on the importance of following theory, on lengthy and deep ('life-transforming') therapy, on assessment and perhaps inadvertent pathologizing, on non-directiveness and objectivity, and on psychological-mindedness, and so on. Many clients, however, have valued simple human qualities such as warmth, engagement, concern and interest; they have sought symptom-relief, value therapists' opinions and guidance and do not necessarily share therapists' cultural and class assumptions (Anderson and Goolishian, 1992; Dupont-Joshua, 1996; Heyward, 1993; Howe, 1993; Krause, 1998; Oldfield, 1983; Russell, Chapter 9).

Bearing in mind that most therapy has been constructed and institutionally fronted by white western males, it is no surprise that it has taken time for women's distinctive views as consumers and therapeutic partners to be heard (Maracek and Kravetz, 1998; McLellan, 1995). It is now also common for consumer guides to advise people considering entering therapy to shop around in order to find a counsellor or therapist with whom they feel an appropriate compatibility. As one client reported:

> It's possible my analyst – I mean the second one, the one I've been with all these years – isn't quite the right personality for me. I mean, she's like a very dry, subtle white wine, whereas I might do better with a full, fruity Burgundy. (Dinnage, 1989: 35)

This statement reflects some of the concerns about factors of client–therapist matching expressed by Bayne and Palmer in their chapters. And, quite simply, there have been clients who have given full voice to their discontentment with their therapists and to regrets about therapies gone awry, and from whom we can – must – learn (Alexander, 1995; Heyward, 1993).

The Dialogical Turn

Elements of what is meant by dialogical therapy can be found in passages by Fritz Perls and later Gestalt writers, most of whom have been influenced by Martin Buber's writings, particularly his influential book *I and Thou*. However, Maurice Friedman (1996; and in Chapter 4) traces a quite distinctive lineage from Buber to his own work and that of Hans Trub, Leslie Farber, Richard Hycner, Ivan Boszormenyi-Nagel, Barbara Krasner and others. While much of this has developed from Gestalt and existentialist backgrounds, Friedman also notes some convergence in the work of psychoanalysts such as Robert Stolorow. Such work is characterized by the centrality of healing through meeting as full human beings. Separate, but I believe related developments include the large group analytic work of de Maré et al. (1991), the critical psychology of Sampson (1993), analyses of intersubjectivity (Benjamin, 1998; Crossley, 1996) and the work of Bohm (1996). Some of this is ironically inaccessible academic material, but nevertheless identifies the potential value of talking to each other exploratively, affirming each other and being changed by the encounter.

Presence

Almost by definition our problems are located in the past and future, in loss, regret and anxiety, and the ability to live in the present constitutes much of the remedy for human suffering. Equally, the ability of therapists to be fully present to their clients, and consequently unusually intuitive, has been noted as perhaps the single most significant therapeutic factor by Carl Rogers among others. Hycner (1991) commends the practice of 'present-centredness' as crucial. Bugental (1987) has noted that rapport is not identical with presence, and it is worth considering how reference to the 'here and now' in therapy as an occasional *technique* differs from existential presence. Although personal and interpersonal presence does not have to be understood spiritually, there are many references to presence in religious texts. Buber's *I and Thou* points to a divine presence, known in Judaism, for example, as 'Shekhinah' (Gunzburg, 1997). It may be that presence, if we could understand it conceptually, is linked with theories of energy fields and their healing qualities. Greater understanding of the differences between occasional fortuitous (heightened) presence and sustained, meditative presence might also advance therapeutic success.

Perhaps not a necessary, but a common ingredient of presence, is silence. All counsellors and therapists encounter moments, sometimes extended episodes, of silence, and varieties of silence, between their clients and themselves. The radical priest Illich (1973: 45) gave a beautiful description of the workings of silence.

> At the pole opposed to despair there is the silence of love, the holding of hands of the lovers. The prayer in which the vagueness before words has given place to the pure emptiness after them. The form of communication which opens the simple depth of the soul. It comes in flashes and it can become a lifetime – in prayer just as much as with people. Perhaps it is the only truly universal aspect of language, the only means of communication which was not touched by the curse of Babel. Perhaps it is the only way of being together with others and with the Word in which we have no more foreign accent.

Is the Relationship the Be All and End All?

I end this chapter with a condensed consideration of some of the objections that have been put forward to the tendency to place the therapeutic relationship at the centre of the entire therapeutic enterprise. Rather than an uncritical assumption that the relationship between client and therapist is central and non-problematic, it may be that questioning will lead to better evidence and better practice.

1 The very term 'therapeutic relationship' is quite loose, overlapping as it does factors that could be ascribed discretely to the personalities of client and therapist, techniques and placebos, timing, chance, and to wider, contextual factors. Furthermore, no one has satisfactorily analysed the relationship into its parts, particularly into those parts responsible for therapeutic change. Even Carl Rogers's core conditions are rather sketchy, perhaps somewhat arbitrarily divided, and do not account in detail for the 'atoms' and variations in change processes. In addition, different therapeutic theories are associated with quite different accounts of relational phenomena. What is bedrock in one (for example the unconscious in psychoanalysis) is absent from or disputed by others (for example in the existentialist, person-centred and behaviour therapies).

2 There is some ironic danger that if the centrality of the therapist–client relationship is accepted as the key factor in human helping, then this may play into the hands of critics such as Hans Eysenck who have long argued that therapy does no more than could be done by friends, relatives, priests and other untrained helpers and healers. Also, if it is central, then much of the theoretical training of therapists may be quite redundant: teach practitioners mainly to relate better and more deeply (Mearns, 1996).

3 Mahrer (1997) argues that it is not the relationship that the client has with the therapist that is significant, but the relationship the client has with his or her own deep, inner, experiencing self. Furthermore, Mahrer believes that much apparent therapy is a caricature of true therapy, resting as it does on 'role relationships' in which each participant (client and therapist) seeks and gains essentially non-therapeutic, distracting role, status and emotional rewards. Mahrer's own preference in the clinical setting is to sit or

recline side by side with clients, with eyes closed; not directly relating to each other but both looking at the same 'third thing' or attentional centre – the client's inner experiencing. A similiar argument to Mahrer's is found in primal therapy – that the process is about putting clients in touch with their own ability gradually to access, feel and integrate historic psycho-physiological pain, and that therapists should be quite interchangeable facilitators of the process rather than symbolically essential, containing figures. Echoes of this position are also found in co-counselling.

4   It is evident that the majority of people, including those experiencing significant distress, deal for better or for worse with their own problems and aspirations without professional help. Furthermore, if one searches for examples of outstanding individuals who have significantly transcended their own psychological impediments, attained high levels of mental health and made notable contributions to society, such examples are more likely to be associated with religion, philosophy, the arts, adversity-transcendence and self-liberation than with psychotherapy and counselling.

5   Most accounts of the therapeutic relationship, including this one, are written primarily from the point of view of the therapist. In spite of a growing number of accounts and critiques from the client's perspective, the dominant explanatory discourse is located on professional (not consumers') terrain, thus giving a distorted and disempowering picture (McLeod, 1997). Yalom's co-authored account (Yalom and Elkin, 1974) with his client, provides an unusual example of co-constructed narrative.

6   It is clear that the psychotherapeutic enterprise focuses, albeit dyadically, on the individual and usually on his or her close relationships. Critics have made the charge that therapy weakens social analysis and political resolve, and fails to note the extent to which self-reliance, self-change, peer-help, dialogue and social action may be potent and necessary. Therapists may also be guilty of a psychologizing misdiagnosis and the raising of false hopes, leading to disappointment. If distress is commonly due to distal rather than to proximal causes (Smail, 1993), then emphasis on intimate therapeutic and other personal relationships may be seriously misplaced (Baker, 1996; Cloud, 1998).

7   In spite of a great deal of inference about common factors from outcome research, we cannot conclusively assume that intense client–therapist relationships are in fact and/or for ever-more the most powerful means of effecting change, or that they are effective for all kinds of presenting concerns (Bellack and Hersen, 1990; Roth and Fonagy, 1996). Given the march of cognitive-behavioural, genetic, psycho pharmacological and related research, we cannot dismiss (except from a position of defensive faith) the possibility of new and quite precise therapeutic agents being discovered.

8   Given powerful trends towards the widespread use of infor-mation, communication and entertainment technology, which already includes therapeutic uses and potentialities, the traditional dominance of the face-to-face, one-to-one therapeutic relationship will increasingly come under pressure. It will force us to ask whether or to what extent actual human presence is essential for therapeutic support, healing and change: where does the relation-ship belong and exactly how does it operate in telephone counsel-ling, computer-assisted therapy, therapy by e-mail, and other forms of as yet embryonic cyber-relational therapy? Technology may even eventually deliver to us the solution to the problems of prescriptive therapeutic matching, connecting clients computer-dating style with the therapist most likely to help them, regardless of where they live.

9   We often forget to note, too, that our access to clients' worlds, and the accuracy and sufficiency of anyone's account of their life, can be very limited. As Havens (1989: 49–50) puts it:

> Let us see the other as a lifetime moving past, a flying arrow or, better, a train seen from outside at night, with its lighted, swiftly passing windows throwing bits of action and personhood out to us. The stream of consiousness described by William James, still less the other's whole movement from past through present to future, is not arrested in an interview. However much patients reflect on themselves before us, that reflection takes place on a continually moving platform. The other is moving, and we are too.
>
> I can say to the train, stop, let me aboard to walk through your compartments, ride with you a while, see the world through your windows. Or I may throw the engineer out and drive the train myself (society says the doctor must do just that if he sees the train headed for a cliff). But I can't really come aboard. It is a sealed train, sealed by the fact that, observe you as I can, hear from you about yourself, some-

times learn your feelings, nevertheless the most cooperative patient in the world must speak from a separate existence only partly sampled and understood even by himself.

10   In what could be interpreted as a rush to idealize the therapeutic relationship, we may forget that in many ways it is often a stylized, asymmetrical (Winstead et al., 1988) and dis-embodied relationship. In other words, it tends to rest uncritically on a particular tradition of office-based and conversation-based, subtly hierarchical factors which marginalize the facts of everyday socio-economic reality, of bodily existence, and exaggerate the significance of the verbal and psychological dimension.

11   Therapists cannot entirely ignore critics who argue that we perhaps make a fetish of relationships generally, leading unintentionally to dysfunctionally enmeshed co-dependencies and, in the case of therapeutic relationships, to new, illusory forms of guru–disciple relationship and therapism (Cloud, 1998; Kaminer, 1992; Weldon, 1999).

12   Steiner (1974) argues from the transactional analysis tradition that we should not assume that individual one-to-one therapy is the relationship of choice, and in fact believes that group therapy is usually superior. For Steiner, dyadic therapy encourages a focus on the intrapersonal nature of personal difficulties and resolutions instead of between-ness. Group therapy more closely approximates to the real interpersonal and social conditions that clients must face. Friedman (1996) raises the question of the possible superiority of family and contextual therapy to artificial or indirect forms of dyadic therapy.

An Invitational Conclusion

At this stage in the development of the fields of psychotherapy, counselling and cognate disciplines, there are grounds for devoting considerable attention to the therapeutic relationship, to the healing that transpires within it, and to investigating the nature of the atoms of influence, healing and change involved. Arguably, this is necessarily an increasingly interdisciplinary field based on many converging clinical and spiritual practices and theories, academic disciplines, critical analyses – and simple human dialogue. It is hoped this book will go some way towards the further understanding, demystification, and enhancement of therapeutic and wholeness-oriented human relationships – and that, as a reader you will benefit from engaging with its arguments as you read them, and responding in whatever ways you can.

References

Alexander, R. (1995) *Folie à Deux*. London: Free Association Books.

Anderson, H. and Goolishian, H. (1992) 'The client is the expert: a not-knowing approach to therapy', in S. McNamee and K.J. Gergen (eds), *Therapy as Social Construction*. London: Sage.

Arkowitz, H. (1992) 'A common factors therapy for depression', in J.C. Norcross and M.R. Goldfried (eds), *Handbook of Psychotherapy Integration*. New York: Basic Books.

Baker, N. (ed.) (1996) *Building a Relational Society: New Priorities for Public Policy*. Aldershot: Arena.

Bellack, A.S. and Hersen, M. (eds) (1990) *Handbook of Comparative Treatments for Adult Disorders*. New York: Wiley.

Benjamin, J. (1998) *Shadow of the Other: Intersubjectivity and Gender in Psychoanalysis*. London: Routledge.

Benson, H. (1996) *Timeless Healing: The Power and Biology of Belief*. London: Simon & Schuster.

Beyebach, M. and Carranza, V.E. (1997) 'Therapeutic interaction and drop-out: measuring relational communication in solution-focused therapy', *Journal of Family Therapy*, 19: 173–212.

Biestek, F.P. (1961) *The Casework Relationship*. London: Unwin University Books.

Bohm, D. (1980) *Wholeness and the Implicate Order*. London: Routledge.

Bohm, D. (1996) *On Dialogue*. London: Routledge.

Bordin, E.S. (1979) 'The generalizability of the psychoanalytic concept of the working alliance', *Psychotherapy: Theory, Research and Practice*, 16 (3): 252–60.

Brazelton, T.B. and Cramer, B.T. (1991) *The Earliest Relationship: Parents, Infants and the Drama of Early Attachment*. London: Karnac.

Brazier, D. (1993) 'The necessary condition is love: going beyond self in the person-centred approach', in D. Brazier (ed.), *Beyond Carl Rogers*. London: Constable.

Buber, M. (1965) *Between Man and Man*. New York: Macmillan.

Buber, M. (1970) *I and Thou* (trans. W. Kaufmann). Edinburgh: T. & T. Clark.

Bugental, J.F.T. (1987) *The Art of the Psychotherapist*. New York: Norton.

Campbell, B. (1975) 'Feelings and survival: an evolutionary perspective', in A. Janov and E.M. Holden, *Primal Man: The New Consciousness*. New York: Thomas Y. Crowell.

Carkhuff, R.R. (1969) *Helping and Human Relations*, vol. 2: *Practice and Research*. New York: Holt, Rinehart & Winston.

Cashdan, S. (1988) *Object Relations Therapy: Using the Relationship*. New York: Norton.

Clarkson, P. (1995) *The Therapeutic Relationship*. London: Whurr.

Cloud, D. (1998) *Control and Consolation in American Culture and Politics: Rhetoric of Therapy*. Thousand Oaks, CA: Sage.

Crossley, N. (1996) *Intersubjectivity: The Fabric of Social Becoming*. London: Sage.

Curtis, J.M. (1981) 'Determinants of the therapeutic bond: how to engage patients', *Psychological Reports*, 49: 415–19.

de Maré, P., Piper, R. and Thompson, S. (1991) *Koinonia: From Hate, through Dialogue, to Culture in the Large Group*. London: Karnac.

Dinnage, R. (1989) *One to One: Experiences of Psychotherapy*. Harmondsworth: Penguin.

Dorn, F.J. (1984) *Counseling as Applied Social Psychology: An Introduction to the Social Influence Model*. Springfield, IL: Charles C. Thomas.

Dossey, L. (1994) *Healing Words*. San Francisco: Harper & Row.

Dryden, W. (1989) 'The therapeutic alliance as an integrating framework', in W. Dryden (ed.), *Key Issues for Counselling in Action*. London: Sage.

Dryden, W. and Feltham, C. (1994) *Developing the Practice of Counselling*. London: Sage.

Duck, S. (1986) *Human Relationships: An Introduction to Social Psychology*. London: Sage.

Dupont-Joshua, A. (1996) 'Race, culture and the therapeutic relationship: working with difference creatively', *Counselling*, 7 (3): 220–3.

Egan, G. (1990) *The Skilled Helper* (4th edn). Pacific Grove, CA: Brooks/Cole.

Egan, G. (1994) *The Skilled Helper* (5th edn). Pacific Grove, CA: Brooks/Cole.

Ehrenwald, J. (ed.) (1976) *The History of Psychotherapy*. Northvale, NJ: Aronson.

Ellenberger, H.F. (1970) *The Discovery of the Unconscious: The History and Evolution of Dynamic Psychiatry*. New York: Basic Books.

Frank, J.D. (1973) *Persuasion and Healing*. New York: Schocken.

Friedman, B. (1992) *Partners in Healing: Redistributing Power in the Counselor-Client Relationship*. San José, CA: Resource Publications.

Friedman, M.S. (1996) 'The dialogical psychotherapy movement', *The Journal of Imago Relationship Therapy*, 1 (1): 43–53.

Fromm, E. (1975) *The Art of Loving*. London: Unwin.

Gelso, C.J. and Carter, J.A. (1985) 'The relationship in counseling and psychotherapy: components, consequences, and theoretical antecedents', *The Counseling Psychologist*, 13 (2): 155–243.

Giddens, A. (1991) *Modernity and Self-Identity: Self and Society in the Late Modern Age*. Cambridge: Polity Press.

Goldberg, C. (1977) *Therapeutic Partnership: Ethical Concerns in Psychotherapy*. New York: Springer.

Greenson, R.R. (1967) *The Technique and Practice of Psycho-Analysis*. London: Hogarth Press.

Grossinger, R. (1982) *Planet Medicine: From Stone-Age Shamanism to Post-Industrial Healing* (rev. edn). Boulder, CO: Shambala.

Gunzberg, J.C. (1997) *Healing through Meeting: Martin Buber's Conversational Approach to Psychotherapy*. London: Jessica Kingsley.

Halmos, P. (1965) *The Faith of the Counsellors*. London: Constable.

Hammond, D.C., Hepworth, D.H. and Smith, V.G. (1977) *Improving Therapeutic Communication: A Guide for Developing Effective Techniques*. San Francisco: Jossey-Bass.

Havens, L. (1989) *A Safe Place: Laying the Groundwork of Psychotherapy*. Cambridge, MA: Harvard University Press.

Hendrick, S.S. (1995) 'Close relationships research: applications to counseling psychology', *The Counseling Psychologist*, 23 (4): 649–65.

Heyward, C. (1993) *When Boundaries Betray Us: Beyond Illusions of What is Ethical in Therapy and Life*. San Francisco: HarperCollins.

Hobson, R.F. (1985) *Forms of Feeling: The Heart of Psychotherapy*. London: Tavistock.

Horvath, A.O. and Greenberg, L. (eds) (1994) *The Working Alliance: Theory, Research and Practice*. Chichester: Wiley.

Howard, G.S., Nance, G.W. and Myers, P. (1987) *Adaptive Counseling and Therapy*. San Francisco: Jossey-Bass.

Howe, D. (1993) *On Being a Client: Understanding the Process of Counselling and Psychotherapy*. London: Sage.

Hurding, R.F. (1985) *Roots and Shoots: A Guide to Counselling and Psychotherapy*. London: Hodder & Stoughton.

Hycner, R.H. (1991) *Between Person and Person: Toward a Dialogical Psychotherapy*. Highland, NY: Center for Gestalt Development.

Illich, I. (1973) *Celebration of Awareness*. Harmondsworth: Penguin.

Josselson, R. (1996) *The Space between Us: Exploring the Dimensions of Human Relationships*. Thousand Oaks, CA: Sage.

Kagan, N. (1980) *Interpersonal Process Recall: A Method of Influencing Human Interaction*. Houston, TX: Mason Media.

Kahn, M. (1991) *Between Therapist and Client: The New Relationship*. New York: Freeman.

Kakar, S. (1982) *Shamans, Mystics and Doctors*. London: Unwin.

Kaminer, W. (1992) *I'm Dysfunctional, You're Dysfunctional: The Recovery Movement and Other Self-Help Fashions*. New York: Addison-Wesley.

Karasu, T.B. (1992) *Wisdom in the Practice of Psychotherapy*. New York: Basic Books.

Kiev, A. (ed.) (1964) *Magic, Faith and Healing*. New York: Free Press.

Klein, J. (1987) *Our Need for Others and its Roots in Infancy*. London: Tavistock.

Krause, I.B. (1998) *Therapy across Culture*. London: Sage.

Langs, R. (1976) *The Bipersonal Field*. New York: Aronson.

Langs, R. (1996) *The Evolution of the Emotion-Processing Mind*. London: Karnac.

Lazarus, A.A. (1993) 'Tailoring the therapeutic relationship, or being an authentic chameleon', *Psychotherapy*, 30 (3): 404–7.

Lewis, C.S. (1963) *The Four Loves*. London: Fontana.

Lomas, P. (1987) *The Limits of Interpretation*. Harmondsworth: Penguin.

Macmurray, J. (1961) *Persons in Relation*. London: Faber.

Mahrer, A.R. (1997) 'Experiential psychotherapy', in C. Feltham (ed.), *Which Psychotherapy?: Leading Exponents Explain their Differences*. London: Sage.

Mair, M. (1989) *Between Psychology and Psychotherapy: A Poetics of Experience*. London: Routledge.

Maracek, J. and Kravetz, D. (1998) 'Power and agency in feminist therapy', in I.B. Seu and M.C. Heenan (eds), *Feminism and Psychotherapy: Reflections on Contemporary Theories and Practices*. London: Sage.

Maroda, K. (1991) *The Power of Countertransference*. Northvale, NJ: Aronson.

May, R. (1992) *The Art of Counselling* (rev. edn). London: Souvenir.

McLellan, B. (1995) *Beyond Psychoppression: A Feminist Alternative Therapy*. North Melbourne: Spinifex.

McLeod, J. (1997) *Narrative and Psychotherapy*. London: Sage.

Mearns, D. (1996) 'Working at relational depth with clients in person-centred therapy', *Counselling*, 7 (4): 306-11.

Mehrabian, A. (1971) *Silent Messages*. Belmont, CA: Wadsworth.

Moore, T. (1994) *Soul Mates: Honouring the Mysteries of Love and Relationship*. Shaftesbury: Element.

Morgan, S. (1995) *Helping Relationships in Mental Health*. London: Chapman & Hall.

Oldfield, S. (1983) *The Counselling Relationship: A Study of the Client's Experience*. London: Routledge & Kegan Paul.

Patterson, C.H. (1974) *Relationship Counseling and Psychotherapy*. New York: Harper & Row.

Robertiello, R.C. and Schoenewolf, G. (1987) *101 Common Therapeutic Blunders: Countertransference and Counterresistance in Psychotherapy*. Northvale, NJ: Aronson.

Robinson, W.P. (1996) *Deceit, Delusion, and Detection*. Thousand Oaks, CA: Sage.

Rogers, C.R. (1951) *Client-Centered Therapy*. London: Constable.

Rogers, C.R. (1957) 'The necessary and sufficient conditions of therapeutic personality change', *Journal of Consulting Psychology*, 21 (2): 95-103.

Roth, A. and Fonagy, P. (1996) *What Works For Whom?* New York: Guilford.

Rusk, T. (1991) *Instead of Therapy: Help Yourself Change and Change the Help You're Getting*. Carson, CA: Hay House.

Rutter, M. (1989) *Sex in the Forbidden Zone*. London: Mandala.

Sampson, E.E. (1993) *Celebrating the Other: A Dialogic Account of Human Nature*. New York: Harvester Wheatsheaf.

Samuels, A. (1985) *Jung and the Post-Jungians*. London: Routledge & Kegan Paul.

Sandler, J., Dare, C. and Holder, A. (1992) *The Patient and the Analyst* (2nd edn, revised and expanded by J. Sandler and A.U. Dreher). London: Karnac.

Sayers, J. (1991) *Mothering Psychoanalysis*. Harmondsworth: Penguin.

Schaap, C., Bennun, I., Schindler, L. and Hoogduin, K. (1993) *The Therapeutic Relationship in Behavioural Psychotherapy*. Chichester: Wiley.

Schwartz-Salant, N. (1998) *The Mystery of Human Relationship: Alchemy and the Transformation of the Self*. London: Routledge.

Sills, C. (ed.) (1997) *Contracts in Counselling*. London: Sage.

Silverman, D. (1997) *Discourses of Counselling: HIV Counselling as Social Interaction*. London: Sage.

Smail, D. (1993) *The Origins of Unhappiness*. London: HarperCollins.

Smith, D.L. (1999) 'Maintaining boundaries in psychotherapy: a view from evolutionary psycho-analysis', in C. Feltham (ed.), *Controversies in Psychotherapy and Counselling*. London: Sage.

Stein, M. (ed.) (1995) *The Interactive Field in Analysis*, vol. 1. Wilmette, IL: Chiron.

Steiner, C. (1974) *Scripts People Live*. New York: Grove Weidenfeld.

Stern, D. (1985) *The Interpersonal World of the Infant*. New York: Basic Books.

Stevens, A. and Price, J. (1996) *Evolutionary Psychiatry*. London: Routledge.

Strong, S. (1968) 'Counseling: an interpersonal influence process', *Journal of Counseling Psychology*, 15: 215-24.

Symington, N. (1994) *Emotion and Spirit: Questioning the Claims of Psychoanalysis and Religion*. London: Cassell.

Szsaz, T. and Hollander, M.H. (1956) 'A contribution to the philosophy of medicine: the basic models of the doctor-patient relationship', *Archives of Internal Medicine*, 97: 585-92.

Tart, C.T. (1975) 'The physical universe, the spiritual universe, and the paranormal', in C.T. Tart (ed.), *Transpersonal Psychologies*. New York: Harper & Row.

Thorne, B. (1991) *Person-Centred Counselling: Therapeutic and Spiritual Dimensions*. London: Whurr.

Ullman, M. (1991) 'An approach to closeness: dream sharing in a small group setting', in H.A. Wilmer (ed.), *Closeness in Personal and Professional Relationships*. Boston, MA: Shambala.

Weldon, F. (1999) 'Mind at the end of its tether', in C. Feltham (ed.), *Controversies in Psychotherapy and Counselling*. London: Sage.

West, W. (1997) 'Integrating counselling, psychotherapy and healing: an inquiry into counsellors and psychotherapists whose work includes healing', *British Journal of Guidance and Counselling*, 25 (3): 291-311.

Wilmer, H.A. (ed.) (1992) *Closeness in Personal and Professional Relationships*. Boston, MA: Shambala.

Winstead, B.A., Derlega, V.J., Lewis, R.J. and Margulis, S.T. (1988) 'Understanding the therapeutic relationship as a personal relationship', *Journal of Social and Personal Relationships*, 5: 109-25.

Yalom, I.D. (1991) *Love's Executioner and Other Tales of Psychotherapy*. Harmondsworth: Penguin.

Yalom, I.D. and Elkin, G. (1974) *Every Day Gets a Little Closer: A Twice-Told Therapy*. New York: Basic Books.

Zeldin, T. (1994) *An Intimate History of Humanity*. London: Sinclair-Stevenson.

Zetzel, E.R. (1956) 'Current concepts of transference', *International Journal of Psycho-Analysis*, 37: 369-76.

2 *The Relationship in Psychodynamic Counselling*

Jeremy Holmes

Without a therapeutic relationship there can be no therapy. This truism applies to all forms of counselling and therapy even if the relationship is seen mainly as an adjunct to the presumed effective component, which might, for example, be a set of homework tasks, practising specific relaxation techniques, or a structural intervention in family therapy. Even in bibliotherapy the books will have been recommended by counsellors with whom their clients have a relationship of some kind. In psychodynamic counselling, however, rather than being a vehicle for the delivery of a specific modality of therapy, the relationship is itself the major focus of therapeutic work. For the psychodynamic clinician, the medium is the mutative element.

Distinctive Features of the Psychodynamic Counselling Relationship

The therapeutic relationship is central to psychic change in two main ways, one common to all therapies, the other specific to psychodynamic work.

Common Factors in Counselling

The therapeutic relationship is perhaps the most important of the 'common factors' which contribute to the effectiveness of all forms of counselling. In entering counselling the client begins to form a relationship with someone who aims to be interested, concerned, neutral, non-judgemental, accepting, consistent, stable, balanced, benign, trustworthy, warm and nurturing – a daunting ideal! This relationship is the route to the other common factors which include being offered an explanatory framework within which the client's distress can be understood, the instillation of hope or 'remoralization', and a set of active steps which can be taken towards change. In psychodynamic work the latter may comprise no more than a contract for regular meetings and an injunction for the client to follow Freud's 'basic rule' – to say whatever is in the client's mind, however irrelevant, embarrassing or personal it may appear to be.

Frank's (1961) notion of the relationship as a key therapeutic factor is supported by research findings focusing on the 'therapeutic alliance'. The strength of this alliance can be measured in objective and subjective ways, each of which show that it is the single most important factor in determining the outcome of therapy. Failure to turn up at appointments, lateness, or attempts to renegotiate the therapeutic contract early in therapy are all poor prognostic signs, and predict dropping out, and/or failure to benefit from treatment. Similarly, when clients are asked to rate their feelings about the therapist and therapy in the first three sessions, those who report positive feelings at this early stage are likely to do well in the course of therapy, while those who are doubtful have, on the whole, a poor outcome. The influence of the therapeutic alliance far outweighs modality of therapy as a determinant of outcome – in other words, it matters far more how good the therapeutic alliance is than which particular type of counselling is offered (Orlinsky et al., 1994).

In view of this, it is important to consider what are the key components of the therapeutic alliance. These can be divided into therapist factors and client factors. The therapist must be a 'good listener', confident in herself and in her methods, respectful of the client, able to maintain boundaries, firm in her limits, while at the same time being flexible enough to adapt her technique to the needs of the particular client. The most important client factors are motivation and positive expectations of change – if the client thinks that therapy is likely to help, it probably will; if not, not. Psychodynamic counselling may be especially vulnerable here, since its methods are far less obvious and dependent on 'common sense' than are, for example, cognitive behavioural or supportive approaches.

The Specific Contribution of Psychodynamics

Despite this, psychodynamic approaches can claim one significant advantage over other modalities of counselling. The majority of clients who seek help through counselling are suffering from relationship difficulties: they want intimacy but cannot achieve it, or feel stuck in relationships which make them unhappy. While psychodynamic approaches may involve talking around these issues, in the end the key to change is the therapeutic relationship itself, which will manifest the very problem of which the client is complaining. Thus the person who finds it difficult to get close to a partner will like as not be hard to reach in counselling; someone who forms clinging dependent relationships in outside life will similarly become dependent on their counsellor. As will be discussed below, these manifestations may be quite subtle, and are best seen as applying to the relationship *as a whole* – that is, to the counsellor plus client – and not necessarily simply to the client himself. For example, a woman who seeks help because of angry outbursts towards her children may be meek and docile in therapy, but leave the counsellor with feelings of bottled up fury at the end of each session.

A central feature then of psychodynamic approaches to the counselling relationship is that the relationship itself becomes an object of scrutiny and a vehicle for change. The minutiae of counsellor–client interaction at both a behavioural and emotional level are the stuff of the treatment: when and why either party is slightly late, or 'forgets' to announce that they will be away next week, the interplay of the client's feelings for the counsellor and her responses – these are all grist to the psychodynamic mill. That is not to say that psychodynamics concentrates exclusively on the therapeutic relationship – the principle, like all rules in counselling has to be applied flexibly and is much more applicable to some clients than to others. There is usually much work to be done in discussing psychodynamic aspects of the client's external life, which has nothing directly to do with the counselling relationship, but in the end the principles learned will also come up in the counselling relationship. There is nothing more convincing to a client than suddenly to see that he is doing to the counsellor exactly what he does to his partner, and to begin to grasp the underlying forces which push him in that direction.

What do we Mean by 'Psychodynamic'?

The discussion has proceeded thus far without defining what is meant by 'psychodynamic'. Freud postulated a 'dynamic' unconscious in the sense that it represents not just thoughts and emotions which happen to be out of awareness (in psychoanalytic terminology 'pre-conscious'), but also those that have a 'certain dynamic character', and are *actively* kept apart from consciousness in spite of their intensity and activity (Freud, 1912: 434). In psychoanalytic metapsychology psychodynamics is intimately connected with repression and splitting.

For Freud the dynamic nature of the psyche was particularly evident in two kinds of clinical phenomena, both of which are still relevant to contemporary counselling. Firstly was the problem of resistance, in which clients failed to respond to therapy despite good rational reasons for doing so, suggesting a part of the mind actively opposed to change, preferring to cling to maladaptive ways of behaving, rather than relinquish the perverse satisfactions of destructiveness or a sick role. Secondly, the phenomenon of post-traumatic amnesia (still the subject of passionate debate a century later) led Freud to postulate an active – and hence dynamic – banishment of painful memories from consciousness. He believed that these repressed, or partially repressed memories of painful experiences continued to influence behaviour and to produce symptoms.

We can illustrate some of these points with an example.

The sequelae of violence

A man in his early 50s was referred for counselling because of depression following a car crash a year previously in which he had been hit head-on by an oncoming vehicle. He was not seriously physically hurt, but had been miserable and unable to cope ever since.

He had previously run a successful building firm, but was finding it increasingly difficult to cope, especially with the paperwork involved in the business. When asked at the start of the assessment interview what he thought about the idea of counselling, he replied that he was highly sceptical, and he didn't think it was for him, but nevertheless, he confessed, he was pretty desperate to get something done about himself.

Before the accident, his life had gone reasonably well, and he was happily married with two grown-up sons, one of whom worked with him in the business. When asked about his childhood he became hesitant and tearful, and said he would 'rather not talk about it'. However he let it be known that his father, a publican, had been extremely violent, and had beaten his sons mercilessly throughout their childhood. He also described how guilty he felt about his depression, and how he felt he should be able to pull himself together: 'in our family illness wasn't tolerated. You were allowed one day in bed if you had the 'flu, and that was it. If you still felt ill after that it was put down as whinging.'

'No wonder you felt hesitant about coming here', said the counsellor; 'seeing someone like me is tantamount to admitting weakness and talking about things as whinging.'

The client then described the accident in detail and how when he saw the oncoming car he knew the driver had 'lost it'. The counsellor suggested that this was particularly traumatic because it might have reminded him of how his father 'lost it', when he was administering the beatings, and that he had been as powerless to stop the accident as he had been to prevent his father's rages. At this point the client seemed visibly to relax and started crying openly, talking about how desperate he felt and revealing his suicidal thoughts.

Several features stand out in this case which illustrate the nature of psychodynamics. Firstly, the client is highly suspicious of the counsellor and the whole counselling process. He invests the counselling relationship with a particular emotional charge – he is wary, confesses that it is not for him – that these imputations of unconscious meaning do not belong to the overt contract of client-with-problem meets counsellor-trying-to-help. A part of the mind is activated by the counselling situation which seems to exert a dynamic influence on the client, irrespective of the 'reality' of the relationship being offered by the counsellor.

Next he tells the counsellor that he would 'rather not talk' about his childhood, while looking worried and sad as he does so.

He seems to be hinting at painful memories which, by not being talked about, can be kept out of awareness, but which threaten to overwhelm his precarious psychic equilibrium. We can easily visualize a 'dynamic' struggle within his mind between the wish to communicate his past pain, and the fear that to do so might lead to some sort of breakdown of his normal modes of coping. Moreover, he points to another part of the mind, a set of expectations and prohibitions derived from childhood, which insists that to show vulnerability is 'bad', and that to maintain a stiff upper lip is the way to gain approval. Here the superego is exerting its dynamic influence on the way he approaches his difficulties.

In a similar vein, the accident itself can be understood in dynamic terms. When he said to himself that the other driver had 'lost it', memories of his father being out of control and his own powerlessness as a little boy were reawakened. That dynamic meant that the accident, by reactivating psychic trauma from childhood, had a significance for the client far beyond the actual trauma inflicted on either his car or his body.

Finally, these factors all combined to influence the counselling relationship, in that the counsellor was viewed with some suspicion and resistance (which lessened as the interview proceeded), the client being braced against counselling being used, like his father's belt, to batter his defences and humiliate him.

Conceptualizing the Counselling Relationship

I shall now pick out five key psychodynamic concepts for more detailed discussion.

Patterns of Defence and Preconception: Malan's Triangles

David Malan, a psychoanalyst particularly interested in brief psychodynamic therapies, encapsulated the essence of psychodynamics in his 'two triangles' – the 'triangle of defence' and the 'triangle of person' (Malan, 1996).

The *triangle of defence* comprises three elements – anxiety, defence, and a 'hidden impulse' – which together describe the balance of forces influencing an individual's psychic life. For example, the client described above had a wish/need to express his distress and rage towards the driver who hit him, and ultimately to his abusive father. These feelings were well hidden –

partially or wholly repressed. But, since the accident, he had not been able to relax: he felt anxious and on edge, and depressed about himself and his situation. His defences, which normally kept strong feelings at bay, thereby preserving psychic equilibrium, albeit at the expense of restricting his emotional life, were partially de-activated. The same theme is played out in the *triangle of person* (the therapist/counsellor, the 'other', and the parental relationship). The client's 'wariness', evident from the moment of meeting the counsellor, linked with his feelings towards his abusive father, and was justified in relation to the 'other' who had caused the crash, but also towards people in general with whom he was cautious in expressing his feelings.

The psychodynamic counsellor is always on the lookout for a common theme – or *focus* (see below) – that brings together the counselling relationship itself, the client's attitude towards significant others in his world, and past patterns of relationship, especially with parents. The search for these underlying patterns or meanings are characteristic of psychodynamic approaches generally.

An important aspect of the psychodynamic approach is an emphasis on the pervasiveness of defences. Clients can be classified according to their use of 'primitive' defences such as splitting or dissociation, intermediate defences such as intellectualization, somatization and repression, or 'mature' defences such as humour and sublimation. Defences serve to maintain the integrity of the personality, albeit often at the cost of restrictions in emotional life. In consequence there is a built-in *resistance* to change and much of the work of psychodynamic counselling may focus on this resistance, and not infrequently is defeated by it.

Transference and Countertransference

Transference, a key concept in psychodynamic counselling, can also be undertood in terms of Malan's triangles. It refers to the way in which patterns of feeling from the past break through into contemporary relationships, thereby distorting individuals' perceptions of themselves and those with whom they are connected. The client we have discussed approached his counsellor *as though* he were his father. He was unaware of this, merely experiencing a strong feeling of unease and wariness as he entered the counselling situation. This kind of transferential response is often intensified at times of anxiety, when people tend to fall back on stereotyped ways of reacting, derived from the past. One of the aims of psychodynamic counselling is to help the client become more aware of these patterns; hence the need to keep a certain level of stress in the counselling relationship (always compatible with a working therapeutic alliance). If the counsellor is over-friendly and puts the client too much at her ease, the likelihood of these transferential patterns emerging may be diminished.

Freud originally conceived countertransference as the mirror-image of transference, describing ways in which the counsellor's reactions to the client can also be shaped by preconceptions and patterns from the past. For example, had the counsellor in the case described himself had a father who was distant and rejecting, he might have found the client's 'wariness' very threatening, and gone out of his way to please him, thereby exaggerating the client's sick-role, rather than helping him to overcome it. This would then have given the counsellor the perverse (even if completely unconscious) satisfaction of seeing the transferential object (who had become in the counsellor's mind a client–father amalgam) disabled and under his control.

This kind of possibility led Freud to argue that therapists and counsellors needed to have their own therapy in order to be aware of these countertransferential forces, which he compared with the 'blind spot' in the visual field – a built-in imperfection in the perceptual system, which, if ignored leads to distortion and lacunae, but once recognized, can be taken account of. Personal therapy is integral to training in psychodynamic counselling.

A significant shift occurred in contemporary approaches to countertransference (Bateman and Holmes, 1995), when it was realized that the counsellor's emotional response to the client was not necessarily a product of countertransference in the classical sense of reflecting the counsellor's own blind spots, but could be a reflection of the inner world of the client. To return to our example: at one point in the initial interview the counsellor felt quite irritated with the client's sullen withdrawal and near-monosyllabic utterances, and an image came into his mind of him shaking the client into life. As he reflected on this he could see how he had been unconsciously 'shaped' by the client's material into feelings and reactions that were typical of the client's description of his relationship with his abusive father. These counter-transference responses were not so much a manifestation of his own emotional life, but rather originated in the *client's* unconscious need to structure the world in familiar ways. Here countertransference, initially seen by Freud as a block to good therapy, is used in the service of deeper understanding of the client.

This new angle on countertransference has important technical implications. In interacting with the client, the counsellor needs simultaneously to be able to attend to his own inner world, using his reactions and fantasies as a clue to possible themes that are relevant to the client – to be a participant observer, or an observing participant. Had the counsellor found, for example, his mind wandering to thoughts of the Middle East conflict while listening to the client, he might have been alerted to the possibility of suppressed aggression and resentment which the client dared not express directly for fear of rejection.

Projective Identification

Discussion of countertranference leads on to the important, if complex and sometimes obscure concept of projective identification (PI) that is central to much contemporary psychodynamic thinking.

The notion of projection is relatively straightforward as a form of emotional perceptual distortion, attributing to others characteristics that more properly belong to the self. The idealization of pop stars or footballers, or the denigration of one's enemies are based on projective processes, in which wished-for – or hated – aspects of the self are transferred on to convenient recipients. In Klein's original formulation, projective identification was seen as an extension of this process in which the infant projects unwanted aspects of the self not just 'on to' but 'into' the 'object' (that is, significant other) (Hinshelwood, 1989). Thus the child feels rage and envy towards the frustrating mother, but these feelings threaten to overwhelm more benign perceptions and so are projected into what becomes a hated 'bad mother', thereby enabling the child to hold on to an image of a 'good mother' within himself. The mother is *identified* with this projection – hence the term projective identification.

In this early formulation PI is essentially a 'primitive' defence mechanism. Subsequent Kleinian authors, especially Bion, extended the concept in three main ways (Hinshelwood, 1989). Firstly, it was realized that PI is a non-verbal method of *communication* of feelings in which the object is induced to experience the subject's own painful affect. Secondly, Bion saw that PI applied not just to negative emotions, but that, as described above under counter-transference, it underpinned normal empathy as well. Thirdly, he described a sequence in which the baby projects painful feelings into the mother who then contains or 'holds' them, 'detoxifies' them within her psyche, and then 'returns' them to the infant who could then re-introject them in a manageable form.

For example a baby might wake crying in the night. The mother goes to him, sees that he is wet, and starts to change his nappy; meanwhile the child continues to scream and cry blue murder. The mother all the while makes soothing remarks such as 'Ah, you are wet', 'Poor old chap', etc. Eventually the changing is over, the child is hugged and pacified and returns to sleep. The child has by PI let his other know how he feels; he blames the 'bad mother' for making him wet, but allows the 'good mother' to soothe him. As this sort of sequence is repeated over and over again, he inter-nalizes the soothing process. Eventually he will learn how to soothe himself, and be able to report on uncomfortable experi-ences: 'I feel furious', 'I am unhappy', etc.

All this is clearly relevant to psychodynamic counselling. The counsellor uses her empathy all the time; she is aware of how, via PI, her emotions and fantasies may reflect the client's unbearable feelings which he can only communicate in this 'primitive' way. The process of counselling is developmental in that the aim is to help the client to move from non-verbal modes of communication and reliance on others to hold and detoxify his distress, towards self-soothing and more direct verbal expression of feelings. In addition, 'bad mother' feelings based on primitive blaming and envy are lessened, and no longer have to be held separate from the 'good mother'.

Patterns of Attachment

Thus far we have been concerned with ways of conceptualizing the inner world of the client, and his perceptions of the counsel-ling situation. But counsellor and client do not just have feelings: they also *behave* in certain ways towards one another. They form a 'real' as well as a transferential relationship. The most compre-hensive account of this aspect of psychodynamic counselling comes from attachment theory (AT) (Holmes, 1993). AT holds that at times of illness or distress people (and other mammals) will seek out caregivers for protection and comfort. This attachment behaviour is assuaged by effective caregiving, which enables the individual then to relax and explore his environment, play, or pursue whatever his goals may be. Attachment patterns may be 'secure' or 'insecure'. In the absence of secure attachment, or (which is much the same thing) the presence of continuing threat, attachment behaviours continue to be activated, and exploration inhibited.

The relevance of this to psychodynamic counselling is that the counsellor attempts to provide conditions of secure attachment, or, to use the language of AT, to be a 'secure base' for clients. Secure base conditions require a warm, safe, predictable environment with an attachment figure (the counsellor) who is empathic, responsive and able to attune to the client's emotional needs, while at the same time maintaining appropriate boundaries. This ideal scenario enables the client, in Winnicott's (1971) famous paradox, to be 'alone in the presence of the other' and so continue with his voyage of self-discovery. Of course reality is not quite like that. Both client and counsellor bring to their relationship a past attachment history. The client is likely to have had insecure attachment experiences which means that he will, at times at least, mistrust his attachment figure. To oversimplify, he will either see the counsellor as unpredictable and so cling to her in the hope of thereby maintaining the attachment bond, or he will fear rejection and so keep a safe distance from her, while maintaining the link which, however attenuated, is still his lifeline.

Furthermore, the counsellor also has her attachment patterns which will influence her response to the client. Research (Dozier at al., 1994) suggests that insecure clinicians tend to see their own needs reflected in the client and so amplify whatever attachment pattern is there, while secure clinicians tend to redress the balance and compensate for their client's habitual patterns. Thus clinging clients will elicit from insecure clinicians more and more care, while secure clinicians will be firm with boundaries with this client group. Conversely insecure clinicians whose clients keep their distance, will go along with this, leading to early drop out or superficial work; conversely secure clinicans will try to get behind their client's avoidance to the warded-off pain it protects.

A key finding of attachment research has been the link between childhood attachment patterns and narrative style in adult life (Holmes, 1996). The way a person talks about themselves and their biography reflects habitual patterns of attachment. Children who have been securely attached are able when adult to talk about themselves and their pain in a coherent fluent way. Their narratives are imbued with emotion, but not overwhelmed by it. By contrast people with an avoidant history of attachment tend to have a dismissive narrative style, in which they have few memories of childhood and describe them in a sparse unelaborated way. Those enmeshed individuals who have physically clung to an inconsistent attachment figure tend by contrast to speak in a way that matches this, clinging on to their misery, as though overwhelmed by it. Some children appear to fail to make coherent attachment patterns at all, especially if their parents have been the subject of major trauma; their narrative styles tend to be incoherent and hard to follow, with breaks in logical continuity of their speech.

The scientific findings of links between childhood attachment and adult narrative provide some evidence to support one of the basic premises of psychodynamic counselling – the importance of early childhood experience as a determinant of adult relationship difficulties. It also informs the listening strategy of the counsellor, who will infer from the client's narrative style what kind of relationship patterns they habitually form and have been subjected to in the past.

The Therapeutic Benefit of a Relationship

What is it about a therapeutic relationship that makes clients feel better – about themselves, their problems, and their life generally? Although there is much that is yet to be understood about this, some sort of formulation is needed if counsellors are to proceed with their work in good faith. Three kinds of answers can be summarized, corresponding roughly to the Bowlby-Winnicott-Bion interpersonal model, that of ego psychology, and, more recently, to a 'theory of mind' approach that is particularly associated with the work of Fonagy (1991).

From the attachment perspective described above, the key contribution of the counsellor is to provide a secure base for the troubled client. In childhood the secure base is vested in the caregiver, and this situation is reproduced in counselling. But in adult life a key component of personal security lies not in external relationships – however important these may be – but in an individual's *sense of self*. Secure base in childhood leads to strong sense of self in adult life, as does effective counselling or psychotherapy. This view can be linked with the ideas of Winnicott and Bion, suggesting that *holding* and *containment* are vital aspects of the ˙counselling relationship. The capacity to hold one's self together, including negative and positive aspects of emotion (the essence of the Kleinian 'depressive position') arises out of positive holding experiences, again, either in childhood or in counselling/ therapy. Psychodynamic counselling 'works' via the capacity of the counsellor to provide a secure base or holding environment, which is then internalized by the client.

A different viewpoint arises out of the ego psychology school of psychoanalysis, which argues that the essence of successful treatment is strengthening of the ego, making it more adaptable and with a greater repertoire of responses: less in thrall to drives and desires on the one hand, or dominated by the prohibitions of the superego on the other. The view that the success of dynamic counselling arises out of clients' *insight* into themselves and their motivations can be linked with this, since self-knowledge is a significant component in enhancing flexibility in one's relationships and dealings with the world generally. A bridge exists here with cognitive counselling, since the notion of *metacognitive monitoring* is another way of viewing this capacity to stand back from one's thoughts and see them for what they are.

This leads on to the third strand – the idea that counselling enhances what Fonagy (1991) calls *reflexive function* – the capacity to reflect upon one's self and one's actions, and those of others. Fonagy suggests that successful relationships require the participants to have a *theory of mind* in relation to their significant others – that is, to believe that those they are close to have feelings and an internal world of their own. They suggest that the development of this theory of mind arises out of empathic parenting. If the parent sees his or her children as sentient beings, with feelings and perspectives of their own, then those children as they grow up will likewise experience others in the same way. Conversely, children who are treated as things rather than subjects, will tend to see others similarly.

In this model, interpretations, the key interventions of psychodynamic counselling, are essentially attempts to formulate aspects of the client's mind – what the counsellor thinks about what the client is thinking (client-centred interpretations), or what the counsellor thinks the client is thinking about what the counsellor is thinking (counsellor-centred interpretations) (Steiner, 1993). This kind of dialogue, or meeting of minds, leads to enhanced reflexive function, greater self-awareness and awareness of others, and hence greater autonomy and capacity for intimacy (Holmes, 1996).

The Psychodynamic Relationship in Practice

How then does the psychodynamic counsellor set about trying to help her client? Psychodynamic techniques follow logically from the theoretical framework outlined above.

Setting and Style

A central requirement for psychodynamic work is a safe, reliable, and reasonably neutral setting, limited by secure boundaries of place and time. Psychodynamic work is seriously compromised if it is carried out in corridors, or in rooms where there are liable to be interruptions, at irregular times, with sessions of variable length, or by a counsellor whose style and dress varies wildly from one meeting to the next. Junior doctors doing psychodynamic counselling need to remove their 'bleeps' before starting sessions! A clear contract for agreed times and length of session (usually, by convention, 50 minutes) is reached at the start of counselling, and if the treatment is to be time-limited, for the number of sessions (the latter to be revised if necessary).

The importance of the reliable and neutral setting is that it provides a stable backdrop against which the turbulence of the patient's unconscious manifestations can be noted and brought into focus. If the counsellor is herself habitually late in starting sessions, the client's possible lateness will not be so apparent, and its meaning will be obscured: thus it would be difficult to distinguish lateness as a retaliation, from, say, lateness as a manifestation of hopelessness.

The same applies to the ending of sessions. Beginner counsellors frequently allow sessions to 'run on', especially if the client brings up an important topic just at the end. This too is contrary to the spirit of psychodynamic work, where the *form* of a client's communication, shaped by the unconscious, may be more important than its *content*. Such clients may feel so anxious about talking about significant topics – perhaps for fear of being rejected or ignored – that they can only bear to do so at the eleventh hour, and that needs to be addressed first, before the topic itself can be tackled. The counsellor needs to feel comfortable about saying 'let's come back to that next week', and ending the session promptly. To cut the client off in this way means that the counsellor has to be self-confident enough to set firm boundaries without feeling she is being aggressive – an issue which may need to be dealt with in supervision or personal therapy.

Similarly, the neutrality and reticence of the psychodynamic counsellor, and the tendency to be reticent ('opaque') about personal details, is not an arbitary uptightness typical of this mode of counselling, but flows from the need to maintain an absolute focus on the client and his or her projections. Self-revelation is tempting to beginner counsellors as a 'joining' technique at the start of counselling, but it is better to start somewhat austere and then relax as the therapy progresses, rather than vice versa. The focus is always upon the client and his or her needs, and self-revelation on the part of the counsellor, whether implicit (striking dress, pictures of children on desk for example) or explicit (for example, 'I know how you feel, I am a widow too') usually (there are always exceptions to the rule) interferes with the client's need to explore him or herself in a context in which cues are kept to a minimum.

The same is true of the opening moves of sessions. After the initial assessment process, most psychodynamic counsellors prefer to remain silent at the start of a session and to wait for the client to initiate, rather than asking 'What sort of week have you had?' or something similar. This ensures that the client's conscious or unconscious preoccupations will form the agenda of the session, rather than merely eliciting a compliant response to the counsellor. There are of course some clients who are so anxious that they will need a little encouragement to start, but here a neutral 'Mmmm' may be better than a specific question.

In general the purpose of the setting is to create a physical and psychic *space* within which the client's fears and fantasies can be expressed, and his imagination flourish. The job of the counsellor is to protect that space both from external disruption, and equally from any sabotaging attempts by the client (for example arriving late, wanting to over-run, bringing partners to sessions unannounced, etc.) – who will in part inevitably be resistant to change. In Winnicottian (1971) terms, this space is 'transitional' space – transitional between reality and fantasy – and the counsellor is a potential transitional object, partly 'real', partly a figment of the client's inner world.

Listening Strategies

One of Freud's first patients defined psychoanalysis as the 'talking cure', but from the counsellor's perspective it is just as much a 'listening cure'. A key skill in psychodynamic counselling is 'active listening', in which the counsellor attends in part to the clients' narrative, in part to the non-verbal aspects of their communications, and in part to their own inner reactions. Freud called this process 'free-floating attention', Reik (1922) 'listening with the third ear'. From the psychodynamic perspective everything that happens in counselling is a potentially relevant communication: not just what the client says, but how it is said, including apparently trivial remarks, such as comments made on the journey from the waiting room to the consulting room, after the session is officially 'over', etc. The counsellor will also monitor her own spontaneous actions and comments, which may be evoked by the client's unconscious needs.

Acting out (events in the client's life that seem directly related to what is happening in counselling, such as forming a new relationship whenever the counsellor is on holiday, or cancelling a session just after the counsellor has missed one), and *acting in* (actions within the session such as leaping up and walking round the room, sitting in the counsellor's habitual chair, etc.) are all grist to the psychodynamic mill, in that their meaning needs to be understood and ultimately interpreted.

The significance of non-verbal communication, and acting out and acting in, is that these aspects are usually under much less conscious control than the stories told directly in the session, and thus reveal the client's unconscious preoccupations, similar to dreams and slips of the tongue. Consider the simple but not unusual scenario of a 'retaliatory' missed session after a break. The client may protest that he has no objections whatsoever to the counsellor being away, that everyone needs a holiday, and so forth, and yet when his subsequent absence is discussed it may emerge that he felt deeply rejected by and furious with the counsellor, and this in turn might link tranferentially with episodes from the past, for example when his mother went into hospital to have another baby, sent him to boarding school, or left him in the hands of a sexually predatory babysitter.

Another aspect of listening has already been touched on in discussion of attachment patterns – the counsellor is always trying to read back from the client's narrative style to possible early attachment relationships, and see how these might be reflected within the counselling relationship itself.

Interpretation

The aim of psychodynamic counselling is to use the relationship to translate into *interpretations* the kinds of dynamic understanding we have outlined so far. But what is an interpretation? We will consider four aspects: what interpretations are *not*, interpretations as linking statements, the use of metaphor, and focality.

Therapists in general make all sorts of remarks and comments to their clients: questions designed to gather information, empathic/reflective remarks, supportive statements, challenges, requests for clarification, suggestions and directions, boundary-related comments ('It is time to stop'), etc. Psychodynamic counsellors generally try to avoid offering support or being directive, the former because too much support dampens the anxiety which may reveal unconscious preoccupations, the latter because the aim is to help the client to make his own decisions, rather than having them imposed upon him.

The aim of an interpretation, by contrast, is to convey to the client possible *meanings* of their feelings or actions. These meanings will be informed by dynamic understanding. Meanings are essentially linking statements. As E.M. Forster said, 'everything is *like* something else'. Malan's triangles provide a useful framework for making such links – between present unhappiness and past trauma (in the case described earlier in this chapter between the head-on collision and the client's father's violence); between the counsellor and a parent (the client wary of the counsellor as he had been of his father); between current 'outside' relationships and what goes on in the counselling relationship.

Perhaps the most potent source of both linking and meaning is the use of *metaphor*. A typical counselling session consists of a number of mini-narratives in which the client describes some problematic situation involving self and others. An underlying principle of the psychodynamic approach is that the choice of narrative, and the scenarios implicit in it, are influenced by unconscious factors typical of the client's basic assumptions about himself and his relationship with others, including the therapist. Thus, to take a simplistic example, if the client is annoyed with his counsellor, he might start a session by talking about his irritation with a colleague at work. The story about the colleague stands as a metaphor for a more general tendency. If asked to describe in more detail his feelings he might say, 'I feel like throttling him!', to which the counsellor might suggest (although this can be overdone), 'Perhaps you feel like throttling me sometimes too.'

Metaphor can often provide a useful reference point for *focus* in counselling. The idea of focus was introduced by Balint (see Malan, 1996) in the context of time-limited therapy, but is more generally a guide to interpretation which tries to bring together different aspects of the clients' problems and their underlying dynamics, including the relationship with the counsellor, into a single theme.

The Bungee Jump

An unmarried, childless, successful businesswoman in her early 30s came into counselling because, although she had 'everything', by which she meant material comfort and worldly success, she was plagued with feelings of emptiness and depression. In addition she felt stuck in her current relationship which she felt was 'going nowhere', and yet which she felt unable to leave. Her account of her life was that she, the youngest and possibly unwanted child of rather narcissistic parents who valued only beauty and success in their children, was throughout her childhood a complete failure and a 'wimp'. Eventually she had dragged herself away from home and spent a year in Australia, travelling and working. On her travels she found herself at a fair where 'bungee jumping' was going on. She realized that she had to force herself to do a jump. She spent two whole days trying to summon the courage, and eventually jumped. This proved a turning point. Soon after she returned home, and began the first steps in her successful career.

In counselling she was a likeable but exasperating client, who talked incessantly, but went round and round in circles, always seeming cheerful and pleasing to the counsellor, but never really picking up on any of his comments.

It became apparent that she was terrified to show feelings of any sort, for fear she would be thought stupid or 'wimp'-like. She would endlessly ruminate about whether or not to leave her boyfriend, seemingly trying to lure the counsellor into giving advice. The counsellor used the bungee jump as a metaphor for her dilemma: in order to progress in life she had finally found a way to overcome her fear, but now, switching off her feelings had become a trap: she was terrifed to allow sadness or anger or even love to surface with her boyfriend (which was perhaps why the relationship felt so sterile), or with the counsellor (which was why he felt so exasperated).

Alliance Rupture, Breaks, and Termination

Failure and loss are inherent in psychodynamic counselling, as in life. Sometimes the counsellor fails to understand the client, and an atmosphere of frustration and misunderstanding builds up. Given that problematic relationships are what bring most clients for help, it would be surprising if these problems were not a feature of the therapeutic relationship as well. *Alliance ruptures* therefore inevitably arise as counselling proceeds, and ability to repair them is a crucial part of the counsellor's technical repertoire. When something goes wrong the counsellor will reflect upon this and work with the client to understand what has happened. This is in itself part of the healing process. If it fails, as it not infrequently does, the client will probably drop out.

Such empathic breaks are part of the minute-to-minute work of sessions. Each session is also of course separated from the next by a break – usually a week. To be suitable for counselling, the client needs to be able to tolerate such gaps in the relationship with the counsellor, and to bring resulting feelings of abandonment, anger and rejection into the sessions when they arise.

In general, how a person handles *loss* is a key part of their psychological make-up, and can often be understood within an attachment framework. The securely attached individual can hold on to the image of the lost object in his mind and thereby tolerate separation, albeit with sadness. By contrast, insecure avoidant people tend to shut down feelings in order not to experience the pain of loss (as did the client above), while insecure enmeshed people cling to their objects and may remain in an inconsolable state of grief when loss ensues.

Within counselling, therefore, the inevitable loss of the counsellor at ending provides a focus for working on previous disappointments and bereavements, and helping clients to let go of their treatment without feeling that all is lost. Where treatment is time-limited, the counsellor will often 'count down' to the ending, so that the client is reminded at each session how many he has left. Where counselling is open-ended, negotiating an ending – including setting a date for highly dependent clients – is an important phase in the counselling relationship, testing for the counsellor as well as the client.

Supervision and Personal Therapy

Freud once said that when two people form a relationship, four others are also involved – the parents of the protagonists. He was referring here to the oedipal idea that the dynamics of relationship patterns must take into account people's position *vis-à-vis* their parents, as well as the current relationship. Similarly, the counselling relationship is part of a network of relationships, past and present, including the counsellor's supervision and her own counselling.

In supervision, there may be a resonance between the client–counsellor relationship, and what goes on between supervisor and counsellor – a sort of transference by proxy. If the supervisor is irritated or bored by the material the counsellor presents, that may reflect feelings which the counsellor has suppressed, perhaps in her anxiety to be 'helpful' to her client. A basic postulate of the psychodynamic approach is that repressed, split-off or suppressed emotion will manifest itself in some way – in this case in the supervisory relationship. In drawing attention to this the supervisor acts as a model of reflexive function, which will feed into the counsellor's technique, and ultimately into her relationship with clients.

Personal therapy for counsellors, as well as helping to identify and overcome blind spots in relationships, similarly provides a model of a therapeutic relationship which the counsellor can draw on in her relationship with her clients. Our own experiences from the past affect our choice of career and the capacity to help clients, but can be crucially modifed by the experience of being clients ourselves. In addition, if we will let them, our clients teach us how to be better counsellors. The psychodynamic perspective reminds us that ultimately counselling is a two-way process in which each party influences the other, with luck, for their mutual benefit.

Future Directions in Psychodynamic Counselling

Building on Freud and Klein, the elements of contemporary psychodynamic thinking were laid down nearly half a century ago by the object relations pioneers such as Winnicott and Balint. For a while the field became relatively static, and in danger of becoming ossified. The past decade, however, has seen a flowering of new ideas and research (Holmes, 1998). The impetus for this has come from three main directions. Firstly, there has been an increasing interest in research on child development and mother–infant interaction, and the parallels between this and counsellor–client relationship (Stern, 1985). This research suggests for instance that the 'real' relationship between counsellor and client has features similar to that between effective parents and their children: responsiveness, empathy, the capacity to be attuned, and also to set limits and contain aggression.

Secondly, psychotherapy research, previously dominated by cognitive-behavioural approaches, has turned its attention to psychodynamic therapies (for example Luborsky and Crits-Christoph, 1990), demonstrating for example how accuracy of interpretation is correlated with good outcomes. Finally, psychodynamics has emerged from its splendid isolation and is beginning to look at the parallels and differences between its own and other psychotherapeutic approaches such as cognitive-behavioural therapy. This cross-fertilization, of which this volume is one example, will produce hybrid vigour which will stand counselling in good stead for the future.

Summary

- All counselling relationships, whether psychodynamic or not, contain unconscious elements.
- The counsellor's own emotional reactions are an invaluable guide to the inner world of the client.
- Personal revelation by the counsellor, tempting as it is as a 'joining' technique, may vitiate clients' ability to explore their feelings in safety.

- Personal therapy and supervision are essential for psychodynamic counsellors.
- Psychodynamic counselling 'works' by providing an empathic and safe 'real' relationship, while helping the client to become more self-aware by the use of interpretations about the ways in which that real relationship breaks down.

References

Balint, M., Ormstein, P. and Balint, E. (1972) *Focal Psychotherapy*. London: Tavistock.

Bateman, A. and Holmes J. (1995) *Introduction to Psychoanalysis: Contemporary Theory and Practice*. London: Routledge.

Dozier, M., Cue, K. and Barnett, L. (1994) 'Clinicians as caregivers: role of attachment organisation in treatment', *Journal of Consulting and Clinical Psychology*, 62: 793–800.

Fonagy, P. (1991) 'Thinking about thinking: some clinical and theoretical considerations in the treatment of a borderline patient', *International Journal of Psycho-Analysis*, 72: 639–56.

Frank, J. (1961) *Persuasion and Healing*. Baltimore: Johns Hopkins University Press.

Freud, S. (1912) 'The dynamics of transference', *Standard Edition*, 12. London: Hogarth.

Hinshelwood, R. (1989) *A Dictionary of Kleinian Thought*. London: Free Association Books.

Holmes, J. (1993) *John Bowlby and Attachment Theory*. London: Routledge.

Holmes, J. (1996) *Attachment, Intimacy, Autonomy: Using Attachment Theory in Adult Psychotherapy*. New York: Jason Aronson.

Holmes, J. (1998) 'The changing aims of psychoanalytic psychotherapy', *International Journal of Psycho-Analysis*, 79: 227–40.

Luborsky, L. and Crits-Christoph, P. (1990) *Understanding Transference - the CCRT Method*. New York: Basic Books.

Malan, D. (1996) *Individual Psychotherapy and the Science of Psychodynamics* (2nd edn). London: Butterworth.

Orlinsky, D., Grawe, K. and Parks, B.K. (1994) 'Process and outcome in psychotherapy: noch einmal', in A. Bergin and S. Garfield (eds), *Handbook of Psychotherapy and Behavior Change* (4th edn). Chichester: Wiley, pp. 270–376.

Reik T. (1922) *Listening with the Third Ear*. London: Allen & Unwin.

Steiner, J. (1993) *Psychic Retreats*. London: Routledge.

Stern, D. (1985) *The Interpersonal World of the Infant*. New York: Basic Books.

Winnicott, D. (1971) *Playing and Reality*. London: Penguin.

3 *The Relationship in Person-Centred Counselling*

Paul Wilkins

> The person-centred approach emphasises the importance of the therapeutic relationship between counsellor and client and the active use of that relationship to highlight and explore aspects of the client's social and emotional functioning which are manifested in the therapeutic relationship. This makes it crucial for the person-centred counsellor to be able to find ways of using as much of that relationship as possible. (Mearns, 1994a: 64–5)

Introduction

The person-centred approach derives principally from the work of Carl Rogers and his associates. Wood (1996: 161) points out that:

> The person-centered approach is not a psychology, a psychotherapy, a philosophy, a school, a movement nor many other things frequently imagined. It is merely what its name suggests, an *approach*. It is a psychological posture, a way of being, from which one confronts a situation.

This approach is, in effect, a way of being in relationship. This relationship can be with the self, another individual, a group or even a nation. It can be applied to many areas of human interaction. For example, it informed Rogers's writing on (adapted from Wood, 1996: 171):

counselling and psychotherapy (e.g. *Client-Centered Therapy*, 1951)
internal process and experience (e.g. *On Becoming a Person*, 1961)
the facilitation of learning (e.g. *Freedom to Learn*, 1969; *Freedom to Learn in the 80s*, 1983)
interpersonal relationships (e.g. *On Encounter Groups*, 1970)
social processes and cultural transformation (e.g. *On Personal Power*, 1977; *A Way of Being*, 1980)

The application of this approach to counselling and psychotherapy (between which there is no distinction) has a specific theory and mode of practice. It is known as person-centred or client-centred therapy, the latter often being the preferred term in (for example) the United States. Older texts (especially those written by people from without the approach) may refer to 'Rogerian' therapy, but this term was resisted by Rogers himself and finds little favour with person-centred practitioners.

The person-centred approach to counselling focuses first and foremost on the relationship between counsellor and client. Mearns (1996: 306) points out that, in his very first book, Rogers used the term 'Relationship Therapy' for what later became person-centred counselling. In the context of therapy, theory is relatively unimportant: it explains the efficacy of practice rather than dictates its nature. 'Explanation' of a client's difficulties matters less to a person-centred counsellor than an accepting understanding of how it is to be that client while being fully present in the relationship. Person-centred counsellors resist the role of expert, intending, rather, to accompany the client on a personal journey. Clients know what is best for them and, in the actualizing tendency, have a motivating force for positive change. This actualizing tendency 'is the foundation on which the person-centered approach is built' (Rogers in Kirschenbaum and Henderson, 1990: 380). Brodley (1987: 1) describes the actualizing tendency as: 'the sole and original motivating principle in human beings which brings about growth, differentiation, development, self-maintenance and change'. Person-centred counsellors trust this 'innate capacity in all human beings to move towards the fulfilment of their potential' (Mearns and Thorne, 1988: 10). They trust it in their clients and they trust it in themselves. Implicit in this trust is an acceptance that both client and counsellor are engaged in a process of growth. As Mearns and Thorne (ibid.) put it: 'At the deepest level there is in all of us a yearning and the wherewithal to become more than we are.' This does not mean that person-centred counsellors use interactions with clients to meet their own needs (although there is an honest acknowledgement that both client and counsellor may be changed in the therapeutic encounter). It is an acceptance of a basic similarity between all people which leads to a humility and a profound disinclination to pursue power or control over others. Brodley (1987: 1) lists a set of person-centred values; those that apply most directly to the counselling relationship are:

- Perceptions are a major determinant of personal experience and behaviour. Thus, to understand a person one must attempt to understand him/her empathically – from the perspective of his/her own perceptions.
- The concept of the 'whole person' is part of the helper's experience of the person in therapy.
- In helping relationships, the pursuit of control or authority over other persons is abdicated. Instead, there is a commitment to share power and control.
- In helping relationships, the helper is committed to honesty in relation to him/herself. This honesty is a major means for the helper to maintain and enhance his mental and emotional health and the health of his relationships.

It is the implementation of these values which gives person-centred counselling its particular qualities.

The Core Conditions

Rogers (1957: 96) was very clear about the importance of the relationship between counsellor and client from the outset. One of his best known hypotheses is actually a description of the characteristics of a successful therapeutic relationship. He wrote:

For constructive personality change to occur, it is necessary that these conditions exist and continue over a period of time:

1. Two persons are in psychological contact.
2. The first, whom we shall term the client, is in a state of incongruence, being vulnerable or anxious.
3. The second person, whom we shall term the therapist, is congruent or integrated in the relationship.
4. The therapist experiences unconditional positive regard for the client.
5. The therapist experiences an empathic understanding of the client's internal frame of reference and endeavours to communicate this experience to the client.

6. The communication to the client of the therapist's empathic understanding and unconditional positive regard is to a minimal degree achieved.

No other conditions are necessary.

Bozarth (1996: 25-6) points out that Rogers intended this statement to be integrative – any therapist who implemented these six conditions would, regardless of orientation, facilitate therapeutic change. With some subtle differences (see Bozarth, 1996: 26), Rogers (1959: 213) restated this hypothesis as an integral part of his 'theory of therapy and personality change'. This second statement does not invalidate the general applicability of the first but it is seen as part of Rogers's statement of the specifics of client-centred theory. Rogers (1961: 61-2) emphasized three of these conditions, which he called *congruence*, *unconditional positive regard* and *empathic understanding*. These became known as the *core conditions*. 'Empathy' is now preferred to empathic understanding, and unconditional positive regard is sometimes called acceptance. Person-centred counsellors seek to employ these core conditions in their relationships with clients *to the best of their ability*.

If, in the therapeutic encounter, the therapist experiences and communicates the core conditions to the client, Rogers (1961: 35) was of the opinion 'that change and constructive personal development will *invariably* [his emphasis] occur – and I include the word "invariably" only after long and careful consideration'.

Congruence

Congruence (also referred to as *genuineness* or *authenticity*) is the quality of harmony between a person's inner experiencing and their outward expression. Although it is possible to be congruent alone, it is as an element in the counselling relationship that its power is most appreciated. Mearns and Thorne (1988: 75) define congruence as: 'the state of being of the counsellor when her outward responses to her client consistently match the inner feelings and sensations which she has in relation to the client'. That is, congruent counsellors are not necessarily *doing* anything; they are *being* totally themselves and fully present. Action is not called for but an openness to experience (internal and external) *is* required. There is something about this full presence of the counsellor, the free flow of their experience, which is therapeutic. Spinelli (1989: 151–2) explains it thus:

> Congruence refers to the therapist's ability to be present and without facade, that is, to be a living embodiment of integration. The congruent therapist acts as a role model for authentic being. Once again, it is not so much what the therapist does as the therapist's willingness to be as real, as transparent, as free of defences, as possible that, Rogers argues, provides clients with the necessary strength and willingness to engage in honest and accurate self-exploration and revelation.

This may be broadly true but, as a person-centred counsellor, I am less concerned with providing my client with a role model and more with being convincingly trustworthy. It is my congruence which will aid my client's trust in me and in the counselling process. The counsellor's congruence dissipates professional mystique and facilitates movement towards an egalitarian relationship.

Towards the end of his life Rogers (quoted in Kirschenbaum and Henderson, 1990: 135), re-emphasized the importance of congruence:

> The first element is genuineness, realness, or congruence. The more the therapist is himself or herself in the relationship, putting up no professional or personal facade, the greater is the likelihood that the client will change and grow in a constructive manner. Genuineness means that the therapist is openly being the feelings and attitudes that are flowing within at the moment. There is a close matching, or congruence, between what is experienced at the gut level, what is present in awareness, and what is expressed to the client.

Mearns and Thorne (1988: 75) relate the congruence of therapists to the inner feelings and sensations which they have *in relation to their clients*. They say that, for the counsellor, congruence poses challenges, such as:

> In response to my client, can I dare to:
>
> - Feel the feelings that are within me?
> - Hold my client when I feel he needs to be held?
> - Show my anger when that is strongly felt?
> - Admit my distraction when challenged about it?
> - Admit my confusion when that persists?
> - Voice my irritation when that grows?
> - Put words to my affection when that is there?
> - Shout when something is seething inside me?
> - Be spontaneous even though I don't know where that will lead?

- Be forceful as well as gentle?
- Be gentle as well as forceful?
- Use my sensuous self in relation to my client?
- Step out from behind my 'professional facade'?

Can I dare to be *me* in response to my client?

They say that this challenge only exists because 'helpers are often incongruent'.

Because congruence is a state of being (and therefore may not involve action), it goes largely unnoticed. The client experiences the counsellor as congruent but that perception is often below immediate awareness. In a way, it is (paradoxically) the absence of incongruity which facilitates the counselling relationship.

There are occasions on which being congruent *does* involve action. Lietaer (1993: 18) discusses 'genuineness' and usefully distinguishes two components. These he calls congruence and transparency. Congruence is the inner side of genuineness and is 'the unity of total experience and awareness'. Transparency is the outer side of genuineness which involves the 'explicit communication by the therapist of his conscious perceptions, attitudes and feelings'. Tudor and Worral (1994: 198) identify four elements to congruence. These they call:

- self awareness
- self-awareness in action
- communication
- appropriateness.

The first two elements reflect the inner side of congruence described by Lietaer but they argue that congruent communication involves more than transparency. They suggest that *apparency*, 'which has a more active, relational, transitive quality' is an important aspect of congruence in person-centred counselling. Being apparent is to do with the *appropriate* communication of the counsellor's experience.

Whatever the term given to it, there is an understanding in client-centred counselling that, sometimes, counsellors will communicate their experience directly to the client. Mearns and Thorne (1988: 81–3) point out that responding congruently isn't the same as self-disclosing and they offer some guidelines. In making congruent responses, counsellors are 'giving genuinely felt responses to the client's experience at that time'. These responses must be relevant to the client's immediate concern and counsellors' feelings requiring a response 'tend to be those which are *persistent* or particularly *striking*'.

Communicating congruently is not without tension. For example, Holdstock (1996: 47–52) considers the problem of the therapist's anger. He wonders if, sometimes, person-centred counsellors are becoming more absorbed in communicating their 'negative' feelings than considerate of the person towards whom they are directed. Gaylin (1996: 389–90) also warns of the dangers of inappropriate disclosure. He says:

> The obvious danger of self disclosure is that it may lead to abuse of the client. I define abuse of the client as that moment when the therapist's feelings for the client, either positive or negative, take the focus off the client and onto the therapist and, consequently, the activities of the therapist become self rather than client serving. The pursuit of therapist genuineness and transparency should never be construed as a license to use the client.

If the Mearns and Thorne guidelines are adhered to this is less likely to be a problem. The purpose of responding congruently 'is to offer the client the chance to make use of the experience of the therapist *if it is meaningful and useful*' (Wilkins, 1997a: 38). It is unlikely that momentary flashes of irritation, sorrow, boredom or, for that matter, joy can be usefully shared (although they should never be blocked or denied) but a feeling that persists may be. For example:

> *A client was telling me something of her family history. I noticed that whenever she spoke of her sister, my mind went blank. It wasn't that my attention wandered, more that although I heard her every word, I was somehow devoid of reaction, neither thinking nor feeling. My client was clearly animated and experiencing a variety of feelings so I could be reasonably certain this was my experience not an empathic response. Because it was recurrent (and in that sense persistent), I eventually told my client of my experience:*
> *'When you tell me about your sister, something funny happens to me. It is as if I can't really hear you. I go blank and there is nothing in my mind at all. I don't know why that is.'*

My client replied:
'I knew you kept going away, that you weren't with me like you usually are. I was beginning to feel quite alone – and a bit cross.'

To be honest, I'm still not exactly sure what was happening in this interaction even after taking it to supervision. What I do know is that my client had noticed my altered state, and that I owned it was important to her and helpful in our relationship.

Congruence may not be noticed but a counsellor's incongruence usually is, although perhaps as a vague uncomfortable feeling rather than as a conscious thought. Of incongruence, Rogers (1961: 51) wrote: 'When I am experiencing an attitude of annoyance toward another person but am unaware of it, then my communication contains contradictory messages. . . . this confuses the other person and makes him distrustful, though he may be unaware of what is causing the difficulty.'

Sometimes the client is more directly aware of the counsellor's incongruence and may react to it. For example (from Wilkins, 1997a: 38–9):

> I was working with a client who had previously been in therapy with another therapist. It was our fourth encounter and our relationship was progressing well. I think that I was well able to be fully present with my client and to be aware of my feelings, his feelings and the differences between us. In the middle of the session, as I made a response to my client, he stopped me and said:
> 'Don't give me that "active listening" stuff. I don't need it and I don't want it.'
> This brought me up short. In my mind, I replayed my recent responses and (to my chagrin) I realised that I had been responding mechanically – I had slipped into my own thoughts. An observer might very well have thought that my responses were accurate and facilitative. In many ways they were no different from those when I am paying attention and genuinely tracking my client's experience but my client knew the difference. He had detected my incongruence. Luckily, we had a good enough relationship for him to bring this to my attention and I was able to acknowledge the legitimacy of his reaction. As a result, our relationship moved on. With a less assured client, a greater inhibition of process may have occurred.

Gaylin (1996: 390–1) points out that however congruent and integrated counsellors may be, 'they will still encounter incongruence'. What matters is that this incongruence is acknowledged and addressed. The proper place for this might be in the counselling relationship (where it should certainly never be denied), in supervision or in the counsellor's own therapy.

Congruence is the most powerful tool the person-centred counsellor has and as such it takes precedence over the other core conditions. Rogers (in Hobbs, 1989: 21) said: 'I feel that empathy is extremely important in making contact with another person but if you have other feelings then congruence takes precedence over anything else.' Similarly, Thorne (1991: 189) writes of congruence and the core conditions: 'Acceptance, empathy and congruence – these three, as always, but the greatest and the most difficult and the most exciting and the most challenging is congruence.' Congruence is important in several ways. A congruent therapist is unlikely to appear as a creature of mystique. Mearns and Thorne (1988: 86) write 'Mystery evokes the illusion of power; transparency dissolves it.' This facilitates trust and (for example) provides a context in which empathy and acceptance gain credence. The counsellor's willingness to be experienced 'warts and all' is equally important. Mearns and Thorne (ibid.: 87) write: 'This openness about apparent weaknesses can introduce whole new possibilities for self-acceptance in the client who spends his life in fear of weaknesses in himself.'

Although person-centred counsellors don't seek to provide their clients with an example to imitate, the congruence of the counsellor is likely to inspire an increased congruence in the client. Because incongruence is one of the characteristics of emotional disharmony, this is of itself desirable. Lastly, congruence in the counsellor offers the client the genuine reaction of another person 'whose integrity can be trusted, and whose professionalism has ensured that as far as possible that [reflection] is not discoloured by the counsellor's own need system' (Mearns and Thorne, 1988: 87). This is extraordinarily powerful; it is the meeting of the deepest, most real, most vibrant and vital self of the counsellor with the client and it is of great potency in the client's quest for transformation. Thorne (1991: 187) puts it well:

> The therapist who wishes to be maximally congruent must be able to face his or her inner world without fear: he or she will not cut off if the going gets tough or if strongly positive or negative feelings surge into consciousness. Indeed such occurrences will be welcomed for they are the stuff of direct personal encounter where the therapist's daring to be real assumes a new potency which can dissolve barriers at a stroke and establish a new level of intimacy. This does not mean that the

therapist imposes upon the client or burdens the client with all his or her feelings and problems. It does mean though that the therapist is prepared to face the complexity of his or her own being in the knowledge that to do so is vital to the client's well-being.

Empathy

The notion of empathy is not unique to person-centred counselling and has been variously defined and valued (see Wilkins, 1997b: 3–5). It is usually seen as the ability to perceive and resonate with the feelings of another person. There is widespread agreement that it is a natural trait but one which often becomes masked. With training and practice, this ability can be rediscovered. Mearns and Thorne (1988: 53) write about empathy as sensitivity towards another and offer the thought that becoming more empathic is about releasing this sensitivity. Vanaerschot (1993: 69–70) writes:

> Being empathic is not a gift that is granted to only a few. Neither is it a technique that can be taught without commitment and involvement. It is a profound human contact capacity that can be refined. And for that purpose, training in communicative skills and working on one's own personality by means of personal therapy must be done together.

Although empathy is widely appreciated in the practice of counselling (and indeed seems to share something with some ideas of countertransference – see Wilkins 1997a: 38), it has a particular meaning in person-centred counselling. Mearns and Thorne (1988: 39) offer the following definition:

> Empathy is a continuing process whereby the counsellor lays aside her own way of experiencing and perceiving reality, preferring to sense and respond to the experiences and perceptions of her client. This sensing may be intense and enduring with the counsellor actually experiencing her client's thoughts and feelings as powerfully as if they had originated in herself.

Vanaerschot (1993: 47–71) writes about empathy from the perspective of the therapist, an observer and the client. She says (p. 48):

> From the therapist's viewpoint, empathy is a special way of knowing. The therapist tries to get to know the client's inner world. But one can never directly know someone else's inner world. 'Knowing' in this context means, that the therapist's inner phenomenological world and state of mind, which he can indeed directly perceive, are as similar as possible, or more, almost identical to the client's.

In the person-centred counselling relationship, the counsellor endeavours to sense moment by moment the experience of another person 'as if' it were their own *and to communicate that sense to the client*. Rogers (1959: 210) stresses the importance of retaining 'the "as if" condition'; that is, counsellors, however accurate their sensing of the other, retain an awareness of themselves in the relationship and do not become swamped or overtaken by the client's experience.

Empathic sensing can take many forms. For example, Neville (1996: 439–53) describes five kinds of empathy which have transpersonal, somatic, imaginative, conceptual and integrative qualities respectively, and McMillan (1997: 205–8) describes 'three major aspects of empathy: *physiological, perspective taking* and *transpersonal*. What is agreed is that sometimes empathic sensing may be as a sensation or visceral feeling such as a pain in the stomach, nausea, a creeping sensation between the shoulder blades; sometimes it will be as an emotion like fear, deep sadness, joy or ecstasy; sometimes a metaphor either as words, pictures or even a sound or smell; sometimes as a clear thought. It may even be some combination of these. The intensity of the 'as if' experience varies. Sometimes there is the faintest glimmer, at others the sensing is immediate, powerful and potent. For example:

> *Working with a client who was describing a childhood of neglect, poverty and abuse, I became aware of the reek of rotting food, urine and stale beer. There was no physical cause of these noxious odours so I told my client of what I could smell. From his reaction, it was clear that I had connected in a very powerful way with his experience. He too was aware of this pungent reminder of his childhood.*

> *I was beginning work with a new client. She was bouncy, vivacious and smiling as she told me about herself. As she spoke, I became aware of a creeping sensation between my shoulder blades and I began to feel full of dread and panic. I had no reason to feel like this. I told my client of my sensations and her whole demeanour changed. She burst into deep, retching sobs. Eventually she told me that was how she felt all the time.*

From the client's perspective, empathy can be very powerful. Rogers (1961: 34) wrote:

It is only as I *understand* the feelings and thoughts which seem so horrible to you, or so weak, or so sentimental, or so bizarre – it is only as I see them as you see them, and accept them and you, that you feel really free to explore all the hidden nooks and crannies of your inner and often buried experiences.

The very experience of being deeply understood can be of itself transformative and there is something too in receiving empathy from another which is encouraging. It is quite common for clients who experience the counsellor's empathy to go deeper, often exploring forgotten issues or recalling suppressed material. Vanaerschot (1993: 54-68) discusses the effect of received empathy on the client. She expands on a number of headings which are:

1. One feels valued and accepted as a person.
2. One feels confirmed in one's existence as an autonomous, valuable person with one's own identity.
3. One learns to accept one's own feelings.
4. Empathy dissolves alienation.
5. One learns to trust one's own experience.

Warner (1996: 128-43) has discussed how empathy 'cures'. She (p. 140) considers that inasmuch as empathic understanding promotes the reprocessing of experience 'it is likely to be valuable to virtually all people throughout their lives'. She also says:

However, I believe that empathic understanding plays a particularly crucial role in therapy with clients who have suffered empathic failure in childhood to the point that their ability to hold and process experience has been severely compromised. . . . The ongoing presence of a soothing, empathic person is often essential to the person's ability to stay connected without feeling overwhelmed.

Acceptance

Acceptance is also called *unconditional positive regard*. Rogers (in Kirschenbaum and Henderson, 1990: 135-6, 225) also referred to 'warmth' and 'prizing' in his discussion of this quality. It is an attitude of the counsellor towards the client. For Mearns and Thorne (1988: 59) it is:

the fundamental attitude of the person-centred counsellor towards her client. The counsellor who holds this attitude deeply values the humanity of her client and is not deflected in that valuing by any particular client behaviours. The attitude manifests itself in the counsellor's consistent acceptance of and enduring warmth towards her client.

Acceptance isn't the same as approval. It is a deeply held belief in the client as a person of worth *regardless* of what is said, done or felt. Rogers (in Kirschenbaum and Henderson, 1990: 136) writes: 'Acceptance involves the therapist's willingness for the client to be whatever immediate feeling is going on – confusion, resentment, fear, anger, courage, love, or pride.'

Mearns (1994a: 3–5) has pointed out that accepting somebody is very different from liking them. Person-centred counsellors *aren't* required to like their clients (but nor should they dislike them). Mearns sees liking as based in shared values or complementary needs – in other words, 'liking' is conditional; the power of acceptance lies in the unconditional valuing of another person. He (ibid.: 54) has also pointed out that person-centred counsellors seek to be 'beside' their clients, not 'on their side'. That is, to be as close to the client's experiencing as possible, not allying with their thoughts and feelings. The first is an accepting position, the second is, or may become, conditional.

Acceptance is very hard to develop. Tolerance will not do, neither will what Mearns (1994a: 4) calls the *portrayal* of acceptance. Because the key to the acceptance of others is the acceptance of self, it involves the person-centred counsellor in major efforts of personal growth. Rogers (in Kirschenbaum and Henderson, 1990: 120) wrote about the challenge of self-acceptance and its value to the counsellor: 'If I can form a helping relationship to myself – if I can be sensitively aware of and acceptant toward my own feelings – then the likelihood is great that I can form a helping relationship with another.'

The major therapeutic effect of the counsellor's acceptance is to undermine the client's *conditions of worth* – which are self-imposed defences arising out of inauthentic interactions with significant others (see Mearns and Thorne, 1988: 7–8). Conditions of worth lead to the subjective experience of fragmentation and restricted growth and development. Behaviour is restricted because of a need to win approval and avoid disapproval. The counsellor's acceptance confronts and challenges the defences and self-concept of the client. The experience of being valued by another is also transformative. Mearns and Thorne (1988: 62) write:

> In a sense the client becomes 'contaminated' by the counsellor's attitude and little by little he begins to experience the same attitude towards himself. It is only when the client begins, however tentatively,

to value himself in this way that real movement can take place, and in the case of so many clients this first self-valuing is the direct outcome of sensing the counsellor's valuing of them and accepting that such an attitude is possible.

Acceptance isn't always easy but it is worth the effort. For example:

A 'difficult' client presented at my place of work. He had previously been seen by one of my colleagues of whom he had little good to say. In his expressed view, the service for which we worked was useless and counselling was worse. And yet he wanted an appointment. With some foreboding, I agreed to meet with him for counselling. I had a sense of being tested to my limits. This was confirmed when he arrived for his first appointment driving an army surplus armoured car and began telling me of his love of the military and hatred of women and black people in particular. All this challenged my liberal attitudes and yet I knew that the efficacy of our relationship depended upon me being accepting, not merely acting the part. As I listened and responded to him, I began to wonder about what life experiences had led him to his extreme views. The tale he told was of mistreatment as a child and a tempestuous relationship with his wife whom he experienced as 'robbing' him of his house and his business. Between sessions, I read about prejudice and how it might arise. Almost without noticing, I slipped from being challenged by my client's way of being to an appreciation of the person of worth behind the views. As this happened, there was a softening in him, sessions began to include humour and a sense of companionship in the counselling enterprise. It was as if, as he accepted himself more, he became more accepting of the world. We only met for six sessions and I'm sure that he remained a misogynist and a racist but there was an easing of his attitudes. I think we were both changed by the process.

Integration of the Core Conditions and the Quality of 'Presence'

Each of the core conditions is powerful but they reach their peak when they are offered in combination. Many times I have myself felt 'stuck' in some behaviour pattern only to have this stuckness almost miraculously dissolve when I have felt the genuine, accepting understanding of another. I know too that when I am accepting of my clients, able to tune into their feelings, however scary or shameful, and to be honestly and openly myself in the relationship, then there is a greater likelihood that they will effect the changes they desire.

Sometimes this integration of the core conditions leads to another quality. This Rogers (in Kirschenbaum and Henderson, 1990: 137) referred to as *presence*. He wrote:

> When I am at my best, as a group facilitator or a therapist, I discover another characteristic. I find that when I am closest to my inner, intuitive self, when I am somehow in touch with the unknown in me, when perhaps I am in a slightly altered state of consciousness in the relationship, then whatever I do seems to be full of healing. Then simply my *presence* is releasing and helpful.

Thorne (1991: 73–81) describes 'the quality of tenderness' which he (ibid.: 182) equates with presence. For both Rogers and Thorne there is a transcendental, spiritual or mystical dimension to this quality. In my experience too there is a sense of transpersonal communion. Mearns (1994a: 7–8) points out that this quality may be 'referred to in mystical language or in terms of existing concepts, whichever is the writer's preference'. He says that presence arises from the combination of two circumstances. The first of these is the blending of high degrees of the core conditions and the second 'is that the counsellor is able to be truly *still* within herself, allowing her person to resonate with the client's experiencing. In a sense, the counsellor has allowed her person to step right into the client's experiencing without needing to do anything to establish her separateness.' However presence arises, it is the ultimate manifestation of the person-centred counsellor's intention to *be* with the client rather than to *do* something to them, for them or even with them. For all that it arises from them, it transcends understanding, accepting and being real with the client.

There is another sense in which it is important to integrate the core conditions in the person-centred counselling relationship. Mearns (1994b: 5–10) considers 'the person centred discipline of attending to the client as a "*whole*" person', and warns of the potential to misunderstand this as an injunction to attend only to the wholeness of the client and not 'the elements and dynamics within the personality'. He (p. 7) writes:

> In working with a client who has such different and opposing parts of her personality, the person centred therapist's task is to manifest the therapeutic conditions in relation to *all* the parts of the personality. This is what is meant by working with the 'whole' person. It is absolutely critical that the therapist *values* each of these parts of the client's personality, *listens* to each of them carefully, and is *congruent* in his relationship with both parts of the personality. A common error in practitioners who are not sufficiently well trained is to *align* more strongly with one part of the personality against the other. The danger in this naive procedure is that the therapist is actually colluding with one part of the personality and implicitly rejecting another part. At the very least this tends to block or elongate the therapeutic process and at the worst it might engender psychosis.

Warner (1995: 1–13) has written of the value of the person-centred approach in working with people who have a multiple personality disorder. Her approach is similar to that advocated by Mearns in that it involves being empathic towards, accepting of and genuine with each of the manifesting personalities but she particularly values empathy in work with this client group. She writes (p. 3):

> We have found that when therapists understand dissociative process and remain empathically connected with clients, a natural process tends to develop in which dissociated memories and personalities emerge on their own. Once this process is established in the thera-peutic relationship, clients seem to have an exquisite sense of timing, allowing just as much dissociated material into consciousness at any given time as they can handle without total loss of day-to-day function-ing. And, they seem to sense the order in which they are able to tolerate working on particular memories and life issues.

Implicit in this statement is the person-centred counsellor's trust in the client to work at a pace and in the way which is most suitable for them. It is this which is meant by the term *non-directive* which is sometimes used in the context of person-centred counselling. It means that the client has control of the content, pace and objectives of counselling – not that the counsel-lor is in some sense passive.

The 'split' in the client's personality need not be pronounced for the views of Mearns and Warner to be valid. Many clients have some aspect of themselves of which they are disapproving. It is important that the person-centred counsellor accepts and empathizes with this disliked, denigrated or otherwise unacceptable aspect in the same way as other facets of the personality. Only then is therapeutic movement possible. For example:

My client was a well respected professional, experienced as well integrated and well adjusted by his family and friends. Most of the time, I too met that part of him but, on occasions he was abusive of me and himself, rejecting of my overtures and, quite frankly, a bit of a pain. My sense was of meeting a sulky, withdrawn and badly behaved little boy. My client was clearly ashamed of this aspect of himself and punitive towards it. I had no real trouble in offering this part of him the core conditions. When he was like this, I could feel his loneliness and isolation and, deeper still, his great fear of rejection. It was as if by behaving in a way which he felt would push others away, he was protecting himself from further hurt. As I responded empathically and acceptingly, it was like coaxing a frightened child out into the open. Gradually, my client too began to experience this side of himself as protective and innocent rather than as damaging and evil. The transformation was profound.

Power and Mutuality

The issue of power is very important in the person-centred counselling relationship. Person-centred counsellors resist being responsible for their clients and seek to facilitate the discovery and expression of the personal power of the client. Thorne (1991: 73) states that person-centred counsellors believe: 'That it is important to reject the pursuit of authority or control over others and to seek to share power', which echoes Brodley's third criterion quoted above. For the counsellor to believe or act as an 'expert' is counter-therapeutic. Thorne (1992: 25) describes Rogers's thoughts about this:

Rogers concluded that the therapist's theoretical knowledge could lead him to suppose that he actually knew more about the client's inner functioning than the client did. Once such a dangerous fantasy was established it became difficult, if not impossible, for the client to put trust in his or her own experiencing and in the validity of his or her own perceptions.

It is from clients' rediscovered trust in themselves that therapeutic change comes and it is, therefore, damaging to do anything which interferes with this process. Impressions of the counsellor as a powerful, authoritative person are not conveyed by assumed knowledge alone. The way in which a counsellor speaks, the language used, the setting in which the session takes place and what happens before and after may all exude institutional power or the supremacy of the counsellor. This is unlikely to be helpful. Mearns and Thorne (1988: 96–7) suggest that person-centred counsellors should be concerned about the 'power game' messages given by the promotional material, the first contact, the waiting area, the quality of reception and the counselling room itself.

It is this awareness that contributes to the person-centred view of counsellor and client as colleagues rather than leader and led and which leads to the aim of developing mutuality in the relationship. Mearns and Thorne (1988: 128) write:

> The establishment of *mutuality* is a central process as the therapeutic relationship develops during person-centred counselling. From the time when mutuality is established, both counsellor and client experience their work as a truly shared enterprise and they can trust each other's commitment to achieve and maintain genuineness in relation to each other. Neither is fearful of the other, and intimacy comes easily in ways which are appropriate to the counselling setting.

This concern with power and mutuality has implications for the structure and context of counselling.

Structure in the Person-Centred Counselling Relationship

Because it is the client who directs the course, content, and often the duration of the counselling relationship, person-centred counsellors are not as concerned with 'assessment', goal-setting and contracts as counsellors of some other orientations. Of course boundaries of time, place and behaviour *are* important, but very experienced and well supported person-centred counsellors may value flexibility over a rigid adherence to such structural elements. Mearns (1994a: 10) writes:

> It is important that person-centred counsellors who are choosing to work with more demanding clientele and in more involving ther-

apeutic contracts are able to be flexible in the way they work while ensuring that they are in full control of the work. Structural aspects of the work like frequency of sessions, length of sessions, the possibility of crisis 'call-outs' and working in settings which are safe for the client rather than familiar for the counsellor, are all factors which may be varied by the experienced and well-supported counsellor.

Many (indeed most) person-centred counsellors *do* see their clients regularly and for about an hour with no other contact, but there is no particular reason why this should be so. For example, if the client is in crisis then a telephone call between sessions, or more sessions, may be helpful. Similarly, a client might benefit more from meeting in a setting other than the counsellor's regular place of practice. This may be for a 'one-off' session, visiting a place of emotional importance, or, in the case of a 'fragile' client, in a place with which they are familiar. What is important is that the counsellor and client work together to decide the best way of working and that any departure from the norm is worked through in and supported by supervision. As in any other approach, part of the client's safety derives from knowing when and where the counsellor will be available but this can be by negotiation and agreement, not imposed by the counsellor. Part of the challenge of person-centred counselling 'is that the counsellor becomes as fully involved as possible with her clients, without being emotionally over-involved' (Mearns, 1994a: 10).

One of the characteristics of the person-centred counselling relationship is that it is impossible to be prescriptive or formulaic about precisely what it is or what it should look like. This is because it relies heavily on the individuality and reality of the counsellor and no two people are the same. Within a framework such as the one outlined above, each person-centred counsellor finds their own way of being in the counselling relationship. The practice of any two person-centred counsellors may look very different from the outside. What is important is that clients are offered the core conditions and that counsellors are true to themselves. If a person-centred counsellor is naturally ebullient and expressive, then that is how to be in the counselling session – similarly for a reserved and quiet counsellor. This doesn't mean that the former can dominate the session or that the latter should never say a word, but that this way of being should be allowed expression in the special context of counselling.

Summary: Key Features of Person-Centred Counselling

- Person-centred counselling focuses upon the relationship between counsellor and client.
- This relationship is characterized by the counsellor's sincere attempt to offer the client the core conditions of congruence, empathy and acceptance. These are necessary and *sufficient* to effect positive personality change.
- Although each of these core conditions is separately powerful, their effect is at its greatest when they are integrated. Such an integration may lead to another quality, known as presence or tenderness. Some practitioners experience this as being of a transcendental or spiritual nature, others are more prosaic.
- Person-centred counsellors work towards an equality of power in the counselling relationship. There is a strongly held belief that the pursuit of authority or control on the part of the counsellor is counter-therapeutic. Similarly, an 'expert' stance is seen as damaging the client's prospect for growth.
- Because person-centred counselling focuses on the relationship between client and counsellor and it acknowledges the importance of the client's innate sense of what is necessary for positive change, there is less concern with formal structures than in some other approaches. This does not mean that person-centred counsellors have licence to behave however they wish, but that (within appropriate professional constraints) they aspire to be flexible, adapting to the client's needs.

References

Bozarth, J.D. (1996) 'The integrative statement of Carl Rogers', in R. Hutterer, G. Pawlowsky, P.F. Schmid and R. Stipsits (eds), *Client-Centered and Experiential Psychotherapy: A Paradigm in Motion*. Frankfurt-am-Main: Peter Lang.

Brodley, B.T. (1987) *A Client-Centered Psychotherapy Practice 1*. http://uhs.bsd. uchicago.edu/%7Ematt/cct.practice.html

Gaylin, N.L. (1996) 'Reflections on the self of the therapist', in R. Hutterer, G. Pawlowsky, P.F. Schmid and R. Stipsits (eds), *Client-Centered and Experiential Psychotherapy: A Paradigm in Motion*. Frankfurt-am-Main: Peter Lang.

Hobbs, T. (1989) 'The Rogers interview', *Counselling Psychology Review*, 4 (4): 19–27.

Holdstock, T.L. (1996) 'Anger and congruence reconsidered from the perspective of an interdependent orientation to the self', in R. Hutterer, G. Pawlowsky, P.F.

Schmid and R. Stipsits (eds), *Client-Centered and Experiential Psychotherapy: A Paradigm in Motion*. Frankfurt-am-Main: Peter Lang.

Kirschenbaum, H. and Henderson, V.L. (eds) (1990) *The Carl Rogers Reader*. London: Constable.

Lietaer, G. (1993) 'Authenticity, congruence and transparency', in D. Brazier (ed.), *Beyond Carl Rogers*. London: Constable.

McMillan, M. (1997) 'The experiencing of empathy: what is involved in achieving the "as if" condition?' *Counselling*, 8 (3): 205-9.

Mearns, D. (1994a) *Developing Person-Centred Counselling*. London: Sage.

Mearns, D. (1994b) 'The dance of psychotherapy', *Person Centred Practice*, 2 (2): 5-13.

Mearns, D. (1996) 'Working at relational depth with clients in person-centred therapy', *Counselling*, 7 (4): 306-11.

Mearns, D. and Thorne, B. (1988) *Person Centred Counselling in Action*. London: Sage.

Neville, B. (1996) 'Five kinds of empathy', in R. Hutterer, G. Pawlowsky, P.F. Schmid and R. Stipsits (eds), *Client-Centered and Experiential Psychotherapy: A Paradigm in Motion*. Frankfurt-am-Main: Peter Lang.

Rogers, C.R. (1957) 'The necessary and sufficient conditions of therapeutic personality change', *Journal of Consulting Psychology*, 21: 95-103.

Rogers, C.R. (1959) 'A theory of therapy, personality, and interpersonal relationships, as developed in the client-centered framework', in S. Koch (ed.), *Psychology: A Study of a Science*, vol. 3, *Formulations of the Person and the Social Context*. New York: McGraw-Hill.

Rogers, C.R. (1961) *On Becoming a Person*. London: Constable.

Spinelli, E. (1989) *The Interpreted World*. London: Sage.

Thorne, B. (1991) *Person-Centred Counselling: Therapeutic and Spiritual Dimensions*. London: Whurr.

Thorne, B. (1992) *Carl Rogers*. London: Sage.

Tudor, K. and Worrall, M. (1994) 'Congruence reconsidered', *British Journal of Guidance and Counselling*, 22 (2): 197-205.

Vanaerschot, G. (1993) 'Empathy as releasing several micro-processes in the client', in D. Brazier (ed.), *Beyond Carl Rogers*. London: Constable.

Warner, M. (1995) 'Dissociated process'. Unpublished paper, Chicago Counseling and Psychotherapy Center.

Warner, M. (1996) 'How does empathy cure? A theoretical consideration of empathy, processing and personal narrative', in R. Hutterer, G. Pawlowsky, P.F. Schmid and R. Stipsits (eds), *Client-Centered and Experiential Psychotherapy: A Paradigm in Motion*. Frankfurt-am-Main: Peter Lang.

Wilkins, P. (1997a) 'Congruence and countertransference: similarities and differences', *Counselling*, 8 (1): 36-41.

Wilkins, P. (1997b) 'Empathy: a desirable quality for effective interpersonal communication?' *Applied Community Studies*, 3 (2): 3-13.

Wood, J.K. (1996) 'The person-centered approach: toward an understanding of its implication', in R. Hutterer, G. Pawlowsky, P.F. Schmid and R. Stipsits (eds), *Client-Centered and Experiential Psychotherapy: A Paradigm in Motion*. Frankfurt-am-Main: Peter Lang.

4 *Dialogical Psychotherapy*

Maurice Friedman

The Existentialism of Dialogue

In my book *The Worlds of Existentialism* (Friedman, 1991) I point to a central and still not sufficiently recognized issue that divides existentialists - whether the *self* is seen as central with the relation between selves as a dimension of the self, or whether the *relation itself* is seen as central, with the self coming into being precisely through that relation.[1]

This same issue carries over into existential psychotherapy. Many existential psychotherapists see the self as the touchstone of reality, even while recognizing the world of intersubjectivity, as does Sartre (Friedman, 1991: 186-200), or that *Dasein ist Mitsein* ('to exist is to be with others'), as does Heidegger (ibid.: 180-6). Heidegger's intersubjectivity remains the vague *we* of his '*Mitsein*' or '*Mitdasein*' - a being with others which expresses itself in solicitude but not in direct dialogue. Heidegger's treatment of death as one's ownmost, ultimate, non-relational reality shows, moreover, that *Mitsein* is not as basic for him as *Dasein*. The dialogical psychotherapist, in contrast, starts with the 'between' as the touchstone of reality.

The Life of Dialogue

Dialogical psychotherapy is based in most cases on Martin Buber's philosophy of dialogue and his philosophical anthropology - the study of the wholeness and uniqueness of the human. In his classic work *I and Thou*, Buber (1958) distinguishes between the 'I-Thou' relationship which is direct, mutual, present, and open, and the 'I-It,' or subject–object, relation in which one relates to the other only indirectly and non-mutually, knowing and using the other. What is essential is not what goes on within the minds of the partners in a relationship but what happens *between* them. For this reason, Buber is unalterably opposed to that psychologism which wishes to remove the reality of relationship into the separate psyches of the participants. 'The inmost growth of the self does not take place, as people like to suppose today,' writes Buber, 'through our relationship to ourselves, but through being made present by the other and knowing that we are made present by him' (Buber, 1988: 61).

Being made present as a person is the heart of what Buber calls confirmation. Confirmation is interhuman, but it is not simply social or interpersonal. Unless one is confirmed in one's uniqueness as the person one can become, one is only seemingly confirmed. The confirmation of the other must include an actual experiencing of the other side of the relationship so that one can imagine quite concretely what another is feeling, thinking and knowing. This 'inclusion', or imagining the real, does not abolish the basic distance between oneself and the other. In contrast to empathy which, in the strict sense of the term, means feeling oneself in the client through giving up the ground of one's concreteness, inclusion does not mean at any point that one gives up the ground of one's own concreteness, ceases to see through one's own eyes, or loses one's own 'touchstone of reality' (my own term for those events in our lives which we carry with us and which affect the basic attitude with which we meet new situations (Friedman, 1972)). Inclusion is a bold swinging over into the life of the person one confronts, through which alone I can make her present in her wholeness, unity and uniqueness.[2]

This experiencing of the other side is essential to the distinction which Buber makes between 'dialogue', in which I open myself to the otherness of the person I meet, and 'monologue', in which, even when I converse with her at length, I allow her to exist only as a content of my experience. Wherever one lets the other exist only as part of oneself, 'dialogue becomes a fiction, the mysterious intercourse between two human worlds only a game, and in the rejection of the real life confronting him the essence of all reality begins to disintegrate' (Buber, 1985: 24).

Buber's I-Thou philosophy is concerned with the difference between mere existence and authentic existence, between being human at all and being more fully human, between remaining fragmented and bringing the conflicting parts of oneself into an active unity, between partial and fuller relationships with others. No one ever becomes a 'whole person'. But one may move in the direction of greater wholeness through greater awareness and fuller response in each new situation.

Dialogical Psychotherapy

By dialogical psychotherapy we mean a therapy which is centred on the *meeting* between the therapist and his or her client or family as the central healing mode, whatever analysis, role playing, or other therapeutic techniques or activities may also enter in. If the psychoanalyst is seen as an indispensable midwife in bringing up material from the unconscious to the conscious, this is not yet 'healing through meeting'. Only when it is recognized that everything that takes place within therapy – free association, dreams, silence, pain, anguish – takes place within the context of the vital relationship between therapist and patient do we have what may properly be called dialogical psychotherapy. Healing through meeting is a two-sided event that is not susceptible to techniques in the sense of willing and manipulating in order to bring about a certain result. What is crucial is not the skill of the therapist but, rather, what takes place between the therapist and the client and between the client and other people – what Aleene Friedman calls 'the healing partnership' (A.M. Friedman, 1992).

To become aware of a person, Buber points out, means to perceive his or her wholeness as a person defined by spirit: to perceive the dynamic centre that stamps on all utterances, actions, and attitudes the recognizable sign of uniqueness. Such an awareness is impossible if, and as long as, the other is for me the detached object of my observation, for that person will not thus yield his or her wholeness and its centre. It is possible only when he or she becomes present for me and I for her as a partner in dialogue.

The Elements of Dialogical Psychotherapy

In an attempt to systematize the second, thematic part of my book *The Healing Dialogue in Psychotherapy* (1985) I have set down ten elements of dialogical psychotherapy. The first is *the 'between'* – the recognition of an ontological dimension in the meeting between persons, or the 'interhuman', that is usually overlooked because of our tendency to divide our existences into inner and outer, subjective and objective. The second is the recognition of *the dialogical* – 'All real living is meeting' – as the essential element of human existence in which we relate to others in their uniqueness and otherness and not just as a content of our experience. From this standpoint the psychological is only the accompaniment of the dialogical and not, as so many psychologists tend to see it, the touchstone of reality in itself. The third element is the recognition that underlying the I–Thou, as also the I–It relations, is that twofold movement of *setting at a distance* and *entering into relation* that Buber makes the foundation of his philosophical anthropology (Friedman, chap. 1 of Buber, 1988; and Buber, chap. 2 of Buber, 1988).

All of the foregoing lead to the fourth element – the recognition that the basic element of healing, when it is a question not of some repair work but restoring the atrophied personal centre, is *healing through meeting*.

This is so because of the fifth element – *the unconscious* – seen, as Buber saw it, as the wholeness of the person before the differentiation and elaboration into psychic and physical, inner and outer (Friedman, 1985; chap. 13). Dialogical psychotherapy's inclusion of the unconscious sets it in contrast to those approaches and interpretations which view relational therapy as interpretation of our conscious, person-to-person relationships only. This understanding of the unconscious applies to dreams too, which from this standpoint are never just the raw material of the unconscious but, upon being remembered, have already entered into the dialogue between therapist and client and between the client and others. The result of this approach is the possibility of having dialogues with our dreams themselves, as with any other person or thing that comes to meet us (ibid.: chap. 14).

The sixth element, *existential guilt*, is not basically inner or neurotic. Rather it is an event of the 'between'. Existential guilt is guilt that you have taken on yourself as a person in a personal situation. Freud's guilt is repressed into the unconscious; you do not know it. But existential guilt you do know. Only it is possible that you no longer identify yourself with the person who committed the injury. It is just here, in the real guilt of the person who has not responded to the legitimate claim and address of the world, that the possibility of transformation and healing lies. Guilt does not reside in the person, says Buber. Rather, one stands, in the most realistic sense, in the relationship that gives rise to the guilt. Similarly, the repression of guilt and the neuroses which result from this repression are not merely psychological phenomena, but real events between persons.

Existential guilt also arises, writes Buber, from injuring the common order of existence, the foundation of which we know – at some level – to be the foundation of our own and of all human existence. Each of us understands – in terms of our family, our friendships, the peoples we work with, our social groups of whatever kind – what it means to injure the social structures in which we live.

Buber puts forward three steps that can be taken toward overcoming existential guilt. The first is illuminating this guilt: 'I who am so different am nonetheless the person who did this.' Secondly, we have to persevere in that illumination – not as an anguished self-torment but as a strong, broad light. If we were only guilty in relation to ourselves, the process might stop there. But we are always also guilty in relation to others. Therefore, we must take the third step of repairing the injured order of existence, restoring the broken dialogue through an active devotion to the world. If we have injured it, only we can restore it. We may not always be able to do so with the person we injured; yet there are a thousand places where we can restore the injured order of existence (Buber, 1988: chap. 6; Friedman, 1985: chap. 15).

Therapy too rests upon the I–Thou relationship of openness, mutuality, presence and directness. Yet it can never be fully mutual. There is mutual contact, mutual trust and mutual concern with a common problem but *not* mutual inclusion. The therapist can and must be on the patient's side too and, in a bipolar relationship, imagine quite concretely what the patient is thinking, feeling and willing. But the therapist cannot expect or demand that the patient practise such inclusion with him or her. Yet there *is* mutuality, including the therapist sharing personally with the client when that seems helpful. For this reason, I call this seventh element *the problematic of mutuality* (Friedman, 1985: chap. 16).

The eighth element, *inclusion*, or 'imagining the real', must be distinguished, as we have seen, from that empathy that goes to the other side of the relationship and leaves out one's own side, and that identification that remains on one's own side and cannot go over to the other. Only the two sides together can produce the ninth element – *confirmation*. Confirmation by the therapist can begin to replace the disconfirmation that the patient has experienced in family and community. This confirmation comes through understanding the patient from within and through going beyond this, as Hans Trüb suggests, to that second stage when the claim of the community is placed on the patient. This claim enables the patient to go back into dialogue with those from whom he or she has been cut off (Friedman, 1985: chaps 10, 11, 12).

The tenth and last element, the *dialogue of touchstones*, includes both inclusion and confirmation. Through his or her greater experience in inclusion and imagining the real the therapist enables the patient to go beyond the terrible either/or of remaining true to one's unique 'touchstones of reality' (Friedman, 1972) at the cost of being cut off from the community or of entering into relation with the community at the cost of denying one's touchstones. The therapist must help the patient bring his or her touchstones of reality into dialogue with other persons, beginning with the therapist (Friedman, 1985: chap. 18).

The Dialogical Psychotherapy Movement

Dialogical psychotherapy has had its representatives and pioneers in many major schools of psychotherapy, most of whom have been directly influenced by Buber but some of whom have not (see Friedman, 1985: Part One). In my book *Religion and Psychology: A Dialogical Approach* (1992b), Part One deals with 'Foundations': the Hebrew Bible ('Biblical, relational, and existential trust'), Hasidism and Hasidic tales ('Hasidic hallowing, helping, and healing'), and Martin Buber's philosophy of dialogue and philosophical anthropology. When I first met Fritz Perls he spoke to me of Buber, who had influenced him and the first Gestalt therapy book. Perls's Gestalt therapy slogan, 'I and Thou, Here and Now' is well known. Yet I would not include him among the founders of dialogical psychotherapy. In the last years of his life he was, as his wife Laura Perls said in a public dialogue with me, a showman who was given over to the 'I-It'.

That psychotherapist who above all others made his lifework and his lifeway that of the life of dialogue is the Swiss psychiatrist Hans Trüb. Trüb tells of how the closed circle of the self was again and again forced outward toward relationship through those times when, despite his will, he found himself confronting his patient not as an analyst but as human being to human being. From these experiences, he came to understand the full meaning of the analyst's responsibility. The analyst takes responsibility for lost and forgotten things, and with the aid of his psychology he helps to bring them to light. But he knows in the depths of his self that the secret meaning of these things which have been brought to consciousness first reveals itself *in the outgoing to the other* (Trüb in Friedman, 1991: 497–505; Friedman, 1985: 30–6, 148, 166–8).

A significant extension of the life of dialogue and of dialogical psychotherapy is the theory of 'will and wilfulness' developed under Buber's influence by the Sullivanian psychoanalyst Leslie H. Farber. Farber sees genuine will as an expression of real dialogue, arbitrary wilfulness as a product of the absence of dialogue. The proper setting of wholeness is dialogue. When this setting eludes us, 'we turn wildly to will, ready to grasp at any illusion of wholeness (however mindless or grotesque)' the will conjures up for our reassurance (Farber, 1966: 111). Wilfulness then is nothing other than the attempt of will to make up for the absence of dialogue by handling both sides of the no longer mutual situation (Friedman, 1985: 80–7; 1992a: 78–82).

A third writer who must be mentioned here is Ivan Boszormenyi-Nagy, who, in his *Invisible Loyalties: Reciprocity in Intergenerational Family Therapy* (1973/1984), written with Geraldine Spark; his *Between Give and Take: A Clinical Guide to Contextual Therapy* (1986), written with Barbara R. Krasner; and his *Foundations of Contextual Therapy*, brings Buber's philosophy of dialogue and philosophical anthropology into family therapy. Particularly important here is Boszormenyi-Nagy's taking over from Buber his notion of an objective order of existence (in Boszormenyi-Nagy's terms 'the just order of existence') the foundations of which we recognize at some level as the foundations of our own and all human existence. Boszormenyi-Nagy also takes over Buber's concept of the injury to that order that produces existential guilt as well as the 'rejunction' which draws on the resources of trustworthiness in the family to accomplish that task of repairing the injured order of existence to which Buber points. You may go to the other end of the world to escape your family and be paralysed by interhuman existential guilt.

When each generation is helped to explore the commitments and responsibility of current relationships, an increased reciprocal understanding and mutual compassion between the generations results. The grandchildren are helped to be freed of scapegoated or parentified roles and they have a model for reconciling their conflicts with their parents (Boszormenyi-Nagy and Spark, 1973/1984: 224, 245, 376). Each person's point of view is confirmed precisely through coming into dialogue with the opposing views of others. The contextual therapist guides the family members to the multilaterality of fairness in which one person's being heard or being held accountable makes it easier to hear others or to let oneself be called to account. The contextual therapist uses multidirected partiality ('inclusion') to get every person to bring in his or her subjective accounts and their understandings of the others, and family members explore their capacity for reworking stagnant imbalances in how each of them uses the other and in how they are available to each other (Boszormenyi-Nagy, 1987: 72-4, 76 ff.; Boszormenyi-Nagy and Krasner, 1986: 400; Friedman, 1985: 102-15; 1992a: chap. 7; Friedman, 1992b: chap. 13).[3]

Illustrations

A simple example of the application of the theory of dialogical therapy is that of a current client who said to me in a recent session that she knows her upsetting meeting with her graduate advisor has much more to do with her own business than his. Most therapists would welcome such an approach. I, in contrast, reminded her of her use of the word 'event' and suggested that it be looked at as such and not just as an occurrence in her intrapsychic life. I asked her to imagine where he was coming from that particular day, why he did not take her seriously, and what he was saying about her and his relationship with her through his actions. In her next session she recounted a 'prophetic' dream that took place before this encounter with her advisor, and shared that she had told this dream to him, thus inviting his response so that her dream turned out to be a self-fulfilling prophecy!

A second fuller illustration is my work with Dawn, a 40-year-old Caucasian woman, who came to see me for four years in individual and couples therapy. Dawn complained that Bob, her husband of ten years, never talked to her but spent his hours at home watching television and that he did not do his share of taking care of the children or of babysitting when she went to graduate school. She told me of a time when she broke the television set in a fit of anger and Bob simply replaced it. Dawn's response to this troubled, tense family atmosphere was symptoms of depression: lack of interest and enjoyment in sex, disturbance of concentration and sleep, low energy, and periods of sadness. The flat affect with which she told me how her children were having night terrors indicated clearly the depth of her depression and its impact upon the family.

What struck me most about Dawn was the enormous contrast between her evident intellectual superiority and her inner sense of her self. Dawn's need to compare herself with others seemed to stem from a basic distrust in her relationships with others. Only this could account for the veritable split between Dawn as an active, well functioning person on the outside and as the inferior person which she saw herself as being.

I saw as the basic goal of our therapy helping Dawn enter into dialogue and a relationship of trust. My therapeutic interventions included exploring her family of origin and pointing out patterns, such as Dawn and her siblings as 'delegated' children (children unconsciously programmed to carry out wishes of the parents that the parents cannot carry out directly (Stierlin, 1974)), encouraging expression of feelings, especially anger, getting her to write down dreams, bringing a divorce mediator to group therapy, sending Dawn to a psychiatrist for medication, discussing school plans, suggesting support groups, sending Dawn for psychological testing, and discussing how her daughter's adolescent acting out had brought back problems with her sister, mother and husband.

Analysis of the past was never the main focus of our therapeutic dialogue, however, but was only done for the sake of re-presenting the past and inviting ever deeper layers of her walled-off self to enter into a relationship of trust. The goal of Dawn's therapy was neither the preservation of her relationship with Bob nor establishing her in a new, long-term relationship after Bob's departure. Nor was it any specific matter, such as overcoming Dawn's anxiety and depression, getting Dawn to be able to write papers, or healing her inner split. What was essential, rather, was the relationship of trust that developed between us over the four years in which we entered and re-entered together into dialogical therapy. My behaviour of support, facilitation, confrontation, silence, questioning, reinforcement, interpretation, and modelling was always grounded in a relational stance.

My approach to Dawn's therapy was at times insight-oriented, at times process-oriented, and at other times support-oriented. But it always evolved from the relationship and returned back to my relationship with her. This was true even when I tried traditional Gestalt therapy techniques, such as asking Dawn to play different roles in her family or move from chair to chair addressing herself from the standpoint of some member of her family that she had just spoken to.

I did not simply impose these actions on Dawn but explored with her when it was helpful. The same is true of my interpretations. I did not offer them as authoritative pronouncements but rather asked her whether they rang a bell, and modified them in dialogue with her. Thus the choice of therapeutic goals and objectives was a shared responsibility between me and Dawn, unlike those therapists who see it as their task to set goals, and unlike those therapists who see it as the task of the client.

Inclusion, or 'imagining the real', was necessary from my side if the habitual mistrust on which Dawn's life and actions were established was to be healed to the point where she could enter a relationship of trust with me and later with others.

What was most impressive in our therapy together is the remarkable change that I have witnessed in Dawn during the years of therapy and the more than six years since it concluded. (We have stayed in touch sufficiently that I have been in a position to judge this.) This was precisely her movement from virtual isolation to being a person-in-relationship, a person ready and open for give-and-take with others. Over the years I witnessed in Dawn a gradual but unmistakable warming, opening, flowering and maturing.

Because I approached Dawn's therapy from the stand-point of the healing dialogue, it seems both fitting and meaningful to me to conclude this account of Dawn's case with Dawn's own evaluation of our relationship in her own words:

When I think about our past therapeutic relationship, the process stands out in my memory rather than the content.

Up until the time I met Maurice, I had always 'picked out' a male authority figure - usually a teacher or psychologist - and put him on a pedestal - obsessed about him a lot - not usually in a romantic or sexual way, although there was an erotic element. I just wanted him to like me and approve of me and to think I was smart and interesting. A real relationship, though, was terrifying to me - I kept my distance and rarely ever talked to them - the greater the attraction, the greater the fear.

When I first met Maurice, I could feel myself wanting to fall into this same pattern with him. However, I could never quite feel intimidated by him - although I think I really wanted to. He was too human for that. I never felt that I had to be interesting or smart, good, bad, happy or sad - it just wasn't something I had to be concerned with. If the therapist can be human and fallible, that gives me permission to be human and fallible too.

This was an entirely new experience for me. I soon found that I was involving myself in relationships with other 'male author-ity figures' with much less fear and anxiety than I had felt in the past. I also became aware that I no longer wanted the kind of superior-inferior, vertical type of relationship that I used to seek out. I think this change is, by far, the most valuable result of my therapy relationship with Maurice. I am, in general, much better able to relate to others in an adult to adult way. I am much less intimidated or awed by position, titles or accomplish-ments. I believe that if I ever again become involved in an intimate relationship with a man it will be on a 'healthier' basis - there will be fewer 'neurotic needs' to deal with.

I think there were a number of reasons why my relationship with Maurice was different. I believe I sometimes intimidated people with my intense 'neurotic needs', and Maurice was never intimidated. I was never able to seduce him into my little games, thank God. He always responded to me as simply 'me' and did not classify me or categorize me or try to fix me because there was something wrong. In our relationship he never objectified me, and he didn't allow me to objectify him. Sometimes when I read books or articles written by Maurice, I can be very impressed, but I'm never 'impressed' with him when I'm with him.

In my relationship with my husband, Maurice helped me to understand that it wasn't Bob or me that was necessarily inadequate – it was our relationship. In my relationship with Maurice, I began to realize that I wanted a 'relationship', that relationship was important and life-sustaining and that Bob and I both deserved to be involved with those with whom we could have a 'relationship'.

Seeking to get my 'neurotic needs' met leads to 'death'. Relationship, with all its imperfections, is 'life' – I know that very well now, and my first teacher in this area was Maurice. But because he doesn't 'need' to be my teacher – I am now able to be my own teacher. Because he doesn't 'need' me to follow in his path, I am free to find my own.[4]

Summary

- The foundation of dialogical psychotherapy is Martin Buber's existentialism of dialogue and his philosophical anthropology.

- At the heart of Buber's philosophical anthropology is that distancing and relating that makes it necessary for each of us to be confirmed by another in order for our inmost becoming to take place.

- Central to confirmation is what Buber calls 'making present' and this depends in turn upon 'inclusion' – that bold swinging into the other that enables us to imagine concretely, to some extent, what the other is thinking, feeling, willing, perceiving.

- Inclusion is not to be confused with empathy, for it is a bipolar action in which you remain on your own side while experiencing the other side of the relationship.

- Inclusion, or 'imagining the real', is central to Buber's distinction between 'dialogue', in which we meet the other in her uniqueness and otherness, and 'monologue', in which the other is only part of our experience.

- In dialogical psychotherapy the meeting between therapist and client is central to the therapy.

- Thus dialogical psychotherapy rests on 'healing through meeting' or the 'healing partnership'.

The distinctive elements of this therapy, as described earlier, are: the interhuman; the dialogical; setting at a distance, and entering into relation; healing through meeting; a wholeness-orientated unconscious; existential guilt; the problematic of mutuality; inclusion; confirmation; the dialogue of touchstones.

Notes

1 This is a point I have expanded in my recent essay on 'Intersubjectivity in Husserl, Sartre, Heidegger, and Buber' (Friedman, 1993).

2 For a comparison and contrast of inclusion, or imagining the real, with the various ways in which Carl Rogers used the term 'empathy', see Friedman, 1985: 197–201.

3 This 'capacity to acquire and retain at least a few trustworthy relationships in the face of increasing dehumanization and alienation in the public world cannot be equated with either altruism or with guilt-laden compliance fueled by superego demands' (Boszormenyi-Nagy, 1987: 255).

Space requirements prevent my discussing other dialogical psychotherapists, but I shall at least mention here the books by Aleene Friedman (1992); Maurice Friedman (1985, 1992a, 1992b); William Heard (1993); Richard Hycner (1991; and Hycner and Jacobs, 1995); Barbara R. Krasner and Austin Joyce (1995); and Mordecai Rotenberg (1991).

4 For a fuller treatment of 'The Case of Dawn' see Schneider and May, 1995: 308–15.

References

Boszormenyi-Nagy, I. (1987) *Foundations of Contextual Therapy: Collected Papers of Ivan Boszormenyi-Nagy, M.D.* New York: Brunner/Mazel.

Boszormenyi-Nagy, I. and Krasner, B.R. (1986) *Between Give and Take: A Clinical Guide to Contextual Therapy.* New York: Brunner/Mazel.

Boszormenyi-Nagy, I. and Spark, G. (1973/1984) *Invisible Loyalties: Reciprocity in Intergenerational Family Therapy.* New York: Harper & Row, Medical Division; Brunner/Mazel (reprint, 1984).

Buber, M. (1958) *I and Thou* (2nd rev. edn with Postscript by author added; trans. R.G. Smith). New York: Chas. Scribners.

Buber, M. (1985) *Between Man and Man.* Introduction by M.S. Friedman, trans. by R.G. Smith. New York: Chas. Scribners.

Buber, M. (1988) *The Knowledge of Man: A Philosophy of the Interhuman.* Ed. with an Introductory Essay (Chap. 1) by M.S. Friedman (trans. M.S. Friedman and R.G. Smith). Atlantic Highlands, NJ: Humanities Press International.

Farber, L.H. (1966) *The Ways of the Will. Essays Toward a Psychology and Psychopathology of the Will.* New York: Basic Books.

Friedman, A.M. (1992) *Treating Chronic Pain: The Healing Partnership.* New York: Insight Books (Plenum Pub.).

Friedman, M.S. (1972) *Touchstones of Reality: Existential Trust and the Community of Peace.* New York: E.P. Dutton.

Friedman, M.S. (1985) *The Healing Dialogue in Psychotherapy.* New York: Jason Aronson. Paperback edition 1994, Northvale, NJ: Jason Aronson.

Friedman, M.S. (1989) 'Martin Buber and Ivan Boszormenyi-Nagy: The role of dialogue in contextual therapy', *Psychotherapy*, 26/Fall: 402–9.

Friedman, M.S. (1991) *The Worlds of Existentialism: A Critical Reader* (3rd edn with new updating Preface). Atlantic Highlands, NJ: Humanities Press International.

Friedman, M.S. (1992a) *Dialogue and the Human Image: Beyond Humanistic Psychology*. Newbury Park, CA: Sage Publications.

Friedman, M.S. (1992b) *Religion and Psychology: A Dialogical Approach*. New York: Paragon House.

Friedman, M.S. (1993) 'Intersubjectivity in Husserl, Sartre, Heiddeger, and Buber', *Review of Existential Psychology and Psychiatry*, 21 (1, 2 and 3): 63–80.

Heard, W.H. (1993) *The Healing Between: A Clinical Guide to Dialogical Psychotherapy*. San Francisco: Jossey/Bass.

Hycner, R.C. (1991) *Between Person and Person: Toward a Dialogical Psychotherapy*. Highland, NY: Gestalt Development Center. Paperback edition 1993.

Hycner, R.C. in association with Jacobs, L. (1995) *The Healing Relationshiop in Gestalt Therapy*. Highland, NY: Gestalt Therapy Associates.

Krasner, B.R. and Joyce, A.J. (1995) *Truth, Trust, and Relationships: Healing Interventions in Clinical Therapy*, with a foreword by Maurice Friedman. New York: Brunner/Mazel.

Rotenberg, M. (1991) *Dia-logo Therapy: Psychonarration and Pardes*. New York and London: Praeger.

Schneider, K.J. and May, R. (eds) (1995) *The Psychology of Existence: An Integrative, Clinical Perspective*. New York: McGraw Hill.

Stierlin, H. (1974) *Separating Parents and Adolescents: A Perspective on Running Away, Schizophrenia, and Waywardness*. New York: Quadrangle/New York Times Book Co.

5 'I'm OK, You're OK – and They're OK': Therapeutic Relationships in Transactional Analysis

Keith Tudor

Introduction

Understanding the nature of the therapeutic relationship, from whatever theoretical orientation, is a crucial endeavour for therapists, as in most therapeutic contexts it is the experience of the relationship which is considered to be therapeutic or healing – 'terapia' meaning healing. In considering the therapeutic relationship from the perspective of transactional analysis (TA), this chapter firstly and principally reviews the concept of relationship, referring to different traditions within TA (which are briefly introduced); secondly it explores the issue of dual relationships and TA's contribution to this controversial area of the therapeutic field; and, thirdly, it extends the (largely individual) concept of *the* therapeutic relationship to a number of therapeutic relationships experienced in groups and transacted as members of communities and, ultimately, of society. In doing so, I am concerned both to represent TA's traditional perspective on the therapeutic relationship, in particular the significance and centrality of the transferential relationship and, at the same time, in discussing dual relationships and therapeutic relating, to develop a critical enquiry which re-emphasizes the Adult–Adult therapeutic relationship in TA. This chapter does not assume familiarity with TA on the part of the reader and TA-specific terminology is defined in boxes inset in the text. For those wishing to gain further knowledge of TA by reading, Stewart and Joines (1987), Stewart (1989, 1992), Lapworth, Sills and Fish (1993) and Clarkson et al. (1996) are all recommended as useful introductory texts; for those who prefer knowledge by experiencing, accredited TA trainers regularly run recognized introductory TA '101' courses.

A Note on Terms

One of the problems in discussing the concept and practice of the (or a) 'therapeutic relationship' is that the phrase is commonly used to describe two different referents: it describes the contact between counsellor and client – in effect a self-defining definition, 'I have a therapeutic relationship by virtue of being *in* therapy'; at the same time it is used to refer to relationships which are therapeutic, thereby allowing the possibility that some therapeutic relationships (in the first sense) are not therapeutic. In a paper defining the process of definition, Money (1997) identifies three modes of defining – stipulative (prescriptive and authoritative), reportive (reflecting common usage) and mythogenic (expressing radical reconceptualizations of concepts) – and three strategies of defining – using words (verbal), pointing (ostensive) and doing (performative) – thus yielding nine types of definition. Drawing on this, we may distinguish between the first, self-defining use of the term 'therapeutic relationship' as a verbal, reportive (VR) definition and the second, based as it is on the experience of the relationship as to whether or not it is therapeutic, as a performative, stipulative (PS) use and application of 'therapeutic relationship'. In this chapter I thus distinguish between the two uses (VR and PS).

In identifying four special fields of application – clinical (that is, psychotherapy), educational, organizational and counselling – TA in effect distinguishes between counselling and psychotherapy, although the basis for the distinction is not clear. The International

Transactional Analysis Association (ITAA) defines TA counselling as:

> a professional activity within a contractual relationship. The counselling process enables clients or client systems to develop awareness, options and skills for problem management and personal development in daily life through the enhancement of their strengths and resources. Its aim is to increase autonomy in relation to their social, professional and cultural environment. (ITAA, 1995)

However, the ITAA does not offer an equivalent definition of psychotherapy. The Institute of Transactional Analysis (ITA) (the national British TA organization) describes TA, among other definitions, as a theory of psychotherapy which 'integrates the internal psychological experience with interpersonal behaviours' (ITA, 1995). Such definitions however, with their different emphases, require further elaboration if TA is to succeed in defining and applying any difference – for instance to the different or additional theory, skills and competencies necessary for qualifying as a Certified Transactional Analyst (CTA) (Clinical) (that is, as a psychotherapist) as distinct from qualifying as a CTA (Counselling). Some TA trainers view counselling as a staging post in psychotherapy training and encourage trainee psychotherapists to become members of and seek accreditation with the British Association for Counselling (BAC); others actively discourage this; still others manifest this distinction and run TA counselling courses. In both the generic literature in the field of counselling and psychotherapy, and specifically within TA, I do not see the theoretical case for such a distinction. In my view the arguments for a difference between counselling and psychotherapy are either superficial, historical, political, administrative or to do with theoretical orientation (see Tudor, 1997a). The BAC (1997) recognizes that there is no generally accepted distinction between the two and, as regards competencies for National Vocational Training it appears that the United Kingdom Council for Psychotherapy (UKCP) is unable to distinguish between counselling and psychotherapy. In this chapter, while I generally use the terms counselling and counsellor for consistency with the 'house style' of the book, I do so on the basis that I am referring to counselling, counselling psychology and psychotherapy; where I use the term psychotherapy it is in the context of the discussion or authors cited. I also generally use the plural pronoun 'they' rather than he or she.

Therapy and Relationship in TA

TA has a rich, if somewhat dispersed literature on the therapeutic relationship. In some personal reflections on TA, Stewart (1996: 198) makes the point that the therapeutic relationship is *presupposed* and 'a sine qua non of effective therapy'. In this section I draw out the various strands of this tradition by acknowledging the influence of three 'schools' within TA: the Classical, the Cathexis and the Redecision schools – see Barnes (1977) and Stewart and Joines (1987) for further reading on these. While all TA practitioners are required for qualification and accreditation to demonstrate that they draw on all traditions within TA, the different schools represent different emphases in thinking, treatment – and therapeutic relationship. All, however, describe the therapeutic relationship (VR) in relation to transference – and it is the counsellor's view of transference which is central to their intention and practice in all therapeutic relationships in TA. Further views about the therapeutic relationship, however, and especially the therapeutic attitude of the counsellor, and views which are agreed by all TA practitioners, may be drawn out from Berne's writing about the philosophy, principles and practice of TA (see Table 5.1).

TA maintains the contractual basis of all relationships between counsellor and client. For a relationship to be therapeutic in TA terms (that is, VR *and* PS), four elements need to be present:

1 *The counsellor subscribes to the philosophy, methods and attitudes described below* (Table 5.1). This locates and identifies the counsellor as a *TA* counsellor.

2 *The client has agreed goals which are therapeutic, that is, which are positive and life-enhancing (and not life-threatening).* This takes account of the fact that the client's initial goals and contract may not be therapeutic and that contracts both reflect and define an ongoing, organic process (see Lee, 1997) and that within TA, suicide, homicide and going crazy are generally viewed as forms of escape from life to be confronted rather than supported.

3 *The client's achievement of their goal/s requires the involvement of a counsellor (as distinct from anyone else such as a friend or partner).* This recognizes the significance, although not necessarily the presence of the counsellor as crucial to the therapeutic process.

Table 5.1   *The implications of TA philosophy and method for the counsellor's attitude to the therapeutic relationship*

TA – Philosophy, method and therapeutic attitude	Implications for the counsellor's attitude to the therapeutic relationship
Basic philosophy	
■ People are OK[1]	Positive and mutual regard/respect (I'm OK, You're OK)[2]
■ Everyone has the capacity to think	. . . and a belief in self-responsibility
■ People decide their own destiny and these decisions can be changed	A belief in personal responsibility and autonomy[3]
Therapeutic slogans (Berne, 1966)	
■ *Primum non nocere* – Above all do no harm	The principle from moral philosophy and ethics of non maleficence
■ *Vis medicatrix naturae* – the curative power of nature	Respect for the client's health, potential for health and for developmental obstructions to health, e.g. defences
■ *Je le pensay, & Dieu le guarit* – I treat them and God cures them[4]	A factual (not false) humility[5]
Therapeutic method	
■ Contractual method (a mutually agreed statement of change)	Commitment to a clearly defined relationship in which there is shared responsibility for the process of change
■ Open communication	Commitment to open communication, e.g. regarding client case notes, case conferences, references, etc.
Therapeutic attitudes (Berne, 1966) A fresh frame of mind:	
■ In good health, physically and psychologically	Respect for self and others
■ Well-prepared, clear and open	Authenticity *as a therapist* (as distinct from as a friend)

[1] A shorthand statement describing the positive essence of people.

[2] In his last book, Berne (1975b) developed this into three-handed life positions – 'I'm OK, You're OK, They're OK' etc., thereby giving eight possible life positions.

[3] Defined within TA as 'the release or recovery of three capacities: awareness, spontaneity and intimacy' (Berne, 1968: 158) and enshrined in the BAC *Code of Ethics* (1997).

[4] Although Berne (1966: 63) defines this as 'getting the patient ready for the cure to happen today', this slogan contradicts much of Berne's other writing on the subject of cure.

[5] He also reminds us that 'the professional therapist's job is to use his [sic] knowledge *therapeutically*; if the patient is going to be cured by love, that should be left to a lover' (p. 63, my emphasis).

4 *The above three elements are defined and agreed by the contractual method* (see Steiner, 1971; Stewart, 1989).

The Classical School
Exponents of the classical school follow most closely the approach to treatment of Eric Berne and his immediate associates. This focuses on the diagnosis of ego states (Parent, Adult and Child);

An ego state is 'a consistent pattern of feeling and experience directly related to a corresponding consistent pattern of behaviour' (Berne, 1966: 364).

---

the use of analytic models to facilitate Adult understanding in the client - the classical school is closest to the psychodynamic tradition - including their life script and the psychological games

---

'A script is an ongoing program, developed in early childhood under parental influence, which directs the individual's behavior in the most important aspects of his life' (Berne, 1975b: 418)

---

they play in order to maintain that script; and the use of contracts to make behavioural changes and to achieve cure (see Berne, 1975a, 1975b).

'A game is a process of doing something with an ulterior motive that (1) is outside of Adult awareness; (2) does not become explicit until the participants switch the way they are behaving; and (3) results in everyone feeling confused, misunderstood, and wanting to blame the other person' (Joines cited in Stewart and Joines, 1987: 242–3).

Berne wrote only briefly about the therapeutic relationship as such (see Berne, 1966). In doing so he suggests that, before and in the first few minutes of each session or meeting with clients, therapists should ask themselves 'some fundamental questions about the real meaning of the therapeutic relationship' (pp. 63–4). He views this firstly with regard to the therapist's own development: ' "Why am I sitting in this room? Why am I not at home with my children. . . . What will this hour contribute to my unfolding?" ' (p. 64). Secondly, Berne suggests reflecting on the client and their motivations: ' "Why are they here? Why are they not at home with their children or doing what their fancy dictates? Why did they choose psychotherapy as a solution? Why not religion, alcohol, drugs, crime, gambling . . .? What will this hour contribute to their unfolding?" ' (ibid.). In his last book Berne (1975b), again briefly, discusses the role of the therapist in terms of the part s/he might play in the client's script e.g. 'the Magician' and suggests that the therapist's first task is to discover what role s/he fits in the client's script – 'and what is supposed to happen between them' (p. 353) – thus emphasizing the bilateral nature of the relationship.

On the basis of its philosophy, TA in practice is essentially an actionistic and highly interventionist form of counselling. It is based on diagnosis of the client and, arising from the contractual method, on having a treatment planning sequence which aims to achieve cure or some specific change in the client. To this end, Berne (1966) identifies eight 'therapeutic operations' (interrogation, specification, confrontation, explanation, illustration, confirmation, interpretation and crystallization) which are used by the counsellor as interventions (and interpositions). As such, and especially in its classical form, TA is often experienced as a confrontational and challenging form of counselling. Berne (1966) regarded 'supportive therapy' as 'intrinsically spurious' and regarded the word 'relationship' as vague or borrowed terminology and asked clients what they meant by the word. From this, 'relating' for its own sake is generally downplayed in TA. Stewart (1992: 74) makes the point that Berne's views on the person of the psychotherapist, the necessary personal and professional training and preparation, as well as their assets, therapeutic attitude and responsibilities – all imply that '*the establishment of a relationship, in and of itself, is not necessarily therapeutic*' – which is consistent with our two definitions of the therapeutic relationship. Berne encouraged clients to make clear the meaning of what he referred to as psychological jargon and 'institutional concepts' such as 'relationship' and especially the 'therapeutic relationship'.

In his first book on the principles of TA, Berne (1975a) outlined his structural analysis of personality. In doing so Berne laid the foundation not only for the transactional analysis of personality, but also for a transactional model of relationships – and of communication (see Figure 5.1).

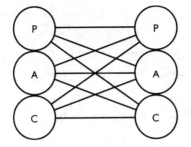

Figure 5.1 *A theoretically ideal relationship (Berne, 1975a)*

'A Parental ego state is a set of feelings, attitudes, and behavior patterns which resemble those of a parental figure. . . . The Child ego state is a set of feelings, attitudes and behavior patterns which are relics of the individual's own childhood' (Berne, 1975a: 75–7).

In defining the Parent and Child ego states, Berne offers a transferential model of relationship: thus a Child to Parent or Parent to Child transaction is, *by definition* transferential, for example:

Counsellor [*to Client*]: Hello . . .
Client [*to Counsellor*]: You're not interested in how I am; you're just concerned with checking that I won't do anything silly. [*A Child reaction to a projected Parent.*]

Counsellor: Hello.
Client: You look tired. Are you OK? Are you sure you're well enough to see me today? [*A Parent reaction to a projected Child.*]

Developing Berne's exploration of the dynamics underlying transference transactions, Moiso (1985) defines the transference relationship in TA terms: '*a relationship in which the patient, in order to reexperience parent–child or primitive object relationships projects onto the therapist his own Parental Ego States. . . .* These are projected onto a screen superimposed on the therapist (Child → projected Parent messages)' (pp. 194–5, original emphasis) (Figure 5.2).

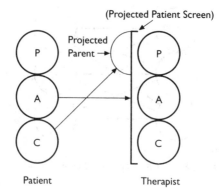

Figure 5.2 *Analysis of transference relationship (Moiso, 1985)*

For further reading on the analysis and use of transference and countertransference in TA see Novellino (1984), Moiso (1985), Barr (1987), Erskine (1991) and Clarkson (1992).

Within TA, especially in its early days, there was a strong tradition of social and radical psychiatry based on the concept of alienation as the essence of all psychiatric conditions which was defined as '*the result of oppression about which the oppressed has been mystified or deceived*' (Steiner, 1971: 5, original emphasis). Steiner and colleagues in the Radical Therapist Collective were at the forefront of critical perspectives and practice in therapy about relationships, particularly those between men and women but also between clients and therapists (see Agel, 1971; Roy and Steiner, 1988; Wyckoff, 1976). This tradition has led to a consistent concern within TA to consider the power issues involved in the therapeutic relationship (see Friedlander, 1987). Boyd (1976: 402), for instance, introduces the concept of 'therapeutic leverage' to describe 'both the here and now attempts of the patient to manipulate the balance of interpersonal power and the second by second maneuvers of the therapist to keep the therapy effective'.

The Cathexis School
This school of TA is based on the work of the Cathexis Institute, founded by Jacqui Schiff, as a centre for the treatment of psychotic clients, including those diagnosed as having schizophrenia

(see Schiff, 1969; Schiff et al., 1975). Based on their analysis of symbiosis, discounting and passivity, they developed the theory

> 'A symbiosis occurs when two or more individuals behave as though between them they form a whole person. The relationship is characterized structurally by neither individual cathecting a full complement of ego states' (Schiff et al., 1975: 5).

> 'Discounting is an internal mechanism which involves people minimizing or ignoring some aspect of themselves, others or the reality situation' (ibid.: 14).

> Passivity is defined as 'how people don't do things (respond to stimuli) or don't do them effectively' (ibid.: 5).

and practice of reparenting the 'crazy Parent' ego state of disturbed clients who, in regression, 'decathect' (that is, withdraw energy) from their introjected crazy Parent, replacing it with their introjections of the positive and consistent (re)parenting of the therapist/s. Another way to understand this process, therefore, is

> 'Reparenting . . . involves the total decathexis of the originally incorporated Parent ego state, and the replacement of that structure with a new Parent structure' (ibid.: 88).

that the therapist replaces the Parent and reparents the Child. Due to the regressive nature of the work and the necessary dependency of the client on the therapist, this work usually takes place in residential settings and requires a high level of commitment on the part of both therapist and client (see Robinson, 1998). These requirements and some of the early methods and techniques used by the Schiff family were – and are – also controversial and have led to much debate within the TA community (see Jacobs, 1994; Azzi, 1998). The particular contribution of the Cathexis school to our understanding of the therapeutic relationship is in terms of parenting – radical reparenting, spot reparenting and self-reparenting.

Counsellors working within the Cathexis school of TA positively use the transference by stepping into the Parent role in order to do the reparenting. In the original Schiffian *radical reparenting* model, the client's historical parent figures are excluded from the Parent ego state because they were - and are still experienced as - so damaging. In clients diagnosed as schizophrenic and in the context of a residential therapeutic community, clients regressed and lived in early developmental stages for extended periods; the therapists then parented them, including holding, feeding - and punishing - so that the client incorporated new, positive experiences of parents into their Parent ego state. In this context regression refers only to 'going back' for extended periods. It is possible to do similar work by 'cathecting young' or 'getting little' for short periods and on an outpatient basis - what Osnes (1974) refers to as *spot reparenting*. Drawing on Berne's (1975a) original work on regression analysis, Osnes suggests that clients go back to an actual and specific experience and relive it up to the point of the original negative parenting (criticism, humiliation, abuse) at which point the counsellor intervenes with a new positive, nurturing message, for example:

> In response to an early experience of physical abuse:
> *Counsellor [to regressed client]*: Your father is wrong. You deserve to be loved [*reconstruction of Parent ego state*]. I love you. You don't have to be afraid [*new message for Child ego state*].

Both radical reparenting and spot reparenting are based on the contractual method. Both take place in groups, the former almost exclusively in residential settings, all of which provide safety, monitoring and regulation - for both client and counsellor. Nevertheless, this work is problematic in that it places a lot of power, authority and influence in the hands of the counsellor, particularly at the moment of reparenting. It thus requires the counsellor to 'know thyself' and 'heal thyself': to be absolutely clear about their motivation for doing this kind of work and to be able to leave any of their own issues to one side: 'a difficulty may arise, however, if unresolved problems in the therapist's ego states are also incorporated' (James, 1974: 33). Working in this reparenting relationship requires the counsellor to work in the transference without identifying themselves with it. Of course, criticisms of this form of therapeutic relationship equally apply to any counselling interventions or transactions which give permission ('It's OK for you to . . .', 'Well done', or a pleased smile) and affirmation ('You think well') as, at best, they may be experienced as patronizing and, at worst, may encourage dependency. Although therapeutic parenting necessarily involves a developmental dependency, even if for only a moment, as with all good parenting it aims to foster independence and autonomy, that is spontaneity, awareness and intimacy. A third form of parenting is *self-reparenting* (James, 1974; James and Goulding, 1998). It differs from radical reparenting in that it takes a more phenomenological and cultural perspective on parenting, parental behaviour and the Parent ego state; it does not exclude the historical parents, seeing something OK about them, and thus restructures rather than reconstructs the client's Parent ego state. Furthermore, in the process of self-reparenting the client's Adult ego state is in charge. Self-reparenting involves a specific procedure which may be facilitated by a counsellor:

1. Awareness of the need for a new Parent which will compensate, supplement or defuse the parent of the old Parent.
2. Historical diagnosis of each childhood figure.
3. Education about parenting.
4. Inner dialogue between the Adult and the inner Child – with a view to discovering what each part of the Child ego state needs.
5. Evaluation of the data by the Adult.
6. Contract on the part of the Adult to be a substitute parent to the inner Child and practice of specific identified parenting behaviour.
7. Recognition of the new Parent (James, 1974).

The Redecision School

This school of TA takes its name from the decisional aspect of TA's basic philosophy (see Table 5.1), and the belief and practice that just as we make decisions about our life, based on our life script, so we may re-decide and change our influences, behaviour, beliefs, experiences, fantasies and feelings. This school is associated with the work of Bob and Mary Goulding who combined TA with techniques from Gestalt therapy such as 'two-chair' work. The Gouldings' main contribution to our understanding about therapeutic relationships is in confronting and redirecting the client's transference to its original source. While recognizing and accounting for the existence of 'transferring from the past' in everything we do and thus in every helping relationship, the Gouldings advocated stepping out of the transference role as far as the client is concerned, for example:

Client [to Counsellor]: I'd like *you* to be my Dad.
Counsellor: Put your Dad there [*pointing to a cushion next to the counsellor*] and tell him what you'd like from him.

Dialogues between two chairs representing the transferred past and the real present, and early scene work replaying scenes from childhood are both techniques used in TA redecision therapy which may be used to work *with* but not *in* the transference. In terms of the therapeutic relationship (PS) *as experienced*, the counsellor acts more as a facilitator and clients are encouraged to take a meta-perspective on their problems (see Goulding and Goulding, 1979).

The different approaches of the different schools of TA to the transference relationship may be viewed as on a continuum:

Working in the transference		Working with but outside the transference
Cathexis school	Classical school	Redecision school

Integrative TA: An Emerging 'School'?
Over the last 15 years in the generic counselling and psychotherapeutic literature, there has been an emerging interest in therapeutic integration; this extends to debates within different 'schools' or 'forces' of therapy and is no less true in TA, although I argue that TA needs to concern itself more with integration *within* TA, that is, '*intra*gration' (Tudor, 1996). Nevertheless, there is a developing integrative *tradition* (it is not yet a 'school' according to Barnes's (1977) definition) within TA (Clarkson, 1992; Erskine and Moursund, 1988; also see Novey, 1996) and indeed, a significant 18 per cent of Certified Transactional Analysts (CTAs) define themselves in the United Kingdom Council for Psychotherapy's (UKCP) register of psychotherapists as 'integrative psychotherapists' (UKCP, 1996). One feature of this is (along with much of the rest of the therapeutic world), an emerging interest in the concept, attitude and practice of empathy. In TA, Clark (1991) links this to Berne's concept of transactions in promoting empathic transactions as a means of deconfusing the Child ego state. Drawing on Gelso and Carter's (1985) components of counselling relationships as an organizing framework for integration – the working alliance, transference and the real relationship – we may identify these components as present in TA:

Deconfusion is the identification and expression of 'unmet needs and feelings in the Child ego state which were suppressed at the time of the script decision in the interests of psychological and/or physical survival' (Clarkson et al., 1996: 241).

- The working alliance (Adult–Adult) – the first stage in treatment planning (see Clarkson et al., 1996) and operationalized in the contractual method of TA. In her therapeutic relationship model, Barr (1987: 135) views this as the 'core relationship' between client and therapist, 'beginning with the client's capacity to recruit and the therapist's recruitability'.
- Transference (and countertransference) (Child–parent, Parent–Child) – central to a TA understanding of the therapeutic relationship (VR and PS) (as elaborated above) and which includes the reparative/developmentally needed relationship (Barr, 1987; Clarkson, 1992) represented by the reparenting work of the Cathexis school.
- The real relationship (Adult–Adult) – reflected in the existential life position 'I'm OK, You're OK' (I+ U+) and the emphasis in TA on the counsellor's authenticity as a counsellor.

My own view is that TA since Berne has over-emphasized the concept of transference and, generally, undervalued and underestimated the importance of the Adult–Adult therapeutic relationship, co-created, defined and negotiated by bilateral contract. This is the subject of a forthcoming paper which emphasizes the transactional (rather than the analytic), and the mutual and bilateral (rather than unilateral) nature of the therapeutic relationship in TA (Summers and Tudor, 1999). A significant application of this is the controversial area of dual relationships.

Dual Therapeutic Relationships

The issue of dual relationships – that is, one person (the therapist) having more than one relationship (for example as a trainer or supervisor in addition to that of a therapist) to a client, or indeed a client (being, say, also a supplier of goods or services) to their therapist – is a 'hot potato' both within TA and in the wider field of counselling and psychotherapy. As far as counsellors in Britain are concerned, at present the dual relationships of counsellor and supervisor and counsellor and trainer are prohibited (BAC, 1997:

B.5.2) while the codes of ethics and practice for supervisors and trainers place responsibility on the supervisor and trainer to be explicit about the boundaries between the two roles (BAC, 1995, 1996). The UKCP's general ethical guidelines do not specifically refer to dual relationships; within its Humanistic and Integrative Psychotherapy Section (HIPS), of which the ITA is a member organization, it is recommended that they are best avoided wherever possible. The HIPS is currently reviewing its recommendations concerning dual relationships. However, given such prohibitions and recommendations, there is surprisingly little written – both within TA and generally – about the logic of the 'no dual relationships' position or its underlying presuppositions. In this section, therefore, I review some of the arguments against and for dual relationships from the perspective of what is or could be therapeutic about such relationships (and thus PS), rather than simply defining dual relationships (in a circular definition) as inherently exploitative and therefore as bad, mad or dangerous even to contemplate (VR).

The History of Counselling is a History of Dual Relationships

While history is no justification for unethical or unprofessional practice, it is worth noting that the founding fathers and mothers of psychoanalysis (none of whom would nowadays be eligible for membership of the training institutes which bear their names or promote their ideas) worked in and with dual and multiple relationships. Freud analysed all his initial trainees; Jung and Reich both had relationships with their clients; and Klein analysed her own children. It is easy to condemn such relationships; it is more complex and rigorous to investigate the therapeutic – or exploitative – nature (or otherwise) of these relationships. Schools (and institutes) in both the analytic and humanistic traditions of psychotherapy have in the past positively advocated and even required dual relationships: trainees being in analysis and supervision with the same training analyst. The argument for this was – and is – based on the applicability of the psychoanalytic method – analysis, suggestion and insight – to the client whether they are (in roles of) a trainee or a supervisee or not: whatever their issues are, these will be played out in all roles in their lives; whatever their own clients' issues are, these may be understood in terms of the client/trainee/supervisee's countertransference.

'Relationship is Confused with Role' (Cox, 1997)

Relationship is defined as 'the state of being related; a condition or character based upon this; kinship' (Onions, 1973: 1786), while a role is a part or character one undertakes. On this basis, the 'relationship' between client and counsellor may equally and perhaps more accurately be defined as a professional role taken on under contract for a specific period of time.

An exercise

Take a moment to write down who you are in your life in terms of relationships — daughter/son, sister/brother, mother/father, partner/ lover, etc.; trainer, tutor, supervisor, therapist, client, etc. More particularly, you might do this in relation to any of the authors of the chapters in this book or, indeed, any writers cited in the book. You might do it in relation to a training, therapy or other group of which you are a member.

Now think about these as *roles*. . . . Is there any difference?

In doing this exercise, some people find that thinking and feeling about roles rather than relationships normalizes or makes usual what we do: I am a husband, father, friend, uncle, brother, son, employer, trainer, colleague, supervisor, therapist, consultant, examiner, client, consumer, etc. These are parts of the whole of me; they define temporal roles, some more long-term or permanent than others. Taking on the *role* of examiner does not necessarily entail a relationship or kinship. This applies equally to personal roles and relationships: there are men who are in the *role* of a father (a man caring for his children) but who are not actively or meaningfully *in relationship* with their children. It is important to distinguish between relationship and role and between professional and personal, and the different types of definition discussed – the verbal, reportive (VR) and the performative, stipulative (PS) – are helpful in doing this (Table 5.2). Table 5.2 does not stipulate a fixed association or definition of relationship or role (as has been discussed and which, of course, are each open to all nine types of definition). It does, however, convey that the difference between relationship and role is commonly between what is received or reported as being so (*the* therapeutic relationship) (VR) and what is experienced as a role (a therapeutic, supervisory, training role) (PS). The thick line between the professional and

Table 5.2 *A framework for understanding professional and personal relationship and role*

	Professional	Personal
Relationship	E.g. therapist, supervisor, trainer (verbal, reportive definitions)	E.g. father (verbal, reportive definition)
Role	E.g. therapist, supervisor, trainer (performative, stipulative definitions)	E.g. a man who cares for his children for a period of time (performative, stipulative defintion)

personal relationship indicates that this dual relationship is un-desirable if not prohibited by most professional therapeutic organizations and associations. Notwithstanding this, counsellors are also personal in their professional role ('I am me wherever I go') and over time the real(ity) relationship (thus PS) is often experienced by both parties as transcending the role relationship.

Dual and Multiple Roles are an Inevitable Part of Life and of Counselling

This appreciation that we have many roles in life leads us to two conclusions and decisions: to avoid dual roles or to meet and deal with them. Trying to avoid or *having* to avoid dual professional relationships (roles) in order to adhere to particular professional codes of ethics and practice may, indeed, be viewed as neurotic:

- As defensive against anxiety or real contact between people: a 'defensive therapy' position.
- As repressive of complexity: 'to simply outlaw the dual relationships of supervisor/therapist does not adequately address the complex issues involved; rather it imposes a rigidity on a complex and often ambiguous profession, reduces the choices and autonomy of the supervisee, and does not necessarily ensure the optimal welfare of a supervisee's clients' (Cornell, 1994: 25).
- As phobic; in a chapter on the problems of dual relationships in the education of counsellors Lloyd (1992) refers to 'dual relationship phobia'.

As members of the same professional body as our therapist, supervisor, client, etc., we are in dual relationship; living in a remote area or being part of a 'minority' community we are likely to be in dual and multiple professional and therapeutic relation-

ships. Codes of ethics and practice which place absolute requirements on us to avoid dual relationships assume choice usually
available only in larger cities and to 'majority' communities. In
terms of anti-discriminatory practice and client autonomy, it may
well be more therapeutic for a gay man to work with a local
counsellor, another gay man, than to travel to another town to see
a second-choice counsellor (for a discussion of the boundaries
between different role relationships and negotiation of different
professional boundaries, see Embleton Tudor, 1997).

The Criticism of Dual Relationships is not Consistent
For the majority of counsellors there is a requirement at some
stage of their training or professional development to be in
therapy themselves. Given that we subscribe to the concept of a
professional and collegial community (see, for instance, BAC,
1997), this requires counsellors to be in a dual relationship/role,
that is, one with a colleague. The logic of completely avoiding
dual roles is that counsellors should be in counselling with non-
counsellors! Neither does the criticism of dual relationships
extend to dual or multiple *therapeutic* relationships (such as
identified by Barr, 1987; Clarkson, 1990, 1995; Gelso and Carter,
1985; Greenson, 1967).

Arguments Against Dual Relationships/Roles – and
Responses
Perhaps the strongest argument against dual relationships is that
they muddy the transferential waters. While, for some counsellors,
depending on their theoretical orientation, such muddying might
be viewed as a good thing, and others might take on the challenge
of working with this complexity, there is a risk to clients (who
might also be trainees or supervisees) of a counsellor exploiting
their client's positive transference. This is a significant phenomenon in the world of counsellor training where a considerable
number of trainees want to train as counsellors with their own
counsellor, whose facilitative qualities and skills they have experienced. Again, I view this situation as an issue of possible exploitation and one which is countered by good training and supervision
both of which could and should address, in this frame of reference, the countertransferential issues involved.

In this context of counsellor training, one major practical argument against dual relationships is the current situation of 'in-

house' certification of counsellors and psychotherapists. Thus a trainer who may also have been a trainee's counsellor and/or supervisor may also be in the position of examining that trainee (client/supervisee). This is a clear merging of interests and, despite the HIPS recommendation about the non-duplication of trainer and examiner roles, reflects the incestuous and exploitative reality of some training organizations. Robertson (1993) identifies various characteristics of abusive mini-cultures of training organizations. This is partially addressed by the presence and role of external examiners, although their role – and relationship – with the training organization arguably needs to be monitored externally. It is also answered by external accreditation systems *in addition to qualification.* In TA, practitioners are examined and accredited totally 'out-of-house' and one of the organizational strengths of TA is its rigorous examination and accreditation of its practitioners, trainers and supervisors. Examinations take place at International Conferences and thus TA practitioners are subject to international, external scrutiny. Also, from a therapeutic point of view, clients who are trainees/supervisees might not expose or work through the pathological and/or dysfunctional parts of themselves for fear of being judged and assessed as trainees/ supervisees.

Most arguments against dual relationships centre on three issues:

1 *The possible exploitation of the client.* This appears to be founded on the evidence that the majority of ethics complaints from clients investigated by professional bodies, and certainly by the ITA, concern dual relationships. However, I consider these to be issues of exploitation, not necessarily of duality. The response to this problem is for the counsellor to have good awareness, training and supervision about issues of power, influence, exploitation and anti-oppressive practice – theory and practice which the social psychiatry tradition of TA informs.

2 *The possible conflict of interests* – indeed, in an unsubstantiated assertion, Bond (1993) equates dual relationships with conflict of interests (see also Herlihy and Corney, 1992). In response, it is clearly crucial for both or all parties to consider precisely what interests are in conflict. In my view, it is the merging (rather than the conflict) of interests and the

possible erosion of boundaries which is more common and problematic in this area (as with the above example from training). The concept of symbiosis is useful in analysing, understanding and working with issues of merger and separation. The possible merging of interests is an argument for establishing and maintaining clear rather than blurred or merged roles: as regards personal and professional roles and relationships, for example not being both partner and therapist (see Table 5.2), or incompatible professional roles, for example not being trainer and examiner. I define incompatibility in relation to:

■ TA philosophy: people are OK, everyone has the capacity to think and people can decide their own destiny.
■ General values of caring professions: integrity, impartiality and respect (see Bond, 1993).
■ Principles from moral philosophy: beneficence, non-maleficence, justice and respect for autonomy.

3 *The possible impairment of the therapist's judgement.* This is not solely a problem of duality but an issue of professional competence and an argument for self-awareness, high-quality training and ongoing supervision. Obviously, some counsellors on some occasions will make a decision based on some impaired judgement. As regards dual relationships the checklist (pp. 111–12) may aid such judgement and ethical decision-making.

Therapeutic Advantages to Dual Therapeutic Relationships

There are two possible advantages of dual therapeutic relationships to be considered. Firstly, as humans we are organized wholes (holons) in multiple roles and relationships, trying to make meaning of our complex lives and worlds. Working within a facilitative and 'holding' dual relationship can help us to make sense of this complexity rather than artificially separating (and splitting) our selves. The counsellor/trainer/supervisor working with dual or multiple roles also has the opportunity to model dealing with, rather than avoiding, complexity.

Secondly, a person is a client/trainee/supervisee/etc. Clients are whole people who are damaged, disturbed or disintegrated in some way; as such their therapeutic issues will have repercussions in all their roles and relationships. Someone who learned to please others will do this as a client, trainee counsellor and supervisee. There is no difference *therapeutically* between the activities of training, supervision, personal therapy and personal development. Indeed, in the training context, there are strong arguments for a trainer, observing a particular therapeutic issue in a person (at that moment in the role of a trainee), to counsel that person on that issue. Writing from a person-centred perspective but making a point which is equally applicable to other orientations, Mearns (1994: 35) argues that 'personal development for professional working is so crucial to the person-centred approach that it cannot be left to the vagaries of individual therapy'. Personal development is an important part of most training in counselling and psychotherapy and takes place in the training group ('check in', group time, reflection time, community meetings, and so on). It may also take the form of demonstration individual therapy sessions in the training group. An absolute ban on dual relationships, therefore, would logically exclude such therapy unless it were redefined as 'personal development'. Within TA, the Gouldings promote dual relationships, for instance between trainer/therapist and trainee/client, arguing that they are protected by the contractual method of TA therapy and, furthermore, that treating (doing therapy with) trainees is the best way to get across the different kinds of contracts as well as the operational method of TA; Bob Goulding summarizes: 'I don't see how we can train properly if we don't treat as part of the training contract (Goulding and Goulding, 1978: 139). In discussion with other Gestalt and TA colleagues, the following arguments are advanced in favour of this dual relationship:

- The trainer/therapist observes problems (e.g. games) which the therapist may not.
- Moving between roles promotes equality and mutuality.
- It is immediate: 'the best way to deal with countertransference is at the moment it occurs in the group' (Goulding and Goulding, 1978: 140).

The dual relationship of trainer/therapist is an established tradition within TA (for a discussion of which see Bader, 1994; Clarkson, 1994; Cornell, 1994) and, indeed, a number of TA practitioners have left the BAC on this very issue – which is ironic in view of the fact that the ITA (1998) has recently prohibited combining the roles of therapist and supervisor to one person and has a guideline suggesting that the combined therapist/trainer role is best avoided as far as is practically possible.

A Dual Relationship Checklist
In an attempt to stem the flood of professional opinion against dual therapeutic relationships, I offer the following ten-point checklist by which clients *and counsellors* could both be protected and take permission to explore the therapeutic value of duality, multiplicity and complexity. I emphasize 'and counsellors' as, in the arguments against dual relationships, little attention is given to the exploitation of counsellors by clients.

1   Distinguish between relationship and role and between professional role and personal role. This provides a framework for assessing congruence and consistency in therapeutic role and relationships.
2   Develop the concept of 'role fluency' (Clarkson, 1994) that is, a fluidity between roles and a fluency in different roles.
3   Reframe the debate from duality to the issue or question of exploitation *both* of clients *and* of counsellors as regards:
    ■   sexual exploitation, that is, no sexual relations (for example ACA, 1995: A.7);
    ■   financial exploitation – the ACA, for instance, discourages bartering (for a discussion of which see Tudor, 1998);
    ■   political – Clarkson (1994) discusses the potential for political exploitation where clients who are also trainees and members of the same professional organization may be involved in voting for their therapist.
4   Subscribe to an accepted professional code of ethics and practice (although the relative permission or prohibition regarding dual relationship will depend on which code of ethics counsellors subscribe to); and have a clear, congruent and communicable personal ethics, which includes being clear about counsellors' personal motivation and issues of power.
5   Be well trained and experienced, especially in dealing with issues of power, oppression, exploitation and abuse.
6   Ensure that all final accreditation procedures are preferably 'out of house' or at least at 'arm's length' so that the trainer

(/supervisor/therapist) is never the marker or sole or deciding marker of a trainee's work for final accreditation (see ITA,
1998).

7   Develop an ability to evaluate clinical, legal and ethical
considerations in counselling (see, for instance, Bader, 1994).

8   Take 'professional precautions': 'when a dual relationship
cannot be avoided, counsellors take appropriate professional
precautions such as informed consent, consultation, and
documentation to ensure that judgement is not impaired and
no exploitation occurs' (ACA, 1995: A.6.a).

9   Appreciate that clients, trainees and supervisees are consent-
ing adults - *and customers*. Some training organizations (and
counsellors) infantilize their clients in how they regard and
treat them (for example through certain conceptualizations
about their development in training), which is not only
patronizing but also fosters inappropriate dependency and
exploitation - and is countered by adopting theories of adult
(rather than child) development in education.

10 Acknowledge the humility of what actually helps and heals,
such as being held, receiving a postcard, a smile or an
acknowledgement at a conference - often outside the boundary of the 'therapeutic hour'; and acknowledge the humanity
of being willing to work with complexity, contradiction and
conflict.

Afterword

In the course of writing this section, at one point I typed 'duel'
instead of 'dual' relationships! - a Freudian slip which reminds me
of the comp'exity of working with duality and duelling relationships.

From the Therapeutic Relationship to
Therapeutic Relating

Finally, in this chapter, I am concerned to indicate ways of applying
the (largely individual) concept of *the* therapeutic relationship to
therapeutic relationships experienced in groups and transacted as
members of communities and, ultimately, of society. I identify two
aspects of this. The first is the movement the client makes from
some form of dependency on one (*the*) therapeutic relationship to
other relationships which are therapeutic. Within the therapeutic

sphere these could be, and often are, other members of a counselling group and, indeed, other counsellors; outside counselling,
these may be new, often intense friendship relationships which
are experienced as therapeutic and which support the client's
change/s. The second aspect of this wider application is the
movement from the nominal (noun) 'relationship' to the activity
(verb) of *relating*.

One of the criticisms of therapy is that is individualizes – and
privatizes – relationships: if you have a problem, go to a therapist.
When the concept of therapy is explained to the eponymous hero
in the film *Crocodile Dundee* he asks the person concerned 'Why?
Don't you have any friends?' Despite the advances in our understanding of the psyche and the nature of healing in the last 100
years (since Freud coined the term 'psychotherapy'), the exclusive
nature of the therapeutic relationship remains an important criticism and challenge to this particular helping and healing activity.
The relationship with your therapist is viewed as *the* therapeutic
relationship and, to some extent, the focus on the concept of the
therapeutic relationship encourages this. By focusing on the verb/
action *relating* rather than the noun *relationship* we shift attention from the relationship between client and counsellor (and
others) to how the client relates and, further, to how they establish and maintain relating which is therapeutic in the rest of their
lives outside the limited contact with their counsellor. In the rest
of this section I highlight a number of ways in which the client
may unfold the therapeutic relationship into therapeutic relating.

*Extending the Frame of Reference of 'Therapeutic
Relationship'*
One of the ways in which the focus on the primary therapeutic
relationship (VR) between client and counsellor may be extended
is in working in groups. Here the contractual method is open to a
series of sub-contracts between the group counsellor and clients
and between clients themselves (Tudor, 1999). Inevitably a client's
goal in group therapy is facilitated by other members of the
group: 'I will respond to each person in the group in each
meeting'; 'I will ask to sit next to someone in the group each
meeting'; 'I will ask for feedback from group members at least
once each meeting': all rely on at least the presence of other
group members if not their active participation for the completion
of the client's contract. In terms of TA approaches to counselling

groups, the Classical school focuses on the analysis of transaction between group members, the Cathexis school draws on others in the group or therapeutic community especially in confrontation and checking reality, while in the Redecision school the approach is more individual therapy *in* the group, with other group members as witnesses and participants in any therapeutic drama or re-enactment.

This sub-contracting may be extended to the introduction of other counsellors, either in the individual setting or to the counselling group. I have made a number of arrangements whereby clients have chosen to work with another counsellor, say a woman or a counsellor with a different cultural background, while retaining a therapeutic contract – and occasional contact – with me. This fosters the (developmental) reality that clients may be nourished by more than one care-giver and that the initial 'primary' counsellor does not have all the answers. It also opens up the primary therapeutic relationship (and, by implication, the counsellor's counselling) to other influences and to outside, independent scrutiny. At times the introduction of another counsellor to a group is largely pragmatic, in the event of, for instance, the illness or unavoidable absence of the group counsellor. The advantage of such occasions however is, again, the introduction of another frame of reference on clients' issues, including how they accommodate or assimilate a new therapeutic relationship, however temporary. Those group counsellors who never introduce a colleague or who never co-lead a group may find it useful to think about the therapeutic advantages of doing so.

The third area of therapeutic relationship outside the primary client–counsellor relationship (and one hardly addressed in the literature) is the effect on existing relationships in the client's life and the development of new, influential therapeutic relationships, possibly with other members of a counselling group but also with other, new friends. One common reported experience of longer-term counselling is that clients change their networks of friendships. This is unsurprising in that people often come to counselling with some disturbance – a life script which supports certain ego state pathology. Their existing friendships and relationships are founded on or at least exist in the context of this disturbance. In the course of counselling and as a result of 'getting better' and/or 'cure' they are likely to review existing relationships/friendships and to view new ones. As a result of an early script decision, one client who had spent most of her life pleasing others changed this and promptly both gave up and lost a lot of her existing friends who had, in effect, relied on her to please them. Given this, it is important that clients have opportunities to apply and practise relationships which are therapeutic (PS) – which is one reason to encourage both alternate meetings of counselling groups without the counsellor (see Wolf and Swartz, 1962; Tudor, 1999) and socializing amongst group members.

Therapeutic Relating
Finally, I propose a shift in our collective thinking about the importance of therapeutic relationship/s to the concept of therapeutic *relating* in all aspects of our lives. This develops the clinical (therapeutic) application of TA in the social sphere (see Garcia, 1998; Jacobs, 1996). In discussing the logical relation between therapy and relationship, Stewart (1996) suggests that the quality which makes relating therapeutic is 'seeking positive intention'. If we learn anything from TA therapy it is how to transact with others with positive, active intention in our everyday lives, independently of a (the) therapeutic relationship. The social contact which members of a counselling group may have outside the group provides an important experience and model for further social contact beyond even these therapeutic relationships. Seymour (1977: 41) argues that the 'I'm OK, You're OK' life position is one of liberation and interdependence, 'characterized by autonomous behavior based on choice'. Developing Seymour's argument and taking Berne's (1975b) three-handed life positions, I take the 'I'm OK, You're OK, *and They're OK*' position as a profound existential – and operational – challenge to include 'them' (whoever 'they' are) in the field of my relating. In practice, in the physical dimension, this means having regard for my environment, both immediate and global, thus: 'think globally, act locally'. In the social dimension, in our relating with others in our public world, this means having respect for and understanding of others and, for instance, not gossiping about 'them' – which is a powerful contract to make, especially in a group and organizational context but, nevertheless, one which I have seen work effectively and improve the social environment (also see Tudor, 1997b). In the psychological dimension, this means having or developing an understanding of the 'they' in our lives and the part both they and we played in our psychological development; it is

easier to blame than to resolve, easier to look back than to look forward. Finally, in the spiritual dimension, this means developing a sense of others as a supportive network or community for our values and aspirations and the meaning we make of our lives.

Summary

- An understanding of the therapeutic relationship in TA is based on the counsellor's understanding of transference and on the contractual method.
- The ego state model of personality is one by which counsellors may distinguish between transference and non-transference transactions.
- TA therapeutic relationships encompass the working alliance and the transferential, reparative (reparenting) and real relationships between counsellor and client.
- Dual relationships are not necessarily exploitative – counsellors need to distinguish between exploitation and duality, and relationship and role.
- The contractual method of TA defines roles and relationships and protects both client and counsellor.
- A dual relationship checklist identifies key issues for the counsellor as regards dual therapeutic roles and relationships.
- Change through counselling requires the client to move from a (the) dependent therapeutic relationship to autonomous therapeutic relating with others both within and, ultimately, beyond the context of counselling.

Acknowledgements

My thanks to Ian Stewart for his supervision and generous encouragement, to Ulrike Müller and Charlotte Sills for their comments on an earlier draft of this chapter and to Mary Cox for her contribution to my thinking about dual relationships.

References

ACA (American Counseling Association) (1995) *Code of Ethics and Standards of Practice*. Alexandria, VA: ACA.

Agel, J. (ed.) (1971) *The Radical Therapist*. New York: Ballantine Books.

Azzi, L.G. (ed.) (1998) 'Regression in psychotherapy' (special issue), *Transactional Analysis Journal*, 28 (1).

BAC (British Association for Counselling) (1995) *Code of Ethics and Practice for Supervisors of Counsellors*. Rugby: BAC.

BAC (British Association for Counselling) (1996) *Code of Ethics and Practice for Trainers*. Rugby: BAC.

BAC (British Association for Counselling) (1997) *Code of Ethics and Practice for Counsellors*. Rugby: BAC.

Bader, E. (1994) 'Dual relationships: legal and ethical trends', *Transactional Analysis Journal*, 24 (1): 64-6.

Barnes, G. (1977) 'Introduction', in G. Barnes (ed.), *TA after Eric Berne*. New York: Harper & Row, pp. 3-31.

Barr, J. (1987) 'The therapeutic relationship model: perspectives on the core of the healing process', *Transactional Analysis Journal*, 17 (4): 134-40.

Berne, E. (1966) *Principles of Group Treatment*. New York: Grove Press.

Berne, E. (1968) *Games People Play*. Harmondsworth: Penguin. (Originally published 1964.)

Berne, E. (1975a) *Transactional Analysis in Psychotherapy*. New York: Grove Press. (Originally published 1961.)

Berne, E. (1975b) *What Do You Say After You Say Hello?* London: Corgi. (Originally published 1972.)

Bond, T. (1993) *Standards and Ethics for Counselling in Action*. London: Sage.

Boyd, H.S. (1976) 'In recognition of dual relationships', *Transactional Analysis Journal*, 6 (4): 401-4.

Clark, B.D. (1991) 'Empathic transactions in the deconfusion of ego states', *Transactional Analysis Journal*, 21 (2): 92-8.

Clarkson, P. (1990) 'A multiplicity of psychotherapeutic relationships', *British Journal of Psychotherapy*, 7: 148-63.

Clarkson, P. (1992) *Transactional Analysis Psychotherapy: An Integrated Approach*. London: Routledge.

Clarkson, P. (1994) 'In recognition of dual relationships', *Transactional Analysis Journal*, 24 (1): 32-8.

Clarkson, P. (1995) *The Therapeutic Relationship*. London: Whurr.

Clarkson, P., Gilbert, M. and Tudor, K. (1996) 'Transactional analysis', in W. Dryden (ed.), *Handbook of Individual Therapy*. London: Sage, pp. 219-53.

Cornell, W.F. (1994) 'Dual relationships in transactional analysis: training, supervision and therapy', *Transactional Analysis Journal*, 24 (1): 21-9.

Cox, M. (1997) 'Dual relationships'. Presentation at European Association for Transactional Analysis Training Endorsement Workshop, Keele (April).

Embleton Tudor, L. (1997) 'The contract boundary', in C. Sills (ed.), *Contracts in Counselling*. London: Sage, pp. 125-41.

Erskine, R.G. (1991) 'Transference and transactions: critique from an intrapsychic and integrative perspective', *Transactional Analysis Journal*, 21 (2): 63-76.

Erskine, R.G. and Moursund, J.P. (1988) *Integrative Psychotherapy in Action*. Newbury Park, CA: Sage.

Friedlander, M.G. (1987) 'Power' (special issue). *Transactional Analysis Journal*, 17 (3).

Garcia, F. (1998) *Building Community through Cooperation*. http://www.usataa.org/community-cooperation.html

Gelso, C.J. and Carter, J.A. (1985) 'The relationship in counseling and psychotherapy: components, consequences, and theoretical antecedents', *The Counseling Psychologist*, 13 (2): 115–243.

Goulding, M.M. and Goulding, R. (1979) *Changing Lives through Redecision Therapy*. New York: Grove Press.

Goulding, R. and Goulding, M.M. (1978) *The Power is in the Patient*. San Francisco, CA: TA Press.

Greenson, R.R. (1967) *The Technique and Practice of Psychoanalysis* (vol. 1). New York: International Universities Press.

Herlihy, B. and Corney, G. (eds) (1992) *Dual Relationships in Counseling*. Alexandria, VA: American Association for Counseling and Development.

ITA (Institute of Transactional Analysis) (1995) *Transactional Analysis: A Humanistic Psychotherapy*. Information sheet. London: ITA.

ITA (Institute of Transactional Analysis) (1998) *Code of Professional Practice and Guidelines for Professional Practices*. London: ITA.

ITAA (International Transactional Analysis Association) (1995) *Transactional Analysis Counseling. Definition*. San Francisco, CA: Training and Certification Council of Transactional Analysts, Training Standards Committee, Counseling Task Force.

Jacobs, A. (1994) 'Theory as ideology: reparenting and thought reform', *Transactional Analysis Journal*, 24 (1): 39–55.

Jacobs, A. (ed.) (1996) 'Transactional analysis and social applications' (special issue). *Transactional Analysis Journal*, 26 (1).

James, M. (1974) 'Self-reparenting: theory and process', *Transactional Analysis Journal*, 4 (3): 32–9.

James, M. and Goulding, M. (1998) 'Self-reparenting and redecision', *Transactional Analysis Journal*, 28 (1): 16–19.

Lapworth, P., Sills, C. and Fish, S. (1993) *Transactional Analysis Counselling*. Bicester: Winslow Press.

Lee, A. (1997) 'Process contracts', in C. Sills (ed.), *Contracts in Counselling*. London: Sage, pp. 94–112.

Lloyd, A.P. (1992) 'Dual relationship problems in counselor education', in B. Herlihy and G. Corney (eds), *Dual Relationships in Counseling*. Alexandria, VA: American Association for Counseling and Development, pp. 59–64.

Mearns, D. (1994) *Developing Person-Centred Counselling*. London: Sage.

Moiso, C. (1985) 'Ego states and transference', *Transactional Analysis Journal*, 15 (3): 194–201.

Money, M. (1997) 'Defining mental health – what do we think we're doing?' in M. Money and L. Buckley (eds), *Positive Mental Health and its Promotion*. Liverpool: Institute for Health, John Moores University, pp. 13–15.

Novellino, M. (1984) 'Self-analysis of countertransference in integrative transactional analysis', *Transactional Analysis Journal*, 14 (1): 63–7.

Novey, T. (ed.) (1996) 'Integrative psychotherapy' (special issue). *Transactional Analysis Journal*, 26 (4).

Onions, C.T. (ed.) (1973) *The Shorter Oxford English Dictionary* (3rd edn). Oxford: Clarendon Press. (Originally published 1933.)

Osnes, R.A. (1974) 'Spot reparenting', *Transactional Analysis Journal*, 4 (3): 40-6.

Robertson, C. (1993) 'Dysfunction in training organisations', *Self and Society*, 21 (4): 31-5.

Robinson, J. (1998) 'Reparenting in a therapeutic community', *Transactional Analysis Journal*, 28 (1): 88-94.

Roy, B. and Steiner, C.M. (eds) (1988) 'Radical psychiatry: the second decade'. Unpublished manuscript.

Schiff, J. (1969) 'Reparented schizophrenics', *Transactional Analysis Bulletin*, 8 (31): 47-63.

Schiff, J.L., Schiff, A.W., Mellor, K., Schiff, E., Schiff, S., Richman, D., Fishman, J., Wolz, L., Fishman, C. and Momb, D. (1975) *Cathexis Reader: Transactional Analysis Treatment of Psychosis*. New York: Harper & Row.

Seymour, N.K. (1977) 'The dependency cycle: implications for theory, therapy, and social action', *Transactional Analysis Journal*, 7 (1): 37-43.

Steiner, C.M. (1971) 'Radical psychiatry: principles', in J. Agel (ed.), *The Radical Therapist*. New York: Ballantine Books, pp. 3-7.

Stewart, I. (1989) *Transactional Analysis Counselling in Action*. London: Sage.

Stewart, I. (1992) *Eric Berne*. London: Sage.

Stewart, I. (1996) *Developing Transactional Analysis Counselling*. London: Sage.

Stewart, I. and Joines, V. (1987) *TA Today*. Nottingham: Lifespace.

Summers, G. and Tudor, K. (1999) 'Co-creative transactional analysis "putting the transactional back into the analysis" '. Manuscript submitted for publication.

Tudor, K. (1996) 'Transactional analysis intragration: a metatheoretical analysis for practice', *Transactional Analysis Journal*, 26 (4): 329-40.

Tudor, K. (1997a) 'Counselling and psychotherapy: an issue of orientation', *ITA News*, no. 46: 40-2.

Tudor, K. (1997b) 'Social contracts: contracting for social change', in C. Sills (ed.), *Contracts in Counselling*. London: Sage, pp. 207-15.

Tudor, K. (1999) *Group Counselling*. London: Sage.

Tudor, K. (1998) 'Value for money?: issues of fees in counselling and psychotherapy', *British Journal of Guidance and Counselling*, 26 (4): 477-93.

United Kingdom Council for Psychotherapy (1996) *National Register for Psychotherapists*. London: Routledge.

Wolf, A. and Swartz, E.K. (1962) *Pschoanalysis in Groups*. New York: Grune & Stratton.

Wyckoff, H. (ed.) (1976) *Love, Therapy and Politics*. New York: Grove Press.

6 The Therapeutic Relationship in Cognitive Therapy

Diana Sanders and Frank Wills

Despite the growing popularity of cognitive behavioural approaches, one common criticism from the worlds of counselling and psychotherapy is that cognitive therapists pay little, if any, attention to the cornerstone of many therapies, the therapeutic relationship. Many counsellors and psychotherapists may have been attracted to the rigour of cognitive approaches to therapy, yet have been put off by the apparent lack of any real consideration of the therapeutic relationship. Literature on cognitive therapy at times gives the impression that the therapeutic relationship is a mere container in which to do the real work, viewing difficulties and issues in the therapeutic relationship as problems to be solved before getting on with the therapy. In recent years, however, cognitive therapy has developed into a wider and more open approach (Wills and Sanders, 1997). The development of therapy in general has provided many useful ideas which help us to understand the underlying processes of therapeutic change within the therapeutic relationship, processes which are now being actively integrated into cognitive therapy by Beck et al. (1990), Layden et al. (1993), Safran and Segal (1990) and Young (1994). As a result of this work, there is a growing cognitive model of the interpersonal process of the therapeutic relationship, as well as substantial focus on how to use the relationship as an active ingredient in therapy.

In this chapter, we look at how cognitive therapy approaches the therapeutic relationship, particularly in its description of the collaborative relationship. We look at how concepts of transference and countertransference have been integrated into the newer interpersonal and schema-focused models of cognitive therapy. We describe ways in which the therapeutic relationship is used in cognitive therapy, 'in the service of therapy' (Safran and Segal, 1990: 41), to conceptualize the client's difficulties and facilitate the counselling process. The chapter ends by discussing how to work with difficulties in the therapeutic relationship, and how such difficulties can be actively used to promote therapeutic change. We make reference throughout the chapter to cognitive conceptualization, or formulation, a working map of the client and his or her difficulties, incorporating past experience, core beliefs or schema arising from the experience, and how such schema and other rules for living are related to the individual's presenting problems. Developing a conceptualization with a client is an integral aspect of cognitive therapy, enabling a fuller understanding of the client's difficulties within their 'frame of reference', and can aid the understanding and resolution of difficulties or issues in the relationship (Persons, 1989; Wills and Sanders, 1997).

What does Cognitive Therapy Say about the Therapeutic Relationship?

Traditionally, and in contrast to other therapeutic approaches, the task of cognitive therapy was seen to be to resolve the client's problems, as far as possible, using the tools of cognitive therapy rather than using the therapeutic relationship *per se*. A good relationship was seen as necessary *but not sufficient* alone for therapeutic change (Beck et al., 1979). If the therapeutic relationship was a car, the cognitive therapist would use it to travel from A to B, whereas the psychodynamic or person-centred therapist would be a collector, spending hours polishing and fine tuning each vehicle. For many clients, particularly those whose problems are amenable to short-term counselling, a mode of transport is called for: it is sufficient for the counsellor to be warm, empathic, respectful and collaborative, for the therapeutic work to proceed. However, for clients with long-term difficulties, more complex problems, personality disorders or interpersonal difficulties, the therapeutic relationship becomes more significant (Beck et al.,

1990; Safran, 1990; Safran and Segal, 1990). For these clients, because their core conflicts are often interpersonal in nature, it is likely that the therapeutic relationship will prove a rich source of information for understanding the client and his or her difficulties. It is also likely that there will be significant issues and difficulties in the therapeutic relationship, and the travellers may well have to turn their hand to mechanics and body-work.

Although the 'necessary but not sufficient' view of the therapeutic relationship has been central to cognitive therapy, more attention is now being paid to the importance of the therapeutic relationship itself. It comes as no surprise that research in cognitive therapy supports what our humanistic colleagues have been saying all along: the quality of the relationship is central. Various studies have demonstrated the importance of non-specific, relationship factors versus technical factors in therapy, showing that a positive relationship makes a significant contribution to the outcome of cognitive therapy (Burns and Nolen-Hoeksema, 1992; DeRubeis and Feeley, 1990; Persons and Burns, 1985; Raue and Goldfried, 1994; Wright and Davis, 1994). In particular, the client's assessment of therapist empathy is positively correlated with recovery from emotional difficulties (Orlinsky et al., 1994). There is also more attention being paid to ways in which the therapeutic relationship itself can be used as an active ingredient in therapy (Beck et al., 1990; Jacobson, 1989). For example, the relationship can provide an arena in which the client can practise alternative or new behaviours, such as being upset with the therapist or expressing emotion rather than avoiding it.

The Core Conditions

> The general characteristics of the therapist which facilitate the application of cognitive therapy . . . include warmth, accurate empathy and genuineness. . . . We believe that these characteristics in themselves are necessary but not sufficient to produce optimum therapeutic effect. . . . the techniques in this book are intended to be applied in a tactful, therapeutic and human manner by a fallible person – the therapist. . . . A genuine therapist is honest with himself as well as with the client. (Beck et al., 1979: 45–9)

The therapeutic relationship is central to cognitive therapy in many ways. It is an often unstated assumption that the core conditions of any therapy, including empathy, genuineness, congruence, and unconditional, non-possessive positive regard (Rogers,

1957) have to be in place before any therapeutic work can proceed. If clients do not feel understood or respected, their inner world cannot be shared with another and the prospect of being able to identify and challenge our strange and illogical thoughts will not get off the ground: Mr Spock of Star Trek constantly challenges the view of mere mortals, but who wants to trust Mr Spock with their innermost secrets? Sharing thoughts and emotions can leave clients feeling vulnerable, their inner world laid open to another. Therefore, the therapist has to show the core conditions of the therapeutic relationship in order for any therapeutic encounter to proceed. Much of the importance of the therapeutic relationship has been implicit rather than explicit in cognitive therapy writings. This does not mean that Beck only paid token attention to these qualities. Throughout his work he stresses the importance of showing the client warmth, acceptance and respect, enabling the client to believe 'this is someone I can trust'. The traditional counselling skills of listening, summarizing and reflecting feelings are vital to cognitive therapy. Such skills also enable the client and therapist to work together to bring out and challenge thoughts and beliefs which are problematic to the client.

It is a common observation of beginner cognitive therapists that the core conditions initially go out of the window as the therapist struggles to offer the client techniques to help identify and challenge thoughts and beliefs. The process of learning cognitive therapy, however, involves both mastering techniques and integrating these into the context of the relationship, a process which develops as the therapist's skills increase. Cognitive therapy also allows adaptation of the core conditions to maximize their helpfulness to the individual client, depending on the client's individual make-up (Wills and Sanders, 1997). For example, too much empathy or warmth may be perceived as threatening to, say, a very depressed client, who believes 'I do not deserve such caring' or 'No one understands me: why is she pretending?'

The Collaborative Relationship

While cognitive therapy uses factors which are common to many other therapies, it is more specific about how such factors are used. Beck (1991), reviewing the development of cognitive therapy, states that the active ingredient of many of the 'common factors' among various psychotherapies, including the therapeutic relationship, is that the end result is cognitive change. Cognitive therapy aims to produce the same result but by a more direct route. 'I certainly consider the therapeutic alliance as a common factor shared with other therapies. But I also believe that the shared and explicit focus on changing belief systems, reinforcing and refining reality testing, and developing coping strategies makes for a more robust therapy' (Beck, 1991: 194). The way such work is achieved is by means of developing a *collaborative relationship* and *collaborative empiricism* (for example Beck et al., 1979, 1985). In the words of Beck:

> The cognitive therapist implies that there is a team approach to the solution of a patient's problem: that is, a therapeutic alliance where the patient supplies raw data (reports on thoughts and behaviour . . .) while the therapist provides structure and expertise on how to solve problems. The emphasis is on working on problems rather than on correcting defects or changing personality. The therapist fosters the attitude 'two heads are better than one' in approaching personal difficulties. When the patient is so entangled in symptoms that he is unable to join in problem solving, the therapist may have to assume a leading role. As therapy progresses, the patient is encouraged to take a more active stance. (Beck et al., 1985: 175)

Collaborative empiricism helps the therapist to 'get alongside' the client, so that the work of 'attacking' the client's problems will not be seen as an attack on the client herself. Again in the words of Beck:

> It is not the therapist's function to reform the patient: rather his role is working with the patient against 'it', the patient's problem. Placing emphasis on solving problems, rather than his presumed deficits or bad habits, helps the patient to examine his difficulties with more detachment and makes him less prone to experience shame, a sense of inferiority and defensiveness. (Beck, 1976: 221)

What does this mean in practice? Beck et al. (1985) spell out two implications.

- *The relationship develops on a reciprocal basis.* Both therapist and client are working together to observe what is going on, to observe and comment on the client's way of being, to offer solutions to the problems and difficulties facing the client. When the client is unable to see the way forward, the therapist may be able to look from a different view and offer this to the client. Similarly, the client can see and offer to the therapist another perspective. There is a feeling in cognitive therapy of both client and therapist rolling up their sleeves and getting on with the work.

- *Avoid hidden agendas.* Cognitive therapy is an explicit therapy. The therapist does not form hypotheses about the client, or interpretations, and keep these to him or herself. Instead, everything is out on the table. If client and counsellor are working to different agendas, then it is unlikely that therapy will proceed smoothly. This means that the therapist admits mistakes, is open to suggestions, and willing to go where the client wants to go, without colluding with the client's difficulties.

A spirit of collaboration gives a 'ping-pong' quality to sessions: the time that therapist and client are speaking may be about equal; the therapist shares his or her thoughts about the client's thoughts, and asks for feedback. This spirit may be clearer when it is absent: when, for example, the therapist tells the client what to do or think. In true collaboration, the therapist is willing to help the client out without being patronizing or disempowering the client. The process of developing such a collaborative relationship involves working with the client to set goals for counselling, determine priorities, maintain a therapeutic focus and structure both within sessions and across therapy as a whole.

Using the Therapeutic Relationship in Cognitive Therapy

As well as defining the core conditions of collaborative cognitive therapy, recent developments have looked at how the therapeutic relationship can be used to conceptualize the client and his or her concerns, to work with difficulties in therapy and to actively promote therapeutic change. Much of this work has arisen from Safran and Segal (1990), who stress that the therapeutic relationship is not something that either is or is not in place, but rather is a quality that continually fluctuates and which can be actively used in therapy. Safran and Segal concentrate on ways in which the therapeutic relationship in cognitive therapy can be used to work on clients' interpersonal schema, in a way which mirrors humanistic ways of working. One way of viewing the therapeutic relationship is illustrated in Figure 6.1. It demonstrates how the relationship is an interaction between the client and the therapist,

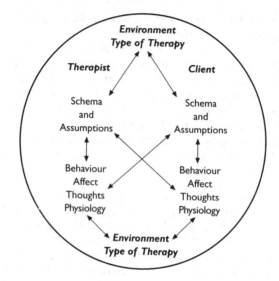

Figure 6.1 *The therapeutic relationship*

with both influenced by the environment in which the therapeutic work takes place. The therapeutic relationship is an arena
in which client and therapist operate according to their schema
and assumptions. While the client is the focus of therapy, the role
of the therapist should not be neglected and understanding the
conceptualization of both the client and the therapist is necessary
to identify and resolve difficulties in the therapeutic relationship. In addition, these difficulties give us greater information and
insight about our client's and our own assumptions and schema,
providing a 'window' on to the client's beliefs, behaviours and
expectations as well as on our own particular psychology.

The Use of Transference to Aid Conceptualization

> In order for the therapist to deal effectively with his or her own role in
> the interaction, it is imperative that he or she have an intellectual and
> an empathic understanding of the cognitive and emotional baggage
> that the patient brings to sessions. (Layden et al., 1993: 117)

While not explicitly forming the cornerstone of cognitive therapy,
the client's reactions to the therapist, and to the therapy allow us
to conceptualize a 'cognitive-interpersonal cycle' and to view

problems or ruptures in the therapeutic relationship as unique opportunities to assess clients' beliefs. What happens in the therapeutic relationship is very likely to mirror the client's psychological make-up and the underlying problems: the core beliefs or schema, and the mechanisms by which the client confirms these schema, are illustrated *in vivo* (Beck et al., 1990; Persons, 1989; Safran, 1990; Safran and Segal, 1990; Wright and Davis, 1994). For example, being late for sessions or not doing homework may be driven by a number of different schema, such as schema relating to extremely high standards, resulting in being disorganized and chaotic outside and being unable to get anything done on time. Alternatively, the client may not be willing to come to sessions on time, or work on tasks between sessions, which may indicate fear of dependency on the therapist or therapy.

The therapeutic relationship is affected by the processes of schema maintenance, schema avoidance and schema compensation, described by Young (1994). We actively engage in behaviours which perpetuate our beliefs – schema maintenance behaviours. In the therapeutic relationship, it is likely that clients will be testing out the therapist to check for a good 'fit' with their assumptions and beliefs, a process which a psychodynamic therapist may describe as a 'transference test'. For example, the belief 'I'm boring' may lead the client to speak or behave in a flat, boring manner, or selectively attend to any tiny cues that the therapist is bored. Schema avoidance describes the affective, cognitive and behavioural processes employed to avoid activating schemas: for example, the client changes the subject, or laughs whenever something painful is being approached. Schema compensation describes the process of acting in a way opposite to that predicted by the schema. For example, the client with issues of dependence (Young and Klosko, 1993) may refuse to trust the therapist, or prematurely discontinue therapy, saying that s/he would prefer to carry on alone (schema compensation).

The client's assumptions and beliefs about relationships may force the counsellor into a 'damned if I do, damned if I don't' situation (Layden et al., 1993). This feeling is characteristic of working with clients whose schema mean that whatever others do, it can be misconstrued in a negative way, resulting in a 'no win' situation in close relationships. The counsellor may also react in a black and white way. The therapist may respond to the client's outbursts and irrational demands by eagerness to end counselling and discharge the client, labelling them as 'impossible to help'. Alternatively, at the other extreme, the counsellor may become a rescuer, going to unusual extremes to help the client or offer the client unrealistic assurances about the counsellor's ability to help, inevitably leading the client to feel disillusioned or betrayed. The therapeutic relationship may 'ping-pong' back and forward between the two extremes of over-distance and over-involvement, mirroring the client's schema and problems. For example, a client who was sexually abused by someone she trusted, learned that it was extremely difficult to trust anyone; at the same time, she learned that the only way to attain love was to be violated in some way. In therapy, the client both craved the therapist's affection and acceptance, but reacted with horror and distrust when the therapist showed signs of caring. When the therapist, in response to the patient's withdrawal, acted in a more reserved way, the client jumped to the opposite extreme, perceiving the therapist as abandoning and neglecting her (Layden et al., 1993).

Countertransference and Cognitive Therapy

The classic psychoanalytic view maintains that 'countertransference' is the sum of the counsellor's reactions to the client's transference, the various feelings that are evoked in the therapist by the client (Jacobs, 1988). Various types of countertransference are described: 'classical' – the counsellor's transference to the client; 'neurotic' – relating to the counsellor's unresolved personal issues; 'role' – the counsellor's response to the role that the client has put him in; or 'complementary' – where the counsellor begins to experience what is going on for the client, which is being unconsciously communicated. In cognitive therapy, counter-transference may be viewed as a valuable means of gaining a deeper understanding of the therapeutic process; it represents the totality of the counsellor's responses to the client, including thoughts, schemas, emotions, actions and intentions (Layden et al., 1993). Counsellors' feelings and reactions are used 'in the service of therapy rather than allowing them to become obstacles in therapy' (Safran and Segal, 1990: 41).

Much of interpersonal communication takes place at a non-verbal level: subtle posture, eye contact, tone of voice or muscle tension. Therefore it can be hard to define why the therapist is reacting in a certain way. The therapist's bodily reactions, images or metaphors can provide useful clues to the client's difficulties.

The counsellor's self-image in the therapeutic relationship can provide important clues as to the client's conceptualization. Feeling like a 'wise owl' has served me well in identifying the client's need for reassurance. If, conversely, the client believes that no one can help, then the client may well treat the therapist with suspicion: a clue to this is if I find myself trying exceptionally hard, and against all odds, to 'sell' the model to the client with my 'estate agent' hat. Supervision is the ideal place to explore these reactions to clients, and therapists often need help and support in working out the most therapeutic responses.

The Therapist's Role in the Relationship

Cognitive therapy also looks at the influence of the therapist on the therapeutic relationship. Rather than assuming that we feel a certain way about a client because this is always an effect of the client's schema, cognitive therapy looks at the effect of the therapist's schema on the therapeutic relationship (Burns and Auerbach, 1996). For example, the concept of empathy involves the therapist's 'experiencing of the patient's . . . emotional states' (Book, 1988: 421). While the therapist's own subjective responses to the client during sessions are of great value, particularly in providing unverbalized information about the quality and nature of the therapeutic relationship, cognitive therapy suggests that such responses say more about the therapist's perceptions, feelings and beliefs than about the client's. Research indicates that therapists' conceptualizations based on their own feelings are not systematically related to what the client is thinking or feeling (Free et al., 1985; Squier, 1990). For example, there may be significant differences between therapists' own estimates of their level of empathy, compared to how empathic the client experienced the therapist to be (Burns and Auerbach, 1996). Burns and Auerbach (ibid.) describe the use of measures such as the Empathy Scale which can be of value in training in cognitive therapy, as well as for experienced practitioners to monitor their therapeutic empathy.

Therapists are only too human, and our own issues may interact with the client's problems. Safran and Segal (1990) stress that therapists need to have a sufficiently flexible, and accepting, self-concept to be able to acknowledge their own feelings in the therapeutic interaction. It is helpful if therapists are aware of their own rules, assumptions and schema which may interfere with their ability either to identify or work with particular client issues or difficulties in the therapeutic relationship. Lists of common unhelpful therapist assumptions are given in Freeman et al. (1990). Assumptions such as 'it is wrong to dislike . . . disagree with . . . feel attracted to . . . be angry with . . . my clients', and 'I must cure the patient', are likely to interfere with the therapeutic relationship.

While examination of the therapist's feelings and beliefs is implicit in many therapies, cognitive therapy describes explicit ways of working with our own psychological make up. Mary Ann Layden (Layden et al., 1993), for example, stresses the importance of cognitive therapists examining their own schema, particularly when working with clients with long-term difficulties in the interpersonal arena and personality disorders, where both client and therapist's schema may be activated in sessions. Cognitive therapy itself provides a number of tools which therapists can use to understand their role in the therapeutic relationship, and supervision and regular analysis of therapy tapes can be very valuable in helping us as counsellors to identify our own issues arising in therapy.

Using the Therapeutic Relationship to Produce Change

Cognitive therapists are paying more attention to ways of actively using the therapeutic relationship to work on the psychological difficulties which are the basis of clients' problems (Persons, 1989). Padesky (1996: 270) describes how the relationship can be used as a 'laboratory for testing beliefs'. For example, the client who finds it difficult to trust anyone, can be encouraged to try trusting the therapist in small ways and observe the results, and use this as a way of both learning new skills and developing new beliefs. Careful self-disclosure from the therapist can offer experimental evidence for clients of the possible impact of their way of being on others in their environment. This is illustrated with 'Sophie'.

> *Sophie would weep in sessions – how difficult everything was, how frightened she was of never being able to cope. With many clients this would evoke empathy and understanding in me. However, with Sophie I would mentally walk out of the door, and feel impatient and non-empathic*

with her tears. I gently fed this back to her, how her crying and calls for help seemed to have the opposite effect to the one she wanted, which in turn made her feel more desperate, and weep more. Her weeping, we conceptualized, was a cry for help rather than an expression of sadness. We then looked at how she might more effectively get the help she wanted. Gradually, the weeping and wailing was replaced by more genuine expressions of sadness and fear, in turn leading to a more genuine and helpful response from others. The therapeutic relationship, for Sophie, was in itself an important arena for change.

Young (1994) has written about how the therapeutic relationship can offer clients limited re-parenting, where their schema can be directly challenged in the relationship with the therapist. The therapeutic relationship can be a corrective experience in itself, particularly for clients with long-term difficulties characteristic of the personality disorders (for example Young, 1994; Young and Klosko, 1993).

Difficulties in the Therapeutic Relationship

To some extent older models of cognitive therapy have tended to give the impression that difficulties in the therapeutic relationship are obstacles to be solved before the real work of therapy can proceed. However, it is now recognized that such difficulties reveal important material about the client, and can be used both to understand the client and her/his mode of relating to others, and to promote therapeutic change. Difficulties in the therapeutic relationship can be used as 'diagnostic cues' to identify schema, particularly those characterizing the personality disorders (Beck et al., 1990; Young, 1994). Safran and Segal (1990) take the view that alliance ruptures often occur when the therapeutic relationship activates an important interpersonal schema. The process of being able to resolve difficulties as they arise can be actively used in therapy, particularly where clients have not had the experience of resolving difficulties with others, or where people in the client's life do not have the time or patience to work things through.

Difficulties in the therapeutic relationship can be broadly defined as anything which threatens the core conditions of the relationship, including therapeutic empathy, listening to the client, keeping the boundaries and keeping a structure within sessions and across therapy. One common relationship difficulty is problems with collaboration. Rather than client and counsellor working together, in an open manner, the counsellor may become 'the expert' and start to offer directive advice; tasks may be set, not negotiated; the client may become 'over-compliant' or 'non-compliant', for example agreeing with the counsellor on homework tasks and then not carrying them out. The client's transference may interfere with the collaborative relationship (Beck et al., 1990; Wright and Davis, 1994; Young, 1994). Beck et al. (1990) identify the kinds of schema underlying problems in collaboration, including themes of distrust and personal shame. In addition, the client may simply not know how to be collaborative, or may fear change.

Difficulties may express themselves as client 'resistance' (Newman, 1994), where the client may not cooperate or may 'go through the motions'. The client may avoid looking at issues of importance previously agreed on, or avoid feeling or expressing any emotion, making the sessions dry and sterile. Problems may arise if the client and counsellor do not share the same conceptualization of the client's problems. The counsellor may have arrived at a working conceptualization of the client's difficulties, and the client may agree in principle with the model but not believe that it applies to them personally. These differences can cause relationship difficulties even before counselling commences. The therapist may have difficulty in empathizing with the client. Problems may arise from the way the therapist is carrying out cognitive therapy, for example, doing the work for rather than with the client; seeing the person as a mass of problems rather than as the person she or he is; or arguing with the client. Both client and therapist may end up in the role of client.

Although it is possible to define and describe difficulties in the therapeutic relationship, in practice, actual difficulties may be missed. The therapeutic relationship involves engagement at the level of emotion and of interpersonal communication which may be non-verbal, and therefore hard at times to describe. However, when difficulties are encountered, something almost intangible occurs: a vague feeling of discomfort, or behaviours that on the surface look straightforward but do not 'ring true', such as the client being persistently late for sessions, always armed with a 'good excuse', or the counsellor feeling reluctant or negative about seeing the client. A helpful marker is the shift from the sessions seeming 'alive', with a sense of counsellor and client working together in an active way, to a 'dead' feeling, where both are 'going through the motions' of counselling without any movement. Only when stepping back and trying to describe and analyse what is occurring, can the difficulties be understood and conceptualized.

Environmental Factors

Various factors external to the client and counsellor may cause difficulties in the therapeutic relationship (Wright and Davis, 1994). These include the type or length of counselling, the situation (such as hospital versus primary care based counselling), pressures to 'cure' people in a fixed length of time, social or cultural factors, financial issues, or effects of the client's real-life social circumstances. Working in the National Health Service, for example, means that the number of sessions per client is frequently limited by service provision rather than always by clients' needs. Difficulties in the therapeutic relationship may reflect a mis-match between the client's needs and the counsellor's style or mode of counselling (Wright and Davis, 1994). For example, the high level of structure, Socratic questioning, or the empirical approach in cognitive therapy may not suit some clients, being so incompatible with their beliefs and assumptions as to make developing a therapeutic relationship extremely difficult. While some clients may want us to be active and directive, others prefer a non-directive or relatively inactive therapeutic style. The client's problems themselves may impinge on the therapeutic relationship: for example, if the client is very depressed and hopeless, the therapist needs to be more energetic and hopeful; panic or phobic clients want the therapist's help in avoiding anxiety, and may therefore resent the cognitive therapist's attempts to elicit anxiety in sessions. Therefore, both individual therapist and client characteristics and the characteristics of the therapy can cause difficulties.

Working with Difficulties in the Therapeutic Relationship

A number of stages are involved in working with difficulties in the therapeutic relationship: assessment and weaving the issues into the conceptualization, then collaboratively sharing and working on the issues with the client.

Assessment: Becoming a Participant Observer

The first step to working with difficulties in the therapeutic relationship is to identify and assess what is going on (Newman, 1994; Safran and Segal, 1990). It can be very difficult to identify problems or difficulties at the time, since we are by definition a participant in the relationship with the client. Both counsellor and client are likely to 'pull' from each other responses that will maintain their schema. Inevitably, the therapist will get sucked in to the client's way of being, leading to a 'dysfunctional cognitive-interpersonal cycle' (Safran, 1990; Safran and Segal, 1990).

Safran and Segal describe a model for both identifying 'rupture markers' when the therapeutic relationship becomes strained or impaired, and intervening, using the context of the therapeutic relationship. The key to assessing difficulties is initially to observe as well as participate in the difficulties. This involves becoming a 'participant observer', using 'decentring' – the process of stepping outside one's immediate experience and thereby not only observing the experience but also changing the nature of the experience itself. Rather than being 'hooked' in the interaction, such as may happen during conversation outside of therapy, the therapist is also aware of being a participant in the encounter. The therapist then 'unhooks' from the interaction to avoid becoming so engaged in the interaction that the client's schema are, yet again, confirmed (Kiesler, 1988). In psychoanalytic therapy, the process is called developing an 'observing ego', 'observing self', or 'internal supervisor' (Casement, 1985). In cognitive therapy, this mirrors the approach of both acting in the situation and thinking the thoughts, and observing the self thinking and feeling (Teasdale, 1996). During the 'hooked' stage, the individual feels, for example, anxious, thinks anxious thoughts and behaves anxiously. During the 'unhooked' or observing stage, the person is able to observe themselves being anxious. In the therapy situation, once the interaction is both experienced and observed, it is possible to discuss what is happening and generate hypotheses for the conceptualization. Newman (1994) suggests a number of questions that the counsellor can use to assess difficulties. Although it is suggested that the counsellor ask these questions about the client, it is also useful for the counsellor to assess his or her own role in the difficulties:

- What is the function of the client's behaviour? What does the client fear would happen if the difficulties were not there?
- How do the problems fit with the client's conceptualization?
- When and under what circumstances has the client been similarly affected in the past?
- What counsellor or client beliefs are feeding the current situation – what schema maintenance behaviours are in operation?
- Does the counsellor or client lack certain skills which make it difficult to collaborate with counselling or resolve the present difficulties?
- Are there environmental factors influencing the counselling?
- Does the conceptualization need revision?

Collaboration

Once difficulties are identified and assessed, counsellor and client work together to conceptualize and deal with the difficulties. The therapist shares her or his thoughts, as appropriate, in the service of collaboratively working with the difficulties. This process must be guided by the conceptualization, and is both an extremely valuable and potentially 'dangerous' stage of therapy. For example, interventions focusing on the relationship can be extremely threatening to clients who have had no experience of being able to discuss or resolve relationship difficulties. Therefore, grounding the interventions in the conceptualization is essential. 'Here and now' examples within the session are valuable to explore difficulties, using guided discovery to identify the client's thoughts and feelings at times of 'alliance ruptures'. The counsellor can ask the client: 'When I said X, it looked as though it was uncomfortable: what went through your mind just then?'

Therapists must acknowledge their own contribution to the experience, and not blame or pathologize the client (Kahn, 1991). Rather than saying, 'I feel like you are trying to control the interaction', the therapist can offer his or her own feelings: 'I feel like I am involved in a struggle with you at the moment. I am not sure what is going on – how does this relate to your feelings right now?' The therapist may wish to say 'I feel like I am giving you a lecture at the moment, and am not sure why this is so', or 'I feel quite puzzled when you tell me you are sad but laugh at the same time'. The therapist's response does not aim to reassure the client, but holds the moment by implying that they can sort out the problem together (Kahn, 1991). Layden et al. (1993) suggest working on the therapeutic relationship in terms of questions the therapist can ask her/himself before offering interventions at the level of the therapeutic relationship: 'How will my patient benefit from this intervention?' and 'How will I benefit from this intervention?' If the answer to the latter is more apparent than the answer to the former, the intervention should be postponed and reflected on, by self-reflection and supervision.

Concluding Comments

- The therapeutic relationship in cognitive therapy has, in the past few years, become a focus of attention in its own right, with the development of cognitive interpersonal models of the therapeutic process, as well as substantial work on how to use the relationship as an active ingredient in therapy.
- The cornerstone of cognitive therapy is the collaborative relationship, within which client and counsellor work to identify and resolve the client's difficulties. Therapeutic collaboration, we believe, empowers the client, giving the message that difficulties are resolvable, and enabling the client's difficulties to be addressed in a parsimonious and empirical way.
- We have described in this chapter ways in which the relationship can be understood and used, using concepts such as transference and countertransference, within a cognitive framework and within a spirit of collaboration.
- One of the strengths of cognitive therapy lies in its use of conceptualization, and we have looked at ways the therapeutic relationship can be woven into the client's conceptualization in order to understand difficulties.
- In line with the empirical philosophy in cognitive therapy, the relationship can in itself be used to test out clients' beliefs, and provide an arena in which clients can practise new ways of being in the world, and test deeply help interpersonal beliefs.
- Supervision and high-quality training are both obvious underpinnings of the technical and interpersonal competence which the approach described in this chapter requires (Burns and Auerbach, 1996; Padesky, 1996).

References

Beck, A.T. (1976) *Cognitive Therapy and the Emotional Disorders*. New York: International Universities Press.

Beck, A.T. (1991) 'Cognitive therapy as the integrative therapy', *Journal of Psychotherapy Integration*, 1: 191–8.

Beck, A.T., Emery, G. and Greenberg, R.L. (1985) *Anxiety Disorders and Phobias. A Cognitive Perspective*. New York: Basic Books.

Beck, A.T., Freeman, A. and Associates (1990) *Cognitive Therapy of Personality Disorders*. New York: Guilford Press.

Beck, A.T., Rush, A.J., Shaw, B.F. and Emery, G. (1979) *Cognitive Therapy of Depression*. New York: Guilford Press.

Book, H.E. (1988) 'Empathy: misconceptions and misuses in psychotherapy', *American Journal of Psychiatry*, 145 (4): 420–4.

Burns, D.D. (1989) *The Feeling Good Handbook*. New York: Plume.

Burns, D.D. and Auerbach, A. (1996) 'Therapeutic empathy in cognitive-behavioural therapy: does it really make a difference?' in P. Salkovskis (ed.), *Frontiers of Cognitive Therapy*. New York: Guilford Press, pp. 135–64.

Burns, D.D. and Nolen-Hoeksema, S. (1992) 'Therapeutic empathy and recovery from depression in cognitive-behavioral therapy: a structural equation model', *Journal of Consulting and Clinical Psychology*, 60 (3): 441–9.

Casement, P. (1985) *On Learning from the Patient*. London: Tavistock.

DeRubeis, R.J. and Feeley, M. (1990) 'Determinants of change in cognitive therapy for depression', *Cognitive Therapy and Research*, 14 (5): 469–82.

Free, N.K., Green, B.L., Grace, M.D., Chernus, L.A. and Whitman, R.M. (1985) 'Empathy and outcome in brief, focal dynamic therapy'. *American Journal of Psychiatry*, 142: 917–21.

Freeman, A., Pretzer, J., Fleming, B. and Simon, K. (1990) *Clinical Applications of Cognitive Therapy*. New York: Plenum Press.

Guidano, V.F. (1991) *The Self in Process: Towards a Post-Rationalist Cognitive Therapy*. New York: Guilford Press.

Jacobs, M. (1988) *Psychodynamic Counselling in Action*. London: Sage.

Jacobson, N.S. (1989) 'The therapist-client relationship in cognitive behaviour therapy: implications for treating depression', *Journal of Cognitive Psychotherapy: An International Quarterly*, 3 (2): 85–96.

Kahn, M. (1991) *Between Therapist and Client: The New Relationship*. New York: W.H. Freeman & Co.

Kiesler, D.J. (1988) *Therapeutic Metacommunication: Therapist Impact Disclosure as Feedback in Psychotherapy*. Palo Alto, CA: Consulting Psychologists Press.

Layden, M.A., Newman, C.F., Freeman, A. and Morse, S.B. (1993) *Cognitive Therapy of Borderline Personality Disorder*. Boston: Allyn & Bacon.

Newman, C.F. (1994) 'Understanding client resistance: methods for enhancing motivation to change', *Cognitive and Behavioral Practice*, 1: 47–69.

Orlinsky, D.E., Grawe, K. and Parks, B.K. (1994) 'Process and outcome in psychotherapy: noch einmal', in A.E. Bergin and S.L. Garfield (eds), *Handbook of Psychotherapy and Behaviour Change* (2nd edn). New York: Wiley.

Padesky, C.A. (1996) 'Developing cognitive therapist competency: teaching and supervision models', in P. Salkovskis (ed.), *Frontiers of Cognitive Therapy*. New York: Guilford Press, pp. 266-92.

Persons, J.B. (1989) *Cognitive Therapy in Practice. A Case Formulation Approach*. New York: W.W. Norton & Company.

Persons, J.B. and Burns, D.D. (1985) 'Mechanisms of action in cognitive therapy: the relative contributions of technical and interpersonal interventions', *Cognitive Therapy and Research*, 9: 539-57.

Raue, P.J. and Goldfried, M.R. (1994) 'The therapeutic alliance in cognitive-behavior therapy', in A.O. Horvath and L.S. Greenberg (eds), *The Working Alliance*. New York: Wiley, pp. 131-52.

Rogers, C.R. (1957) 'The necessary and sufficient conditions of therapeutic personality change', *Journal of Consulting and Clinical Psychology*, 21: 95-103.

Safran, J.D. (1990) 'Towards a refinement of cognitive therapy in the light of interpersonal theory', Parts 1 and 2. *Clinical Psychology Review*, 10: 87-121.

Safran, J.D. and Segal, Z.V. (1990) *Interpersonal Process in Cognitive Therapy*. New York: Basic Books.

Squier, R.W. (1990) 'A model of therapeutic understanding and adherence to treatment regimens in practitioner-patient relationships', *Social Science and Medicine*, 30 (3): 325-39.

Teasdale, J. (1996) 'The relationship between cognition and emotion: the mind-in-place mood disorders', in D.M. Clark and C.G. Fairburn (eds), *Science and Practice of Cognitive Behaviour Therapy*. Oxford: Oxford University Press, pp. 67-93.

Wills, F.R. and Sanders, D. (1997) *Cognitive Therapy: Transforming the Image*. London: Sage.

Wright, J.H. and Davis, D. (1994) 'The therapeutic relationship in cognitive behavioural therapy: patient perceptions and therapist responses', *Cognitive and Behavioural Practice*, 1: 25-45.

Young, J.E. (1994) *Cognitive Therapy for Personality Disorders: A Schema-Focused Approach* (rev. edn). Sarasota, FL: Professional Resource Press.

Young, J.E. and Klosko, J.S. (1993) *Reinventing Your Life*. London: Penguin.

7 The Relationship in Multimodal Therapy

Stephen Palmer

Multimodal therapy incorporates a number of strategies and methods, such as modality profiles, that are not normally used in other forms of therapy including similar approaches such as cognitive-behavioural or rational emotive behaviour therapy. How these are applied in the counselling session without having any detrimental effects on the therapeutic alliance and relationship will be considered in this chapter. Some of the techniques such as tracking, bridging and second-order modality profiles actually may circumnavigate so-called client 'resistance'. Flexible interpersonal styles of the counsellor which match client needs can reduce attrition (that is, premature termination of therapy). This approach is known in multimodal therapy as being an 'authentic chameleon'. Case examples will be used in this chapter to illustrate some of the main strategies and methods used in multimodal therapy.

The Basic Approach

Multimodal therapy was developed by Arnold Lazarus (1989) after he had become disillusioned with the relapse rates of his clients after they had received behavioural therapy. He devised a client assessment template in which seven discrete but interactive dimensions or modalities are routinely examined. The modalities are: **Behaviour, Affect, Sensation, Imagery, Cognition, Interpersonal, Drugs/Biology**, giving rise to the useful acronym **BASIC I.D.**

(Palmer and Lazarus, 1995). Lazarus asserted that all of human personality could be included within the seven modalities. The approach considers each client as unique, having a combination of qualities and characteristics with a different story to tell. By focusing in on the clients' personal experiences the approach takes an idiographic perspective. In addition, multimodal therapy employs a systematic assessment procedure which overcomes the undisciplined approach of many eclectic or integrative practitioners.

The multimodal framework is underpinned by a broad social and cognitive learning theory (Bandura, 1969, 1977, 1986; Rotter, 1954), while also drawing on group and communications theory (Watzlawick et al., 1974) and general system theory (Bertalanffy, 1974; Buckley, 1967). However, the counsellor can choose not to obsessively apply these theories to each client. In fact sometimes 'no therapy' is prescribed. For example, Lazarus advised a client to

> Use the money that you would have spent on therapy to have someone clean your house, have your hair done, and take tennis lessons. You will still have some money left over to meet friends for coffee or a snack. Be sure to engage in these activities on four different days each week, and after doing this for two months, please call and let us know if you are enjoying life more, if you feel less tense, less anxious and less depressed. (Lazarus, 1995: 327)

This resulted in an amelioration of her problems. This example illustrates the pragmatic and active stance taken in multimodal therapy.

Technically speaking, 'multimodal therapy' *per se* does *not* exist, since multimodal counsellors, as technical eclectics, draw from as many other approaches or systems as necessary. To be accurate, there is a multimodal assessment format and a multimodal framework (see Lazarus, 1989, 1997; Palmer and Dryden, 1995). The comprehensive assessment and extensive framework enables counsellors to choose, in negotiation with their clients, the most appropriate counselling programme (see Palmer, 1997a; Palmer and Dryden, 1991). Therefore, depending upon clients' expectations, if they needed mainly a 'listening ear' the counsellor might take a non-directive approach; if the client needed or expected a directive approach then this would also be offered (Palmer, 1999).

From the multimodal perspective, a good relationship, a constructive working alliance and adequate rapport are usually necessary but often insufficient for effective therapy (Dryden and Lazarus, 1991; Fay and Lazarus, 1993; Lazarus and Lazarus, 1991a; Palmer, 1999). The counsellor–client relationship is considered as the soil that enables the strategies and techniques to take root. The experienced multimodal counsellor hopes to offer a lot more by assessing and treating the client's BASIC I.D., endeavouring to 'leave no stone (or modality) unturned' (Palmer, 1997a).

Some clarification may be necessary at this stage. It is often suggested by practitioners that the therapeutic relationship is more important than techniques. But is it? Are effective counsellors using techniques without labelling them as such? Counsellors from some approaches claim not to use any techniques. When helping a client either to feel an emotion or to discuss an issue/problem, this often brings about improvement. However, in both examples the counsellor may have helped the client to focus on the cognitive modality, expressing and subsequently reappraising their cognitions which are intrinsically bound up with the emotion (for example, the cognition 'I am worthless'), and cognitively-problem solving the particular issue/problem (for example, 'Perhaps I could spend more time studying and therefore increase my chances of obtaining a good exam result'). In both examples cognitive shifts and improvements may occur, yet the counsellor may strongly deny using cognitive techniques and interventions. Hence, is it really just the relationship which leads to improvement as some practitioners would suggest?

Taking this argument a stage further, many people gain great benefit from bibliotherapy, that is, reading self-help material. Although the person is probably 'relating to' the book, is the reader really engaging in a 'therapeutic relationship' with a counsellor? Of course not, yet many report a substantial improvement. The books may suggest the application of behavioural techniques by the reader (e.g. Marks, 1980), or cognitive-behavioural techniques (e.g. Palmer and Strickland, 1996), or may instruct the reader directly or indirectly by use of stories or metaphors as in the case of *Aesop's Fables* (Aesop, 1993). Again, are the readers benefiting from the non-existent 'therapeutic relationship' or more accurately from the techniques, insight and sometimes wisdom they imbibe from the books? Although this discussion and brief detour may raise more questions than answers, I hope it demonstrates that practitioners could benefit from keeping an open mind on these issues.

Multimodal therapists often see themselves in a coach/trainer–trainee or teacher–student relationship as opposed to a doctor–patient relationship, thereby encouraging self-change rather than dependency. Although the counsellor and client are equal in their humanity, the counsellor may be more skilled in certain areas. Therefore it is not automatically assumed that clients know how to deal with their problems and have the requisite skills. If they did, then they presumably would not need counselling in the first place for many of the problems discussed in the average counselling room.

Assessment Procedures

In the beginning phase of counselling the multimodal counsellor is collecting information and looking for underlying themes and problems. Moreover, the counsellor determines whether a *judicious referral* may be necessary to a medical practitioner or psychiatrist if the client presents problems of an organic or psychiatric nature. A referral may also be recommended if a productive match between the counsellor and client is not possible. As more data is gathered it may become apparent that the client would benefit from attending, for example, couples therapy, family therapy, group therapy or an anxiety/stress-management group. This issue would then be discussed with the client. Therefore in practice the multimodal therapist may be considered as less possessive than others.

The multimodal counsellor generally examines each modality in a thorough, systematic manner (Palmer, 1992). However, the counsellor needs to take a flexible approach to avoid overwhelming the client with too many questions, or this could have a detrimental effect upon the therapeutic relationship. The worst-case scenario would be if the client began to feel interrogated or undermined by questions which could appear intrusive. On the other hand, some clients would expect a counsellor to ask wide-ranging questions about their problem(s) and to them this would indicate that the counsellor was being professional and taking a real interest in their difficulties.

An in-depth BASIC I.D. and life-history assessment can be undertaken by asking the client to complete the Multimodal Life History Inventory (MLHI) as a homework assignment (Lazarus and Lazarus, 1991b). This 15-page questionnaire helps the counsellor and client to assess the problems and develop the counselling programme without too much time being taken up in the counselling session. The MLHI asks many questions that may not be directly related to the client's presenting problem. Thus the counsellor needs to determine whether the client will find the questionnaire unnecessarily intrusive and subsequently counterproductive to the therapeutic alliance. Often this is a matter of judgement based on clinical experience. Many counsellors have told me that they would find the 15-page questionnaire 'off-putting', yet in my clinical experience this has not been a problem (the notable exceptions I recall have with been counsellors in therapy!).

Some clients may only need an in-depth assessment of key modalities in which they are experiencing difficulties, for example, a client suffering from a simple phobia. In fact, in some of these cases a Modality Profile would not need to be devised, as the main exposure intervention might occur in the first session and the client would not require any further treatment. Flexibility on the counsellor's (and possibly client's) part is the name of the game.

Most counsellors would first discuss the presenting problems or issues, for example, 'You said that your son makes you feel guilty. How exactly does he do this?' 'When do your headaches occur?' (Palmer, 1999). However, when focusing on a particular problem, the multimodal counsellor may rapidly traverse the entire BASIC I.D. to ensure that the relationship between each modality is noted; for example, when feeling guilty (Affect) the client may be demanding that she should be a perfect parent (Cognition) and in her mind's eye have a poor self-image (Imagery). In addition a multimodal counsellor discerns which specific modalities are being discussed and which ones are being avoided or overlooked, as otherwise useful information may be missed. However, it is not assumed that the client is intentionally avoiding discussing a particular modality.

Assessment in Practice

Initially, I normally listen with little interruption to the client telling me his or her problems and difficulties. On average this takes between 15 and 20 minutes before repetition creeps in. I then explain that we may find it helpful if I write up their problems on a whiteboard or flipchart, focusing on seven specific areas which will hopefully ensure that I have not overlooked any relevant aspect. With their agreement I examine each BASIC I.D. modality in turn usually starting with Behaviour.

In a recent case study (Palmer, 1999) I illustrated the typical conversation that I have with a client to lead gently into formulating her modality profile (or problem list). The client, Paola, is Italian, lives in England and is married to a white English male. They have two children who see themselves as English. She works part-time as a bank clerk. When writing up a modality profile with the client, to prevent possible confusion I usually avoid using psychobabble; therefore 'Affect' becomes 'Emotion' or 'Feelings' and 'Cognitions' becomes 'Thoughts/beliefs'. The following dialogue illustrates how the subject can be introduced in the counselling session.

> *Stephen*: We may find it useful if we write up on the whiteboard some of the problems you have just mentioned. In my experience, it would ensure that I have not overlooked any important issues that you want to cover. Is that okay?
>
> *Paola*: It sounds a good idea.
>
> *Stephen*: Perhaps we could just focus on a number of the behavioural problems you raised. [*Counsellor writes 'Behaviour' on the whiteboard.*] These are literally anything you actually 'do' or 'avoid doing'. You mentioned binge-eating. [*Counsellor writes 'binge-eating' on the whiteboard.*] Any other behavioural problems?
>
> *Paola*: My procrastination and poor time management go together! [*Laughs*] [*Counsellor writes them on the whiteboard.*]
>
> *Stephen*: Any others?
>
> *Paola*: No. I think these are my main problems.
>
> *Stephen*: Let's now focus on the emotions you mentioned. [*Counsellor writes 'Emotion' on the whiteboard.*]
>
> *Paola*: I get anxious at work about meeting important deadlines.
>
> *Stephen*: I suppose if we were being really accurate you are anxious about *not* meeting important deadlines! Let's suppose that I could guarantee that you could reach your important deadline, would you be anxious then? (*Counsellor refining the presenting problem.*)
>
> *Paola*: No. You're right.
>
> (*Counsellor writes redefined problem on the whiteboard.*)

The assessment continues in a similar manner covering all of the modalities. It is recommended that the counsellor leaves sufficient space on the whiteboard (or flipchart) for the inclusion of additional issues if they arise during the session. At the end of the counselling session, the counsellor writes up the modality profile

Table 7.1 Paola's modality profile

Modality	Problem
Behaviour	Binge-eats
	Procrastinates
	Poor time management
Emotion (Affect)	Anxiety about not meeting important deadlines
	Shame after binge-eating
	Depressed about missing her parents and family
	Feels guilty after speaking to mother
Sensations	Palpitations and shaky when anxious
	Empty feeling before binge-eating
Imagery	Images of making a fool of herself at work
	Images of losing control
Thoughts/beliefs (Cognitions)	I must perform well
	I must not let my parents down, or I'm worthless
	We should be together as a family
	I can't stand difficulties
Interpersonal	Rows with husband and children
	Passive with work colleagues and boss
	Allows mother to manipulate her
Drugs/biology	High blood pressure
	Migraines when under pressure

and in the next session can provide the client with a photocopy. Table 7.1 illustrates a modality profile which lists the problems of Paola.

Interaction between Modalities

Notice the interaction between the different modalities on Paola's problem modality profile. For example, when she is anxious (Affect) about deadlines, she procrastinates and applies poor time management (Behaviour); she has palpitations and is shaky (Sensations); has images about making a fool of herself (Imagery); holds beliefs that she 'must perform well' (Cognitions); and possibly gives herself migraines (Drugs/biology). In the counselling session, the counsellor will normally show the client how the different modalities interact and thereby increase her levels of anxiety which then subsequently interferes with her ability to perform. The sharing with the client of insights which help the client to understand the problem then leads smoothly into the intervention stage. This is considered as a very important aspect of the therapist's work. This psycho-educational aspect of the approach hopefully enables the client to take charge of their counselling programme.

Role Map

The therapist is encouraged to really get to know the client and his or her problems. Although the modality profile and a completed MLHI help this process, I now also recommend the use of a simple sociological role map to remind the counsellor of the client's idiographic centre which focuses on his or her different roles. I originally undertook role maps with ethnic minority clients in an attempt to understand the different factors involved, as recommended by Ridley (1995), but more recently have found them useful for the majority of clients.

Figure 7.1 is Paola's role map (Palmer, 1999). It illustrates Paola's various roles which contribute to the total picture. Ridley (1995) suggests that counsellors should explore the client's unique frame of reference based upon conjoint membership in these roles. He

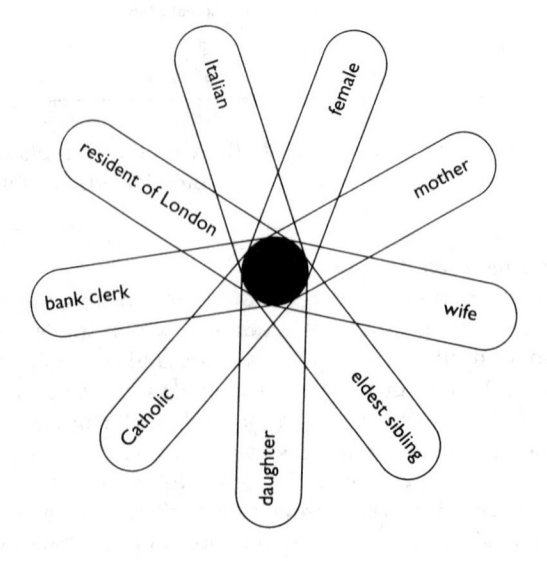

Key
● The idiographic centre

Figure 7.1   *Paola's idiographic role map*

suggests that to obtain an insightful look at the client, counsellors need to focus their attention on the centre of the diagram. The idiographic experience of the client, in our example Paola, sets her apart from every other Italian, female, mother, wife, daughter, eldest sibling, Catholic, bank clerk, and resident of London. Every role should not be ignored as each contributes to understanding Paola. I have found that if I refer back to the role map before the counselling session starts, it enables me to see the client in her or his social, familial and cultural context, literally at a glance. Again this may be reflected in the conversation with the client during the session and demonstrates to the client that the counsellor is taking an active interest in relevant aspects of his or her life.

The Relationship and Therapeutic Approach

Even before the initial counselling or assessment session it is important, if at all possible, to put clients at their ease. When they make the first contact with the counselling centre, they are sent information about the counsellor, the approach and any fees. If they are keen to read about the approach or techniques in depth then we may recommend suitable bibliotherapy (for example Palmer and Burton, 1996; Palmer and Strickland, 1996). We also offer them the opportunity to read a checklist covering relevant issues that they may wish to consider about counselling, such as discussing their goals and expectations of therapy with their counsellor (see Box 7.1). This checklist, it is hoped, helps them ask relevant questions about the counsellor, the therapy and how the therapy may help them. Thus they will enter therapy giving informed consent.

During the early counselling sessions the counsellor closely observes the client's reaction to her or his interventions, strategies, and comments. This helps the counsellor to determine the most appropriate interpersonal approach to take. This was summarized by Palmer and Dryden (1995: 24) as below:

1 Monitor the client's response to directive and non-directive interventions.
2 Discover whether the client responds well to humour.
3 Decide whether the client prefers a formal or informal relationship.
4 Establish how the client responds to counsellor self-disclosure.

Issues for the Client to Consider in Counselling or Psychotherapy

1. Here is a list of topics or questions you may wish to raise when attending your first counselling (assessment) session:
a. Check that your counsellor has relevant qualifications and experience in the field of counselling/psychotherapy.
b. Ask about the type of approach the counsellor uses, and how it relates to your problem.
c. Ask if the counsellor is in supervision (most professional bodies consider supervision to be mandatory; see footnote).
d. Ask whether the counsellor or the counselling agency is a member of a professional body and abides by a code of ethics. If possible obtain a copy of the code.
e. Discuss your goals/expectations of counselling.
f. Ask about the fees if any (if your income is low, check if the counsellor operates on a sliding scale) and discuss the frequency and estimated duration of counselling.
g. Arrange regular review sessions with your counsellor to evaluate your progress.
h. Do not enter into a long-term counselling contract unless you are satisifed that this is necessary and beneficial to you.

If you do not have a chance to discuss the above points during your first session, discuss them at the next possible opportunity.

General Issues

2. Counsellor self-disclosure can sometimes be therapeutically useful. However, if the sessions are dominated by the counsellor discussing his/her own problems at length, raise this issue in the counselling session.
3. If at any time you feel discounted, undermined or manipulated within the session, discuss this with the counsellor. It is easier to resolve issues as and when they arise.
4. Do not accept significant gifts from your counsellor. This does not apply to relevant therapeutic material.
5. Do not accept social invitations from your counsellor. For example dining in a restaurant or going for a drink. However, this does not apply to relevant therapeutic assignments such as being accompanied by your counsellor into a situation to help you overcome a phobia.
6. If your counsellor proposes a change in venue for the counselling sessions without good reason, do not agree. For example, from a centre to the counsellor's own home.
7. Research has shown that it is not beneficial for clients to have sexual contact with their counsellor. Professional bodies in the field of counselling and psychotherapy consider that it is unethical for counsellors or therapists to engage in sexual activity with current clients.
8. If you have any doubts about the counselling you are receiving then discuss them with your counsellor. If you are still uncertain, seek advice, perhaps from a friend, your doctor, your local Citizens Advice Bureau, the professional body your counsellor belongs to or the counselling agency that may employ your counsellor.
9. You have the right to terminate counselling whenever you choose.

Footnote: Counselling supervision is a formal arrangement where counsellors discuss their counselling in a confidential setting on a regular basis with one or more professional counsellors.

Box 7.1 *Issues for the client to consider in counselling or psychotherapy* (adapted from Palmer and Szymanska, 1994)

It is hypothesized that the matching of counsellor behaviour with client expectations will aid the development of a good therapeutic alliance and help to build up trust. This may have other benefits too such as decreasing the rate of attrition. Arnold Lazarus describes the counsellor who attempts to decide the relationship of choice as an '*authentic chameleon*' (Lazarus, 1993). The counsellor shows different aspects of him- or herself to the client that help the relationship, such as being formal or informal, willing to self-disclose and share experiences (if appropriate), the use of humour, as well as the use of directive and non-directive counselling interventions and skills.

The appearance of the counsellor may also be considered as important in relationship building. Clients of different age groups and from diverse cultural and social backgrounds have different expectations of helping professionals. For example, the wearing by the counsellor of formal clothing such as suits may prove anxiety-provoking for many adolescents who associate these with authority figures (Palmer and Dryden, 1995). The latter may be put at their ease more readily by the counsellor wearing informal attire, whereas high-flying business people may consider casually dressed counsellors as unprofessional.

The Multimodal Life History Inventory explores the client's expectations of counselling, which helps to guide the counsellor in matching the counselling programme and his or her inter-personal approach with these expectations. For example, one of my clients, Sue, responded to the 'Expectations Regarding Therapy' section of the MLHI in the following manner (Palmer and Dryden, 1995: 24):

Q: In a few words, what do you think therapy is all about?
A: Having the opportunity to talk through problems with a non-partial (*sic*) listener. Hopefully be given a new way of thinking about things/rationalizing problems.
Q: How long do you think your therapy should last?
A: As long as it is useful to me and productive.
Q: What personal qualities do you think the ideal therapist should possess?
A: Warmth and friendliness, and be non-judgemental, sincere and professional.

This indicated that she would probably be responsive to cognitive strategies, interventions and techniques. I decided to ensure that I was not overly warm and friendly in case this was misinterpreted as unprofessional and insincere. I attempted to maintain a careful balance and obtained feedback by asking Sue to complete an evaluation questionnaire focusing on the counsellor's skills and approach. Sometimes it becomes apparent that the client and counsellor are poorly matched and a poor therapeutic alliance may ensue. This would be likely to affect negatively the therapeutic outcome. If this is anticipated the counsellor has to decide whether it would be preferable to refer the client to another, better suited counsellor, or to have a go and review the therapy after a few sessions.

From Assessment to an Individual Counselling Programme

Table 7.2 summarizes the most commonly used techniques and interventions in multimodal counselling (Palmer, 1997a: 158). These techniques are selected by negotiation with the client. This generally happens in the first or second counselling session although it is often an on-going process. The counsellor attempts to fit the therapy to the client and not vice versa. If a client believes that massage, herbal medicine or yoga might help him or her to deal with stress or tension, then a *judicious referral* to a qualified practitioner would be seriously considered as a primary intervention or as an adjunct to counselling. This would therefore not necessarily prevent the multimodal counsellor from continuing to see the client. For further in-depth information about these techniques including indications and contra-indications, I refer the reader to *Counselling for Stress Problems* (Palmer and Dryden, 1995).

Completed Modality Profile

We return to Paola's problem modality profile (see Table 7.1). In fact it was incomplete as it only showed her problem list broken down into the BASIC I.D. modalities. This illustrated the assessment stage. The next stage is to move from assessment to developing the counselling programme. In the counselling session the full modality profile would be developed with the cooperation of the client. It would include strategies, techniques and interventions that the client was willing to use. Although the counsellor may demonstrate his or her expertise by suggesting useful interventions and explaining the rationale for their application, clients

Table 7.2 *Frequently used techniques/interventions in multimodal therapy and training*

Modality	Techniques/interventions	Modality	Techniques/interventions
Behaviour	Behaviour rehearsal	Cognition	Bibliotherapy
	Empty chair		Challenging faulty
	Exposure programme		inferences
	Fixed role therapy		Cognitive rehearsal
	Modelling		Coping statements
	Paradoxical intention		Correcting misconceptions
	Psychodrama		Disputing irrational beliefs
	Reinforcement programmes		Focusing
	Response prevention/cost		Positive self-statements
	Risk-taking exercises		Problem-solving training
	Self-monitoring and		Rational proselytizing
	recording		Self-acceptance training
	Stimulus control		Thought-stopping
	Shame-attacking	Interpersonal	Assertion training
Affect	Anger expression		Communication training
	Anxiety/anger management		Contracting
	Feeling-identification		Fixed role therapy
Sensation	Biofeedback		Friendship/intimacy
	Hypnosis		training
	Meditation		Graded sexual approaches
	Relaxation training		Paradoxical intentions
	Sensate focus training		Role play
	Threshold training		Social skills training
Imagery	Anti-future shock imagery	Drugs/Biology	Alcohol reduction
	Associated imagery		programme
	Aversive imagery		Life-style changes, e.g.
	Coping imagery		exercise, nutrition, etc.
	Implosion and imaginal		Referral to physicians or
	exposure		other specialists
	Positive imagery		Stop smoking programme
	Rational-emotive imagery		Weight reduction and
	Time protection imagery		maintenance programme

will often have their own ideas which could be included on the profile. In my clinical experience clients will frequently recommend coping strategies such as exercise, assertiveness training, time-management training, meditation, massage, nutrition improvement, yoga, hypnosis and relaxation to help them deal with stress and anxiety. Again, this reinforces the notion that clients can help themselves and that the counsellor is willing to take their ideas seriously. Lazarus (1973) found that if client expectations are met,

Table 7.3 *Paola's full modality profile*

Modality	Problem	Counselling programme
Behaviour	Binge-eats Procrastinates Poor time management	Stimulus control; find triggers Dispute self-defeating thinking Time management and assertion skills; bibliotherapy
Emotion (Affect)	Anxiety about not meeting important deadlines Shame after binge-eating Depressed about missing her parents and family Feels guilty after speaking to mother	Anxiety management; dispute beliefs; rational coping statements Self-acceptance training Counsellor support and rational discussion Self-acceptance training and coping statements
Sensations	Palpitations and shaky when anxious Empty feeling before binge-eating	Relaxation training; positive imagery Focus on self-defeating beliefs; assess for low frustration tolerance
Imagery	Images of making a fool of herself at work Images of losing control	Coping imagery; time projection imagery Coping imagery
Thoughts/beliefs (Cognitions)	I must perform well I must not let my parents down or I'm worthless We should be together as a family I can't stand difficulties	Dispute self-defeating beliefs; develop forceful coping statements; self-acceptance training; increase tolerance levels to difficulties; thought stopping; bibliotherapy
Interpersonal	Rows with husband and children Passive with work colleagues and boss Allows mother to manipulate her	Time-limited communication; dispute unhelpful beliefs; coping imagery Assertiveness training Assertiveness and communications skills; focus on underlying beliefs which trigger her guilt and depression
Drugs/biology	High blood pressure Migraines when under pressure	Liaise with physician; possible medication; relaxation training; bibliotherapy Dispute self-defeating beliefs; relaxation training; biofeedback

then this will usually lead to a better outcome. He demonstrated that if clients believe that hypnosis will help, then this method was more effective than another technique named 'relaxation', even though the latter was still essentially the same hypnosis intervention. I have also reported a similar experience with a client (see Palmer, 1993; Palmer and Dryden, 1995: 28-9).

It is useful if clients have undertaken relevant bibliotherapy which includes how different techniques can be applied, as this helps them to take charge of their counselling programme and select appropriate interventions (for example, Marks, 1980; Palmer and Strickland, 1996).

Table 7.3 is Paola's full modality profile (Palmer, 1999). Once the modality profile is developed the client and counsellor mutually agree which intervention to use first. Notice that in Paola's modality profile, relaxation training occurs three times. This would be a relatively easy place to start the counselling programme as Paola would be able to listen to a relaxation tape daily. Another initial assignment could be to read a section on thinking errors and thinking skills in a self-help book (for example Palmer and Strickland, 1996). She could then keep a record of the thinking errors she makes in the course of the day which could be reviewed during the next session.

It is usually a good idea to review therapeutic progress every five or six sessions. The modality profile aids this review and is updated as problems are overcome and added to as new information is obtained. Near the end of the counselling programme, the counselling sessions are spaced out to encourage clients to deal on their own with problems as they arise, with the goal of reaching total independence of the counsellor. Clients may return for 'booster sessions' after a longer period of time, such as six to twelve months. This helps to reduce the idea that they have been abandoned, which can occur in a minority of cases.

Other Strategies

Bridging

Many clients have preferred modalities which they may use to communicate with the counsellor. For example a counsellor may ask a client how he or she feels (affect modality) about a particular event occurring. The client may respond by describing (cognitive or imagery modality) the event to the counsellor, thereby avoiding saying which emotion was experienced. A multimodal counsellor would not want to threaten the therapeutic alliance by confronting the client directly on this issue, that is by repetitively asking the client how he or she felt about the event in question (Palmer and Dryden, 1995). Multimodal counsellors will deliberately use a 'bridging' procedure to initially 'key into' the client's preferred modality, before gently exploring a modality that the client may be intentionally or unintentionally avoiding, such as the affect/ emotions (Lazarus, 1987). Bridging is undertaken if it might be clinically useful to examine the avoided modality. The following example demonstrates the technique of 'bridging' (adapted from Palmer and Dryden, 1995: 37-8):

> *Counsellor*: When you heard the news, how did you feel about it?
> *Client*: I remember the telephone ringing. I answered it and it was James. He told me how it happened. Jill had run out of school and straight into the road and there just wasn't enough time for the car to stop. Fortunately, the ambulance came quickly and she was rushed off to hospital. I left for the hospital immediately. When I arrived, my daughter was there too. [*This story continued with the client using the cognitive modality.*]
> *Counsellor*: Jan, as you describe what happened, you looked very tense. I wonder if you have any sensations in your body at the moment? [*Bridging manoeuvre has now commenced.*]
> *Client*: Funny enough, I do! I have a vague headache. It's at the back of my head.
> *Counsellor*: If you don't mind, I would like you just to concentrate on your headache for the moment. [*Pause*] How does it feel now?
> *Client*: It feels much worse. I feel that it's going to explode.
> *Counsellor*: Do you recall having this sort of headache before?
> *Client*: Yes. [*Pause*] In fact, I've had it since James told me the news.
> *Counsellor*: How's your headache now?
> *Client*: It's getting worse.
> *Counsellor*: Are you feeling any emotion at the moment?
> *Client*: [*Pause*] I'm sad about what happened. [*Cries*]
> *Counsellor*: It may be helpful if we explore how you feel.

The counsellor allowed Jan to tell her 'story' from her perspective without interruption. The bridging manoeuvre commenced when the counsellor asked the client if she was feeling any sensations. At this point the client was able to move away from the cognitive modality to the sensory modality, eventually bridging into the affect modality. This method did not directly challenge the client and still allowed the counsellor to explore the desired modality.

Experienced counsellors who practise other approaches probably use this technique intuitively although they may be unaware of what they are doing. However, the multimodal counsellor does not leave important issues to chance and is aware of the specific technique for the job in hand.

Bridging often helps counsellors to make progress with clients who may have been unfairly described as 'difficult' or 'resistant' by previous therapists. Counsellors who insist that their clients should 'get into their gut feelings' against the wishes of their clients are likely to experience higher rates of attrition. In fact, in some circumstances clients who have already suffered from abusive relationships may find these directives by the counsellor equally abusive. In addition, by insisting that they 'get into their gut feelings' the counsellor may unwittingly stimulate a re-enactment of the earlier trauma where the abuser held the power (see Palmer and Dryden, 1995). This could negatively affect the therapeutic alliance.

Tracking
'Tracking' is another procedure regularly used in multimodal therapy in which the 'firing order' of the different modalities is noted for a specific problem (Lazarus, 1989). For example, when asked by his manager to give a presentation to the Board of Directors John experienced a panic attack. In the counselling session the counsellor helped John to analyse, step by step, exactly what had occurred. The counsellor wrote on a whiteboard the firing order of modalities as follows:

Firing order	*Modality*	
1	Cognition:	'I can't stand giving presentations. It would be awful if I screwed up.'
2	Imagery:	Picture of an audience laughing at him.
3	Sensation:	Physical symptoms of anxiety, e.g. palpitations, hyperventilation, dry mouth, clammy hands.
4	Behaviour:	Avoidance. Made excuses why he could not give the presentation.

This was a C-I-S-B sequence. John was encouraged to give the presentation. The counselling programme was linked to the sequence of the firing order of the modalities. The intervention was as follows:

Intervention sequence	Modality	Intervention
1	Cognition	Rational coping statement: 'I've stood it before; I can stand it again. If I screw up it won't be the end of the world.'
2	Imagery	Coping image of dealing with negative feedback from the Directors.
3	Sensation	Breathing relaxation exercise.
4	Behaviour	Do NOT avoid the situation.

The rationale for the use of each technique was explained to John. The importance of applying them in the C–I–S–B sequence to help completely short-circuit the anxiety was emphasized. John practised daily repeating his rational coping statement (cognitive modality). The counsellor and John considered a variety of different ways he could deal with a negative response from the Directors. His coping imagery incorporated these ideas so that he could literally see himself dealing with potential difficulties (imagery modality). When practising he would use the coping imagery after saying out aloud his rational coping statement. The counsellor taught him a breathing relaxation exercise (sensation modality) just in case the two other interventions were insufficient to alleviate his anxiety. The counsellor had to remind John that as long as he continued to avoid (behaviour modality) giving presentations, he would carry on experiencing anxiety about undertaking them. It was better in the long run to face his fears and learn how to deal with them. In fact, John found that he did not need to use the sensation intervention.

Tracking avoids instructing clients to use techniques that may fail to work in their individual case. By the time they experience the negative emotion such as anxiety, using an intervention which is last in the firing order is less likely to work efficiently. In John's case his self-defeating cognitions largely exacerbated his stress and the negative imagery triggered the panic. However, other individuals in a similar situation might experience a different modality firing order. John favoured his cognitive modality in a variety of stressful situations. He would be known as a 'cognitive reactor'. Other individuals might be 'sensory reactors' or 'imagery reactors' depending upon which modality fires first. Often the client's structural profile (see later) indicates the type of reactor. This information helps the counsellor in determining the most appropriate intervention for a particular client (Palmer and Dryden, 1995).

In my clinical experience, clients who have been unsuccessfully treated by other counsellors for anxiety or panic attacks are often rather sceptical about any further treatment. They may even report that their panic attacks appear to 'come out of the blue'. By undertaking the tracking procedure in the first multimodal counselling session clients not only gain great insight into their condition, they also become aware of the counsellor's expertise and their faith in the subsequent counselling programme increases. Competence or expertise is therefore regarded in multimodal therapy as a crucial bonding agent in the therapeutic relationship in many cases.

Structural Profiles

In longer-term therapy, structural profiles are drawn to elicit additional clinical information (see Figure 7.2; Palmer 1997b: 155). They also provide data that indicate whether the client and counsellor are sufficiently matched, which increases the chances of a positive therapeutic outcome (see Herman, 1991).

The structural profile is obtained either by asking clients to complete page 14 of the Multimodal Life History Inventory or by asking them to rate subjectively, on a score of 1–7, how they perceive themselves in relation to the different modalities. Typical assessment questions are (adapted from Lazarus and Lazarus, 1991b):

Behaviour: How much of a doer are you?
Affect: How emotional are you?
Sensation: How 'tuned in' are you to your bodily sensations?
Imagery: How much are you into mental images or pictures?
Cognition: How much of a 'thinker' are you?
Interpersonal: How much of a 'social being' are you?
Drugs/biology: To what extent are you health conscious?

If we consider the example in Figure 7.2, Kate perceives herself as a 'thinker' and a 'doer' as she rated herself at 7 on both the cognitive and behaviour modalities. Her low interpersonal score of 2 was due to her perceiving herself as a 'loner'. Once the structural profile had been discussed with Kate, then her 'desired' structural profile was developed (Palmer, 1997b). She was asked in what way she would like to change her profile during the course of therapy (see Figure 7.3). The counsellor ensures that a

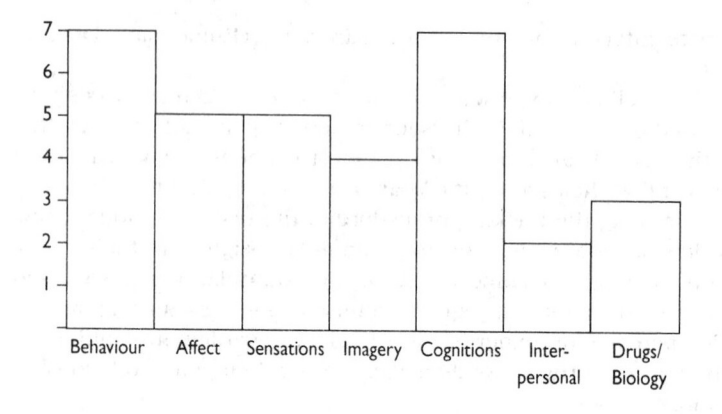

Figure 7.2   *Kate's structural profile*

record of each specific goal or target is noted. If there is sufficient room then each goal can be written directly on to the profile or, if not, is written in the client's records. The client is given a copy for his or her own records, as a reminder of what he or she would like to achieve during counselling. This helps to keep clients working towards their goals.

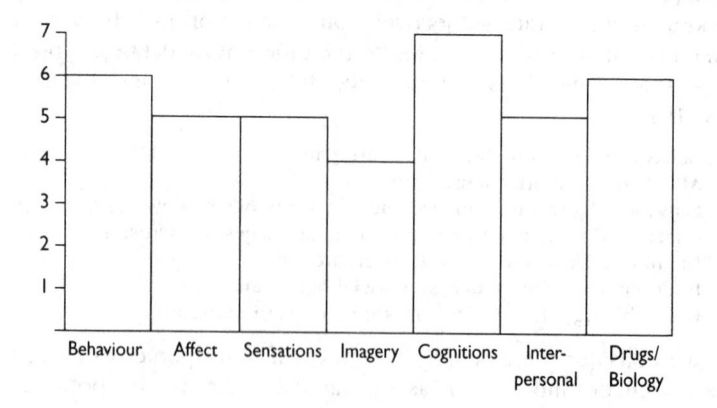

Figure 7.3   *Kate's desired structural profile*

If the counsellor has contracted with the client to review regularly his or her therapeutic progress, then comparing the actual structural profile and the desired structural profile can form part of that review. At this stage clients will often want to revise their desired structural profiles.

Counsellors who undertake marital or couples counselling have found that using structural profiles can provide valuable information (Lazarus, 1989). In addition, the profiles can be compared in the session and used to highlight difficulties that a couple may be experiencing.

Herman and associates (Herman, 1992, 1994; Herman et al., 1995) have undertaken extensive research into structural profiles. Herman has found that when counsellors and clients have wide differences on their structural profiles, therapeutic outcomes are unfavourably affected (Herman, 1991). This indicates that it could be used to match client to counsellor in a counselling centre.

Second-Order Modality Profile

A second-order modality profile assessment is undertaken if a client is experiencing difficulty overcoming a particular problem and the selected strategies applied have been unsuccessful. For example, if Paola continued to experience high blood pressure, then the new profile would focus specifically on all issues possibly connected with high blood pressure, for example, rows or cognitions that exacerbate stress such as 'I must perform well.' In cases where a client has a medical condition it is important for the counsellor to liaise with the client's physician.

The strategies described in this section help the counsellor to tailor the approach to each individual client and unconditionally accept the uniqueness of each person. In addition they enhance the effectiveness of a counselling programme.

For further information on multimodal therapy I would recommend the literature that describes the approach in depth (see Lazarus, 1989, 1997; Palmer, 1997b; Palmer and Dryden, 1995).

Deserted Island Fantasy

This technique, developed by Lazarus (1989) can give the counsellor interesting insights into how the therapeutic relationship with the client may unfold over a period of time. He asks clients to envision themselves on a deserted island with a designated companion (someone the client does not already know) and inquires how they will while away the time. This technique can yield much information. However, since the counsellor could draw incorrect conclusions about the potential relationship, this method has to be used with caution. It is probably better suited for clients entering long-term therapy and would not necessarily be used in brief therapy settings.

'Overcoming Apparent Resistance'

Multimodal counsellors are trained not to assume immediately that clients are 'resistant' if they do not wish to undertake an agreed task, such as a role play exercise. Counsellors are encouraged to understand why the client is reluctant to do the task and examine whether they are expecting too much too soon and/or whether or not they have adequately prepared the client. For example, an *in-vivo* (real-life) exposure programme may have been recommended by the counsellor to help the client deal with agoraphobia. However, this may prove to be an overwhelming exercise for the client as it can trigger very high levels of anxiety. The client could have been more adequately prepared to undertake an exposure programme after first practising coping imagery and a breathing technique. The motto for the counsellor to remember would be 'challenging but not overwhelming' (see Palmer and Dryden, 1995). By being prepared in this systematic manner the client is more likely to undertake the assignment and attrition is less likely to occur.

Strategies and techniques such as second-order modality profiles, bridging and tracking can all be used to overcome apparent resistance.

To reduce the rate of attrition and aid the therapeutic alliance, multimodal counsellors are encouraged to consider five key factors when deciding how to respond and what techniques to use with each unique client in therapy (see Palmer, 1997a, c; 1999):

1   client qualities
2   counsellor qualities
3   counsellor skills
4   therapeutic alliance
5   technique specificity

These five interacting factors may help to determine the choice of interventions and the interpersonal style of the counsellor. Careful consideration should be given to each of them during the course of therapy. The interaction of the client–counsellor qualities may determine therapeutic outcome. For example, if the client is passive, slow talking and takes time to think ideas through, whereas the counsellor is very active-directive, fast talking and quick thinking, the latter's approach will discourage the client from speaking and talking in the session. As the client retreats into his or her proverbial shell, the counsellor may respond by becoming more active-directive, which in turn encourages the client to become even more passive (Palmer, 1999). In this example, it would be preferable for the counsellor to adjust his or her interpersonal style and become less active-directive, thereby encouraging the client to participate in the counselling process. Another example would be that a client is likely to realize quickly that a counsellor is prejudiced and intolerant of others' opinions. The client is likely to start feeling rejected if his or her comments are dismissed. This could lead to unnecessary attrition.

The counsellor may have knowledge of a broad range of strategies, techniques, interventions and skills but be unable to demonstrate or apply them effectively in therapy. Therefore the strategies selected for a client's counselling programme may also be determined (and limited) by the counsellor's therapeutic skills or skills deficits. However, with appropriate training and supervision these type of problems may be overcome.

The therapeutic alliance is underpinned by many different factors. Some clients expect counsellors to provide a listening ear, whereas others want their counsellors to demonstrate their clinical expertise. Some clients want a clear explanation of how the therapy works and can be applied to their problems. Others want support through a difficult period. It is the counsellor's responsibility to help build up and maintain a satisfactory therapeutic alliance and relationship by adjusting their interpersonal style and pitching their interventions at the correct level for a particular client. This is often a process of trial and error although, as discussed previously, counsellors can ask their clients what exactly they expect from the counsellor and the therapy. The building up of trust is not always straightforward and the counsellor may have to demonstrate certain behaviours, attitudes and skills to aid this process. If the counsellor asks the client to undertake overwhelming assignments this could very easily harm a good working relationship.

Technique selection should be guided by the latest research findings. The counsellor needs to ask a number of reflective questions (Palmer, 1999: 197-8):

a. Have I assessed the client/problem correctly? Have I identified the antecedents or maintaining factors correctly?

b. Does the research indicate that this is the correct intervention/ technique for this particular problem or disorder?

c. Even if the intervention/technique has been shown to be the most effective one to use for this specific problem, will it trigger too high a level of anxiety for this client? If it does, should I use a less anxiety provoking intervention/technique?

d. Does the client understand the rationale for this intervention/ technique?

e. Does the client trust my therapeutic judgement?

f. Am I sufficiently skilled to undertake or demonstrate this intervention, technique or skill? If not should I choose a different method, obtain more training, seek relevant supervision, or refer the client elsewhere?

g. Am I expecting too much change, too soon?

h. Would this intervention/technique suit the client's personality?

i. Does this intervention/technique help the client to achieve his or her goals?

j. Are there any indications or contraindications for the use of this intervention/technique with this particular client?

If a therapeutic impasse appears to have been reached, the counsellor, instead of believing the client is 'resistant', can ask him or herself the following questions in addition to the previous ones (see Palmer and Dryden, 1995: 39):

k. Is there a client–counsellor mismatch? Is a referral necessary?

l. Is the client ashamed to express emotion or disclose personal information about him/herself or his or her family in the counselling session?

m. Is the client avoiding certain issues because they are so painful to even think about or discuss?

n. Is a significant other(s) interfering or undermining the client's goals of counselling?

o. Was the homework assignment perceived by the client as relevant?

p. If the client does not wish to undertake the homework assignment what is holding him/her back or preventing him/her from doing it? Can this barrier be circumnavigated?

q. If the client improves and overcomes his/her target problems would this detrimentally affect relationships with significant others as perceived by the client?

r.   Does the client trust me? Do I need to work on strengthening the therapeutic alliance before we tackle more difficult issues?

These issues can also be considered during supervision when difficulties arise. If counsellors tape-record their counselling sessions for supervision purposes they and their supervisors are in a good position to examine carefully the counsellor's responses to so-called 'resistant' clients.

Conclusion

Multimodal counsellors take Paul's (1967: 111) mandate very seriously: '*What* treatment, by *whom*, is most effective for *this* individual with *that* specific problem and under *which* set of circumstances?' But in addition to applying the strategies or techniques of choice, as discussed earlier, the multimodal counsellor also attempts to be an authentic chameleon who also considers the *relationships of choice* (Lazarus, 1993). As I've stated elsewhere (Palmer, 1997b: 164):

> In the first therapy session the multimodal therapist may tentatively experiment with different styles of interaction with the client to discover the interpersonal approach that may benefit the therapeutic relationship. Decisions are made on when and how to be directive, non-directive, supportive, cold, warm, reflective, gentle, tough, formal, informal or humorous. Would the client prefer the therapist to take the stance of a coach or trainer rather than that of a warm, empathic counsellor? These issues are all considered important in forming a good therapeutic alliance with the client (Bordin, 1979).

The counsellor steers clear of placing clients on a Procrustean bed and treating them alike but will look for broad, tailor-made combinations of effective strategies and techniques to bring to bear upon the problem. The methods are carefully applied within an appropriate context and delivered in a manner or style that is most likely to have a positive impact and a good long-term outcome (Palmer, 1997c).

Issues

- Actively listen to the client.
- Become an authentic chameleon: adapt your interpersonal style to that which maximizes the therapeutic relationship and

aids successful therapeutic outcome throughout the entire counselling programme.

■ Adapt the therapy to the client; avoid attempting to fit the client into the therapeutic box. Avoid placing clients on a Procrustean bed.

■ Consider the five key areas when deciding how to respond and what techniques to use with each unique client in counselling: client qualities; counsellor qualities, counsellor skills; therapeutic alliance; and technique specificity.

■ Ensure that clients understand the rationale for the techniques and interventions applied.

■ Be flexible. Learn to be both active-directive and non-directive.

■ Negotiate challenging but not overwhelming assignments (see Palmer and Dryden, 1995).

■ Avoid labelling clients as 'resistant'. Counsellors need to consider how they are personally contributing to any difficulties encountered in counselling.

■ Refer when necessary.

References

Aesop, (1993) *Aesop's Fables*. London: Tiger Books International.

Bandura, A. (1969) *Principles of Behavior Modification*. New York: Holt, Rinehart & Winston.

Bandura, A. (1977) *Social Learning Theory*. Englewood Cliffs, NJ: Prentice Hall.

Bandura, A. (1986) *Social Foundations of Thought and Action: A Social Cognitive Theory*. Englewood Cliffs, NJ: Prentice Hall.

Bertalanffy, L. von (1974) 'General systems theory', in S. Arieti (ed.), *American Handbook of Psychiatry* (vol. 1). New York: Basic Books.

Bordin, E.S. (1979) 'The generalizability of the psychoanalytic concept of the working alliance', *Psychotherapy: Theory, Research and Practice*, 16 (3): 252-60.

Buckley, W. (1967) *Modern Systems Research for the Behavioral Scientist*. Chicago: Aldine.

Dryden, W. and Lazarus, A.A. (1991) *A Dialogue with Arnold Lazarus: 'It Depends'*. Milton Keynes: Open University Press.

Fay, A. and Lazarus, A.A. (1993) 'On necessity and sufficiency in psychotherapy', *Psychotherapy in Private Practice*, 12: 33-9.

Herman, S.M. (1991) 'Client–therapist similarity on the Multimodal Structural Profile Inventory as predictive of psychotherapy outcome', *Psychotherapy Bulletin*, 26: 26-7.

Herman, S.M. (1992) 'Predicting psychotherapists' treatment theories by Multimodal Structural Profile Inventories: an exploratory study', *Psychotherapy in Private Practice*, 11: 85-100.

Herman, S.M. (1994) 'The diagnostic utility of the Multimodal Structural Profile Inventory', *Psychotherapy in Private Practice*, 13: 55-62.

Herman, S.M., Cave, S., Kooreman, H.E., Miller, J.M. and Jones, L.L. (1995) 'Predicting clients' perceptions of their symptomatology by multimodal structural profile inventory responses', *Psychotherapy in Private Practice*, 14: 23-33.

Lazarus, A.A. (1973) 'Multimodal behavior therapy: treating the BASIC ID', *Journal of Nervous and Mental Disease*, 156: 404-11.

Lazarus, A.A. (1987) 'The multimodal approach with adult outpatients', in N.S. Jacobson (ed.), *Psychotherapists in Clinical Practice*. New York: Guilford Press.

Lazarus, A.A. (1989) *The Practice of Multimodal Therapy* (first published 1981). Baltimore: Johns Hopkins University Press.

Lazarus, A.A. (1993) 'Tailoring the therapeutic relationship, or being an authentic chameleon', *Psychotherapy*, 30 (3): 404-7.

Lazarus, A.A. (1995) 'Multimodal therapy', in R.J. Corsini and D. Wedding (eds), *Current Psychotherapies* (5th edn). Itasca, IL: Peacock Publishers.

Lazarus, A.A. (1997) *Brief but Comprehensive Psychotherapy*. New York: Springer Publishing.

Lazarus, A.A. and Lazarus, C.N. (1991a) 'Let us not forsake the individual nor ignore the data: a response to Bozarth', *Journal of Counselling and Development*, 69: 463-5.

Lazarus, A.A. and Lazarus, C.N. (1991b) *Multimodal Life History Inventory*. Champaign, IL: Research Press.

Marks, I.M. (1980) *Living with Fear*. New York: McGraw-Hill.

Palmer, S. (1992) 'Multimodal assessment and therapy: a systematic, technically eclectic approach to counselling, psychotherapy and stress management', *Counselling*, 3 (4): 220-4.

Palmer, S. (1993) *Multimodal Techniques: Relaxation and Hypnosis*. London: Centre for Multimodal Therapy.

Palmer, S. (1997a) 'Multimodal therapy', in C. Feltham (ed.), *Which Psychotherapy?* London: Sage.

Palmer, S. (1997b) 'Modality assessment', in S. Palmer and G. McMahon (eds), *Client Assessment*. London: Sage.

Palmer, S. (1997c) 'A multimodal approach with ethnic minorities'. Paper given at the First International Counselling Psychology Conference, British Psychological Society, Division of Counselling Psychology, Stratford-upon-Avon, 1997.

Palmer, S. (1999) 'Developing an individual counselling programme: a multimodal perspective', in S. Palmer and P. Laungani, *Counselling in a Multicultural Society*. London: Sage.

Palmer, S. and Burton, T. (1996) *Dealing with People Problems at Work*. Maidenhead: McGraw-Hill.

Palmer, S. and Dryden, W. (1991) 'A multimodal approach to stress management', *Stress News*, 3 (1): 2-10.

Palmer, S. and Dryden, W. (1995) *Counselling for Stress Problems*. London: Sage.

Palmer, S. and Lazarus, A.A. (1995) 'In the counsellor's chair. Stephen Palmer interviews Arnold Lazarus', *Counselling*, 6 (4): 271-3.

Palmer, S. and Strickland, L. (1996) *Stress Management: A Quick Guide*. Dunstable: Folens.

Palmer, S. and Szymanska, K. (1994) 'How to avoid being exploited in counselling and psychotherapy', *Counselling, Journal of the British Association for Counselling*, 5 (1): 24.

Paul, G.L. (1967) 'Strategy and outcome research in psychotherapy', *Journal of Consulting Psychology*, 331: 109–18.

Paul, G.L. (1985) 'Can pregnancy be a placebo effect? Terminology, designs and conclusions in the study of psychosocial and pharmacological treatments of behavioral disorders', in L. White, B. Tursky and G.E. Schwartz (eds), *Placebo: Theory, Research and Mechanisms*. New York: Guilford Press, pp. 137–63.

Ridley, C.R. (1995) *Overcoming Unintentional Racism in Counseling and Therapy*. Thousand Oaks, CA: Sage.

Rotter, J.B. (1954) *Social Learning and Clinical Psychology*. Englewood Cliffs, NJ: Prentice-Hall.

Watzlawick, P., Weakland, J. and Fisch, F. (1974) *Change: Principles of Problem Formation and Problem Resolution*. New York: Norton.

8 *The Counselling Relationship and Psychological Type*

Rowan Bayne

Can clients and counsellors be 'matched' in some way, thereby improving the quality of their relationship and the effectiveness of the counselling? This tantalizing idea is implied by such metaphors as 'in tune', 'on the same wavelength' and 'a meeting of minds' and, conversely, 'no contact' and 'speaking a different language'. However, such metaphors point to rather than explain an experience and the idea remains intuitively compelling but vague. Moreover, there are hundreds of characteristics which could be central to a good 'match', for example attitudes, pace, sense of humour, multicultural factors, intellectual qualities, personality traits and types, values, interests (see Dryden and Feltham, 1994: 48-56). There are, thus, far too many characteristics and combinations to investigate; it would take too long and be too expensive (Stiles, Shapiro and Elliott, 1986: 168).

Psychological type theory (Myers, 1980) suggests that personality characteristics are the most important aspect of matching. In terms of Paul's classic question (1967: 111), '*What* treatment, by *whom*, is most effective for *this* individual with *that* specific problem, and under *which* set of circumstances?' (italics in original), type theory proposes focusing on the '*whom*' and the '*this* individual', and on the relationship between them, and it spells out which aspects of personality are the most generally influential (in theory) and also the likely clashes and benefits in each combination of 'psychological types'.

In this chapter, I first discuss one of the main concepts in psychological type theory – 'preference' – and then apply four pairs of preferences to the counselling relationship. Three brief sections come next: on the validity of type theory, on its potential for integration with other approaches to counselling, and on three questions concerned with applying type theory to the counselling relationship:

1. Is similarity of psychological type always or even usually best? (The brief answer is no, that's too simple.)
2. Does a counsellor need to know the client's psychological type to use the theory? (No.)
3. How flexible in adapting to a client is it reasonable to expect a counsellor to be? (It depends.)

Then I touch on a more complicated level of type theory, called type dynamics, and on three other factors affected by type which can in turn have an effect on the counselling relationship: the counsellor's room, the choice of techniques and ways of presenting them.

The Preferences

The concept of preference is at the heart of psychological type theory. It can be defined as 'feeling most natural and comfortable with'. For example, some people prefer extraversion to introversion, and for them action tends to be more natural than reflection. For introverts the opposite is true. Everyone both reflects and takes action, though to markedly varying degrees, but an introvert's extraversion, for example, usually exists in a relatively pale, undeveloped form. It is not 'them' in the same way that their introversion is, not their 'real personality'.

Carol Shields provides a vivid illustration of this idea in relation to the preference for 'thinking' versus 'feeling' in her novel *The Box Garden*, though she does not use these terms and there is no evidence that she knows about Jung's theory of psychological type, Myers' clarification and development of it, or the Myers-Briggs Type Indicator. Her character Charleen is musing about the way another character, Eugene, always finds 'the most kindly interpretation' of other people's behaviour: 'kindness after all comes to him naturally . . . gentleness, generosity and compromise are not for him learned skills', and she contrasts Eugene's natural 'kindness' (a central element of the preference for feeling in type theory) with her own inclinations.

> For me, kindness is an alien quality; and like a difficult French verb I must learn it slowly, painfully, and probably imperfectly . . . it does *not* wake with me in the morning; every day I have to coax it anew into existence, breathe on it to keep it alive; practise it to keep it in good working order. And, most difficult of all, I have to exercise it in such a way that it looks spontaneous and genuine; I have to see that it flows without hesitation as it does from its true practitioners, its lucky heirs who acquire it without laborious seeking, the lucky ones like Eugene. (p. 104)

Here Charleen depicts herself as someone who, despite intense regular practice, has to work very hard to develop and maintain an aspect of her 'feeling'. In type theory, this means that she is likely to be someone who prefers thinking. (Tables 8.2 and 8.3 give more information on what these terms mean in type theory.) It is unfortunate that she seems not to value her thinking; gender stereotypes and cultural values are likely to be relevant. That she *does* prefer thinking is supported by two other pieces of evidence: the tone of her musings is analytic, and seems naturally so, and in a companion novel, *Small Ceremonies*, Charleen's sister reflects that Charleen 'for all her sensitivity, has a core of detachment' (p. 18).

The distinction between preference and non-preference is therefore made – both by Shields and in type theory – in terms of effort. Usually, frequency of behaviour is also a distinguishing feature; for example introverts behave sometimes in extraverted ways but generally in introverted ways. However, some introverts, usually because of their upbringing or careers, behave mainly as extraverts but – crucially – feel that 'something is not right'. Type theory predicts that if they then start to behave introvertedly more of the time, they will quickly feel more natural and comfortable.

I have singled out people who prefer introversion but the same assumptions apply to all the preferences. There are eight of these, in bipolar pairs (Table 8.1). Table 8.2 indicates their meaning in general terms and Table 8.3 gives several characteristics associated with each preference. There are 16 possible combinations of the preferences and therefore 16 psychological types, for example

ISTJ or ENFP. At the most basic level of type theory, ISTJs are people who prefer a combination of introversion, sensing, thinking and judging. Further, given normal development of their type, they are less comfortable with extraversion, intuition, feeling and perceiving.

Table 8.1   *The four pairs of preferences*

Extraversion (E) or Introversion (I)
Sensing (S) or Intuition (N)
Thinking (T) or Feeling (F)
Judging (J) or Perceiving (P)

Table 8.2   *Some general characteristics associated with the preferences*

E	More outgoing and active	
	More reflective and reserved	I
S	More practical and interested in facts and details	
	More interested in possibilities and an overview	N
T	More logical and reasoned	
	More agreeable and appreciative	F
J	More planning and coming to conclusions	
	More easy-going and flexible	P

The relationship between psychological type and behaviour is a substantial one. People who prefer thinking, for example, tend to behave more often and more naturally, in 'thinking' ways than they do in 'feeling' ways (Bayne, 1995; Hammer, 1996; Myers et al., 1998). However, there are four limiting factors. Firstly, people sometimes behave uncharacteristically. Such factors as politeness, stress, and beliefs about a situation (for example about the role of client or counsellor) affect our behaviour. The validity evidence for type theory shows that usually this uncharacteristic behaviour lasts only for short periods. Then the real personality, including the preferences, reappears.

The second limiting factor applies in particular to conversations. It is that the personalities of each person involved tend to have some effect on each other. Thorne's (1987) research on conversations between introverts and extraverts illustrates this point well. She recorded 52 ten-minute conversations: 13 between two introverts, 13 between two extraverts, and 26 between an extravert and an introvert. One or two weeks later she asked the participants to rate a replay of their conversation. Thorne found first that the extraverts tended to be seen as cheerful, enthusiastic and talkative and the introverts as reserved, serious and shy. (This is also evidence for the validity of this part of type theory.) Turning to the participants' experience of the particular kind of relationship, introverts were on average less comfortable with introverts than with extraverts (no direct and positive matching effect on the basis of similarity here), while the extraverts felt comfortable with both introverts and extraverts.

Thorne also analysed the conversations themselves in detail, and this is where the impact of each person's personality on her partner's behaviour comes in. She found that extraverts usually had more upbeat and expansive conversations, introverts more serious and focused ones, and that these tendencies were stronger for Es with other Es and Is with other Is and weaker for Es with Is. Thus the participants in the mixed pairs adapted to each other. For example, some of the Es said they did not feel so pressed to say nice things by their I partners, and many of the Is said they felt refreshed by their E partners.

The third limiting factor on the relationship between type and behaviour is that each person's preferences are more or less well developed, and that generally we develop all eight preferences, that is both the four preferences of a type and their opposites, to varying degrees as we get older. The fourth factor is that people's behaviour is affected by personality characteristics other than those emphasized in type theory, such as anxiety for example, and by intellectual and cultural variables. However, most people behave in characteristic ways most of the time, and these are generally related to their psychological type.

The Preferences in the Counselling Relationship

Table 8.3 lists some of the main ways of behaving associated with each preference. They apply, of course, with some minor changes of wording, to counsellors as well as to clients. From a type theory perspective, counsellors can usefully consider whether or not to modify their behaviour to 'match' the client – for instance to be

Table 8.3 *Behaviour associated with the preferences (from Bayne, 1998)*

People who prefer:	Tend to:
Extraversion	be more active be less comfortable with reflection be optimistic and energetic
Introversion	be more at ease with silence be less comfortable with action be more private
Sensing	be concrete and detailed like a 'practical' approach not see many options be uncomfortable with novelty
Intuition	take a broad view jump around from topic to topic see unrealistic options see lots of options overlook facts like novelty and imaginative approaches
Thinking	avoid emotions, feelings and values in early conversations need rationales and logic be critical and sceptical want to be admired for their competence be competitive
Feeling	focus on values and networks of values need to care (e.g. about a value, a person or an ideal) be 'good' clients or patients want to be appreciated
Judging	fear losing control find sudden change stressful need structure need to achieve work hard and tolerate discomfort
Perceiving	avoid decisions need flexibility avoid discomfort

more active with an extraverted client - or whether or not to discuss any differences with their client - for example, 'I wonder if you find me too quiet. Would you like me to speak more often?' This is a standard strategy in counselling generally (see Dryden and Feltham, 1994). Type theory adds greater clarity about some of the content.

Type theory does not say that counsellors should always try to match or 'talk the language of' a client, as the following examples illustrate. First, an ENFP counsellor and an ISFJ client. One of Provost's (1993) clients was depressed. She also saw herself as a slow learner and was impatient with complexity. She described her life as 'dull and devoid of fun'. Provost, an ENFP, controlled her own natural, relatively bold approach: 'Our relationship was a series of gentle pushes, cautious tries, and sometimes retreats' (1993: 52). Provost suspects that if she'd tried to work at her own pace the client would have clung to the familiar ways or left. Occasionally, she'd try a paradoxical suggestion: 'You're not ready to change – let's be more cautious.' Provost also helped this client appreciate her (the client's) strengths, for example organization (developed J) and warmth and caring (developed F), and they agreed some specific goals, for example to try out some additional learning strategies and to become more playful and flexible. Provost adds that she learned to be more patient from this client, and that 'mutual respect and fascination with each other's processes were important elements in our counseling relationship' (p. 52).

Second, an ISTJ counsellor with an ENTP client. The ISTJ counsellor let go of her natural cautious and systematic approach and let herself be more flowing with her client some of the time, leaping into passages of fantasy and frequent changes of topic. Nevertheless, from time to time she used her STJ strengths to review, organize and structure and to challenge the reality of some of the proposed actions. She sometimes used her dry sense of humour (a less obvious ISTJ characteristic) to do this. At the same time, she appreciated the client's love of possibilities and indeed enjoyed it for short periods, and she joined in some debates (NTs tend to enjoy these), but again only up to a point. Then she would say something like, 'I notice we're back into seminar mode. Shall we try some counselling? . . . Where we'd got to was. . . .'

The general strategy for improving the counselling relationship is then for counsellors to be aware of their preferences (which can also be biases), and where appropriate to clarify the effects of their preferences with clients, using ideas but not necessa ily terms from type theory. Greater awareness of type differences can make an appropriate and comfortable degree of flexibility more likely. Type can also help the counselling relationship by reducing the likelihood of negative judgements of clients by counsellors, and of counsellors by clients.

The next four sub-sections illustrate the use of each pair of preferences in the counselling relationship, drawing mainly on the characteristics listed in Table 8.3.

E and I

Nocita and Stiles (1986) contrasted two views of introverts in one-to-one counselling: (a) that they tend to find it *less* comfortable than extraverts because they are expected to self-disclose, and (b) that they tend to find it *more* comfortable than extraverts because they are used to reflecting on their inner experience. You may like to consider which view seems more likely to be true.

Nocita and Stiles's (1986) main finding was a substantial relationship between introversion and discomfort. Introverts tended to rate their counselling sessions as 'tense, rough and difficult' and their mood after a session as 'sad, angry and afraid' (p. 235). Discomfort is not necessarily a bad thing, unless it leads to premature ending of the counselling. Nocita and Stiles suggest that counsellors look particularly carefully for signs of discomfort in introverts and take it into account.

More generally, extraverts tend to want to do something or talk about a problem, introverts to withdraw from it or concede. One strength of a model of counselling such as the integrative one outlined in Table 8.4 is that it includes both kinds of response, and both Es and Is can find the principle of reflection and under-

Table 8.4   *An integrative model of counselling (basic version) (from Horton and Bayne, 1998)*

Stage One: Explore
The counsellor accepts and empathizes with the client and is genuine. The client explores her or his emotions, thoughts, behaviour and experiences related to a problem.

Stage Two (if necessary): Understand
The counsellor suggests, or helps the client to suggest, themes and patterns or other ways of looking at the problem, and to decide what, if anything, the client can do about it.

Stage Three (if necessary): Act
The counsellor helps the client to decide exactly what to do, taking costs and benefits for self and others into account, and to evaluate the results afterwards.

standing before action a useful one. Indeed, each of the preferences is likely to be used most comfortably and skilfully at one or more of the stages. For example, most counsellors (and clients) who prefer judging feel more 'at home' with Stage Three than with Stage One.

S and N
Most clients and counsellors who prefer sensing will naturally include many details that intuitive types tend to ignore. Conversely, intuitive types are generally more comfortable with the 'big picture' and with interpretations and possibilities that sensing types tend to ignore.

T and F
Clients and counsellors who prefer thinking tend to want reasons, analysis and logic more than warmth and harmony. A client who prefers thinking is likely to talk less about emotions, especially early in counselling. Such behaviour can be interpreted as resistant, shallow or rigid. Type theory proposes another possibility: that the client prefers to analyse logically first. The counsellor with a thinking client can challenge later on if necessary (with good timing) by suggesting that emotions are relevant too.

Feeling types tune into the relationship itself more, and notice detachment and other qualities more quickly. This is *not* saying, for example, that thinking types don't appreciate some warmth and acceptance, but that they tend to need it less and to want to move on to analysis quite quickly. For counsellors who prefer thinking, it may be helpful to see a feeling client's values as her or his reasons – despite the relative absence of logic! What matters most to feeling types is how much they care about something. Muten (1991) suggests that Fs are prone to feeling 'silently wounded' (p. 457) especially with a T counsellor, and to leaving counselling for this reason. (Here I have translated the terms used by Muten from the five-factor model of personality to type theory terms.)

J and P
Clients and counsellors who prefer perceiving want to be flexible and keep their options open. The potential clashes here with judging types, who need to plan and make decisions, are obvious.

The main reactions and prejudices, according to type theory, are that Is (clients or counsellors) may feel overwhelmed, hurried or invaded by Es, Es may see Is as dull and slow; Ss may be seen as boring by Ns, Ns as grandiose by Ss; Ts may be viewed as obsessed with reasons and unsympathetic by Fs, Fs as lacking any logic and too soft by Ts; Js may be considered pushy and rigid by Ps, Ps as aimless and disorganized by Js. Each of these unhelpful reactions and perceptions may also appear when counsellor and client share one or more preferences. Moreover, they can be misinterpreted as resistance. An extreme example of this is the view of Miller (1991) and Muten (1991) that Ps make poor clients (Bayne, 1995). Here I have again translated from the five-factor model to type theory terms.

Overall, as in intimate relationships (Jones and Sherman, 1997), there is *no* best combination of types for a counsellor and a client. Rather, it is a matter of how constructively the two people can use their differences and/or similarities. Type theory also illustrates how difficult empathy can be and how multifaceted it is. At the same time it can help counsellors to be empathic more quickly and deeply, and it suggests a way of integrating the various theories of empathy (Churchill and Bayne, 1998).

The Validity of Type Theory

The validity of type theory and its main measurement technique, the Myers–Briggs Type Indicator (MBTI), are supported well by research (Bayne, 1995; Hammer, 1996; Myers et al., 1998). In particular, relationships between the MBTI and measures of five-factor theory, which has come dramatically to the fore in mainstream personality research, are sufficiently close for type theory to draw on much of the research and some of the writing on that theory (Bayne, 1995).

In contrast, the research so far on matching clients and counsellors, on a variety of characteristics including personality, has produced weak and conflicting results (for example Bergin and Garfield, 1994; Nelson and Neufeldt, 1996). In particular, the Myers–Briggs was at one time seen as 'promising for predicting efficacious client–therapist matches' but has 'fallen out of favour' (Beutler, Machado and Neufeldt, 1994: 236). However, I think that this research failed to be a fair test of the theory because it was too simple and assumed that matching means similarity of type (cf. Quenk and Quenk, 1996).

Type Theory and Integration with Other Approaches to Counselling

Of all the approaches to counselling, type theory and multimodal therapy (see previous chapter) seem the most similar. I think they support and may complement and clarify each other. For present purposes, however, the differences between them are more important: type is usually used informally and flexibly whereas my impression is that multimodal therapy is highly structured. Moreover, type puts more emphasis on the *counsellor's* personality and on her or his *relationship* with the client.

A further difference between type and multimodal therapy is that type seems easier to integrate with other counselling orientations. Indeed, there are two distinct orientations within it, the psychodynamic (Quenk and Quenk, 1984; Spoto, 1995) and the humanistic and cognitive (Provost, 1993; Bayne, 1995, 1998). However, its main initial value lies in the basic level of type theory: its descriptions of the four pairs of preferences. A respect for client differences in these respects can readily become part of most approaches to counselling. In addition, it can make referral more effective and less threatening.

In the next section I sketch some answers to the three questions raised in the introduction.

Questions and Replies

(1) Is similarity of psychological type always or even usually best?

Similarity can be counter-productive – for example the relationship can be too cosy. Clients sometimes (see final section, on other factors) benefit from techniques that do not fit their preferences, for example a guided fantasy with a client who prefers S, or challenging an irrational belief with a client who prefers F. Type theory can then provide an explanation of any difficulties. More generally, no one knows at the moment whether similarity is *usually* best. I think awareness of differences, respect for them, and ability to work with them, are more important, but that for some clients, similarity is best at some points in their lives and a counsellor of a different psychological type is best at others.

(2)   Does a counsellor need to know the client's psychological type to use the theory?

While I find it is often useful to know a client's type (and my own type and therefore the likely clashes between me and the client), it can be both easier and more empathic to respond to whatever preference or 'language' a client is expressing at that moment. The client's language may switch quickly (it is affected by type but also by the topic, the other person and stress) and the counsellor can then switch too, or notice the switch and deliberately decide not to. The different languages are fairly easy to observe accurately: those that have a primary focus on facts or on possibilities, those that are more logical and businesslike or more warm and personal, etc. (see Table 8.3).

(3)   How flexible in adapting to a client is it reasonable to expect a counsellor to be?

I suspect that counsellors of some types are likely to be more flexible than those of other types, but for each individual counsellor the answer is: as flexible as you can be, taking into account your skills, level of stress and the availability of other suitable counsellors (see the 'authentic chameleon' issue, discussed in the previous chapter). Lazarus criticized Ellis, Rogers and others for always being the same - in Rogers's case 'constantly offering his carefully cultivated warmth, genuineness and empathy to all his clients' (Dryden, 1991: 18). I think Lazarus is wrong about 'carefully cultivated' - Rogers seems a natural F - but right in his view that clients want and need different styles of relationship.

Type Dynamics

This section introduces a complicating factor, both for observing the client's 'language' and for applying the theory. It stems from the idea that four of the preferences (S, N, T and F) are organized hierarchically within each person's personality. The first or dominant function is usually the most developed, the auxiliary or second function the next most developed and so on. This theory of personality structure is referred to as 'type dynamics'.

   The complicating factor is that each of us can become 'gripped' by our fourth function, which is the opposite of the dominant. This is most likely to happen when we are tired, ill or very stressed (Quenk, 1996). For example, someone whose dominant function is F but who is in the grip of T will be one or more of the following:

- very critical of self or others (feeling useless, incompetent)
- analysing compulsively (and with a strange energy)
- immobilized.

The other functions are thought to express themselves *in the grip* by such reactions as:

F   Have an emotional outburst, and be startled or frightened by it and the way it seems to take over. Feel attacked, wounded, violated or unloved – that no one cares.

S   Overdo something tangible, for example, over-eat, count compulsively, make lots of lists.

N   See only gloomy possibilities and feel trapped.

There is a different 'feel' about someone in the grip. However, it seems to be fairly rare, and normal strategies for coping with stress can be used. For further discussion, see Provost (1993) and Quenk (1996).

Other Factors

There are three other factors affected by type which usually have little or no effect on the counselling relationship but which occasionally are crucial. Firstly, the manner of the initial contact and aspects of the counsellor's office or room are likely to appeal to some clients and deter others (Sabini, 1988). I am thinking here of formality/warmth, seating, tidiness, etc. I think it is worth applying type theory to any information you give to potential clients – your room and your clothes, etc. Ideally, ask people of different types for their reactions but otherwise ask such questions, where applicable, as 'Is there enough detail?', 'Enough warmth?', and 'Enough reasoning?' (see Table 8.3).

Secondly, counsellors' choice of techniques is influenced by their type (Erickson, 1993; Bayne, 1995). Type theory suggests that clients be asked to use a technique which emphasizes their fourth function only when there is a good level of trust and when they are not stressed. Thus, for example, guided fantasies draw on intuition (N) and cognitive techniques draw on thinking (T). The theory suggests taking extra care in using them with clients who prefer sensing and feeling respectively. Palmer (1997) provides a list of counselling techniques and the modalities in multimodal counselling, several of which correspond to type theory. Thirdly, the timing is important, and so too is the way techniques are presented, for example playfully (for clients who prefer sensing plus perceiving), with expert attention to evidence and theory (N and T), warmly (F), and/or systematically and in detail (S and J).

Conclusions

- Type theory takes client variation in personality seriously. It suggests different styles of relationship for different clients (and at different 'stages' of a counselling relationship with the same client).
- It helps people accept their own strengths and corresponding weaknesses, and those of other people.
- It suggests ways of matching clients and counsellors, although there are probably no 'best combinations'. Other factors matter too, for example how similarities and differences in type are responded to, type development, the client's needs and the counsellor's flexibility.
- It suggests ways in which counsellors can empathize more deeply and more quickly. It makes empathy a more tangible idea and also illustrates how difficult and multifaceted it is.
- It can make referral more acceptable by reducing feelings of failure, rejection or inadequacy on the part of both clients and counsellors.
- It illuminates many aspects of the counselling relationship, but still leaves much that is mysterious.

Note: If you wish to check or discover your psychological type in the Myers–Briggs sense, the MBTI plus feedback from a qualified practitioner is generally the best starting point (Carr, 1997). Contact Oxford Psychologists Press (01865 510203).

Acknowledgement

A very warm thank you to Ian Horton for his detailed and incisive comments on a draft of this chapter.

References

Bayne, R. (1995) *The Myers-Briggs Type Indicator: A Critical Review and Practical Guide*. Cheltenham: Stanley Thornes.

Bayne, R. (1998) 'Psychological type (the Myers-Briggs)', in R. Bayne, P. Nicolson and I. Horton (eds), *Counselling and Communication Skills for Medical and Health Practitioners*. Leicester: British Psychological Society.

Bergin, A.E. and Garfield, S.L. (eds) (1994) *Handbook of Psychotherapy and Behavior Change* (4th edn). New York: Wiley.

Beutler, L.E., Machado, P.P.P. and Neufeldt, S.A. (1994) 'Therapist variables', in A.E. Bergin and S.L. Garfield (eds) *Handbook of Psychotherapy and Behavior Change* (4th edn). New York: Wiley.

Carr, S. (1997) *Type Clarification: Finding the Fit*. Oxford: Oxford Psychologists Press.

Churchill S. and Bayne, R. (1998) 'Psychological type and different conceptions of empathy in experienced counsellors', *Counselling Psychology Quarterly*, 11 (4): 379-90.

Dryden, W. (1991) *A Dialogue with Arnold Lazarus. 'It Depends'*. Milton Keynes: Open University Press.

Dryden, W. and Feltham, C. (1994) *Developing the Practice of Counselling*. London: Sage.

Erickson, D.B. (1993) 'The relationship between personality type and preferred counseling model', *Journal of Psychological Type*, 27: 39-41.

Hammer, A.L. (ed.) (1996) *MBTI Applications: A Decade of Research on the Myers-Briggs Type Indicator*. Palo Alto, CA: Consulting Psychologists Press.

Horton, I. and Bayne, R. (1998) 'Counselling and communication in health care', in R. Bayne, P. Nicolson and I. Horton (eds), *Counselling and Communication Skills for Medical and Health Practitioners*. Leicester: British Psychological Society.

Jones, J.H. and Sherman, R.G. (1997) *Intimacy and Type. A Practical Guide for Improving Relationships for Couples and Counselors*. Gainesville, CA: Center for Applications of Psychological Type.

Miller, T. (1991) 'The psychotherapeutic utility of the five-factor model of personality', *Journal of Personality Assessment*, 57: 415-33.

Muten, E. (1991) 'Self-reports, spouse ratings, and psychophysiological assessment in a behavioral medicine program: an application of the five-factor model', *Journal of Personality Assessment* 56 (3): 449-64.

Myers, I.B. (with Myers, P.B.) (1980) *Gifts Differing*. Palo Alto, CA: Consulting Psychologists Press.

Myers, I.B., McCaulley, M.H., Quenk, N.L. and Hammer, A.L. (1998) *Manual: A Guide to the Development and Use of the Myers-Briggs Type Indicator* (3rd edn). Palo Alto, CA: Consulting Psychologists Press.

Nelson, M.L. and Neufeldt, S.A. (1996) 'Building on an empirical foundation: strategies to enhance good practice', *Journal of Counseling and Development*, 74: 609-14.

Nocita, A. and Stiles, W.B. (1986) 'Client introversion and counseling session impact', *Journal of Counseling Psychology*, 33 (3): 270-3.

182   *Rowan Bayne*

Palmer, S. (1997) 'Modality assessment', in S. Palmer and G. McMahon (eds), *Client Assessment*. London: Sage.

Paul, G.L. (1967) 'Strategy of outcome research in psychotherapy', *Journal of Consulting Psychology*, 31: 109–18.

Provost, J. (1993) *Applications of the Myers-Briggs Type Indicator in Counseling: A Casebook* (2nd edn). Palo Alto, CA: Center for Applications of Psychological Type.

Quenk, N. (1996) *In the Grip. Our Hidden Personality*. Palo Alto, CA: Consulting Psychologists Press.

Quenk, A.T. and Quenk, N.L. (1984) 'The use of psychological typology in analysis', in M. Stein (ed.), *Jungian Analysis*. London: Routledge.

Quenk, N.L. and Quenk, A.T. (1996) 'Counseling and psychotherapy', in A.L. Hammer (ed.), *MBTI Applications. A Decade of Research on the Myers-Briggs Type Indicator*. Palo Alto, CA: Consulting Psychologists Press.

Sabini, M. (1988) 'The therapist's inferior function', *Journal of Analytical Psychology*, 33: 373–94.

Shields, C. (1976) *Small Ceremonies*. London: Fourth Estate.

Shields, C. (1977) *The Box Garden*. London: Fourth Estate.

Spoto, A. (1995) *Jung's Typology in Perspective* (2nd edn). Wilmette, ILL: Chiron Publications.

Stiles, W.B., Shapiro, D.A. and Elliott, R.K. (1986) 'Are all psychotherapies equivalent?' *American Psychologist*, 41 (2): 1165–80.

Thorne, A. (1987) 'The press of personality: a study of conversations between introverts and extraverts', *Journal of Personality and Social Psychology*, 53: 718–26.

9 *Professional and Socio-Cultural Aspects of the Counselling Relationship*

Janice Russell

Introduction

Within post-modernity, the notion of the relationship as an ideal form to be analysed, scrutinized and deliberately striven for is big business. A preliminary search on the Internet under the heading 'relationship' generated over one and a half million sources. Articles abound in popular magazines and so on which purport to help us to establish more open and meaningful relationships, in which we can be assertive yet sensitive, able to share all with our nearest and dearest. Within academic discourse, 'the relationship' has been viewed sociologically as intrinsically connected to the reflexive project of self, the search for identity in a rapidly changing world order. Giddens's notion of the pure relationship epitomizes a shift away from people relating to each other functionally to achieve some other ends, for example to work together, raise children together, to an end in itself (Giddens, 1992). Elias (1978) has documented a historical shift away from the concepts of self and relating as influenced by external factors, towards a tendency to increasingly intrapersonal exploration, while Lasch (1978) has contended that the self to be discovered and realized through the medium of relating to another has become increasingly narcissistic and self-serving. Meanwhile, MacIntyre (1981) has suggested that ideal types have sprung up in society to be reified and emulated, of which one is the Therapist. The Therapist is attributed an elevated status dependent on his/her expert knowledge of how one should be and relate in the world, a knowledge which reflects their ability to get it right for themselves and then to teach others.

It is not surprising then that counselling has sprung up as an expert system (Giddens, 1991) designed to help people find their personal identities and to learn better how to relate to others. In this respect, counselling is a self-serving occupation: counselling psychology discourse contributes to the notions of what *should* constitute an ideal relationship, that is, we should be authentic, expressive and self-determining, and then attracts clients who feel that they are currently unable to achieve this standard. The counselling relationship is posited both as a *medium* for seeking this superior standard of being, and, in some schools of counselling, as a *model* of how a successful relationship might look. Great claims are made for this mysterious entity; that it should be appropriately boundaried, that it should be intimate, that certain matches should be made or avoided, that it is really only a medium for other, more primal relationships to be worked out within, and so on. Whatever the theoretically informed details, we do seem to accept that 'it', that is, the counselling relationship, exists.

In this chapter, I offer a sociological perspective on the 'counselling relationship'. I wish to make the point, however, that there is no such 'thing' as a counselling relationship, and as soon as we approach this concept as if 'it' had specific and unique characteristics, then we invite trouble. There are, in reality, many ways of relating within counselling which will generate fruitful outcomes for the client. As I have suggested elsewhere, counselling is a diverse activity which fulfils a variety of individual and social functions which affect how counsellor and client may relate to each other (Dexter and Russell, 1998). I will be using the term 'counselling relationship', then, as a useful concept, not a totally distinguishable or consistent entity.

I propose, then, to explore and critique some of the claims made for the counselling relationship. Firstly, I will outline the nature of such claims, specifically in relation to the concept of intimacy, and suggest what paradoxes these yield. Secondly, I will suggest that the norms ascribed to the counselling relationship are based on various assumptions of selfhood which are culturally specific, with all the possible ramifications of such assumptions. Thirdly, I will look at one of the greatest myths of how 'the counselling relationship' is formulated, namely that of mutual self-disclosure. In conclusion, I will suggest the benefits of more sociological critique of counselling for the whole counselling movement and for specific counselling contracts.

The Bigger Picture – the Nature of the Counselling Relationship

The counselling relationship is portrayed as unique. This is not meant in the individualized sense, that is, that every relationship between two or more people is unique and non-replicable (although this is one of the arguments of the 'anti-competences' school of thought), but in the sense of the counselling relationship as a genre. We may identify several features which distinguish it from other means of relating. Primarily, it is a relationship which is created for a specific purpose and not on the grounds of mutual attraction as say a courtship, a friendship, or even the choice of a favourite hairdresser. Once established by a contractual agreement, any further form of relating is purported to require rules which are quite unlike the rules of other developing relationships where reciprocity is part of the normal sequence of events (Duck, 1988: 44). Confidentiality and its limits must be agreed, the purpose, that is the ultimate well-being or development of one person, must be defined, the theories which underlie the counsellor's approach must be disclosed, and terms must be set which establish certain rules or parameters which neither party must cross. These are posed mainly in relation to limits of how the two parties involved actually relate, and it is seen as unethical to procure either friendship or sexual relationships via the counselling dyad. What is more, the counselling relationship may be paid for by the client, and its provision might provide the main means of income for the counsellor.

Given these parameters, the claims made for the nature of the counselling relationship have changed over this century. Traditional psychoanalysis revered the 'blank page' non-persona of the therapist, despite some rebellion against such neutrality – one notable example being Sandor Ferenczi, who went so far as to take analysands on vacation to fufil the relationship demands of a successful analysis (Stanton, 1990). Since then, types of therapies and counselling have multiplied, and debate still rages about whether we can distinguish between psychotherapy and counselling, while a general trend is for practitioners and theorists to argue that how the counsellor/therapist and client relate to each other is of paramount importance. Within humanistic schools of counselling which make some claims to client-centredness, great claims are made for the counselling relationship regarding its *intimate* nature. This claim far outstrips the requirement to operate the 'core conditions' (Rogers, 1957), even if we could establish *their* absolute necessity, which as far as I am aware, is theoretically impossible. Research which I have conducted suggests that some counsellors believe that there is no possible therapeutic change without intimacy being a feature of the counselling relationship (Russell, 1997).

Intimacy does seem, though, to be a term which is rather bandied about, with theoretical and practical approaches to counselling often relying on *implicit* notions of intimacy, despite an increasing literature which aims to address directly the accomplishment of intimacy through therapeutic means (Dowrick, 1992; Lerner, 1989). Such texts present intimacy as an *individual* accomplishment. In other words, the level of ability to achieve intimacy with others is rated as a personal attribute. Sociological approaches to the consideration of intimacy (Giddens, 1991, 1992; Sennett, 1977, 1988; Simmel, 1950), however, present intimacy as a *social* phenomenon, and are more concerned with the social processes which influence or produce the accomplishment of intimacy. These may be to do with how public space is organized, how institutions such as marriage are designed and valued, the demands on relationship created through patterns of work, and so on.

In the *Oxford English Dictionary*, intimacy is defined as 'the state of being intimate', while 'intimate' is defined as 'close in acquaintance, familiar . . . essential, intrinsic, closely personal' (*OED*, 1982). The word derives from the Latin *intimus*, to mean inner or inmost. So we have within counselling an extremely interesting situation. Received wisdom dictates that the relationships formed between counsellor and client are intimate, intensely personal, and yet need to adhere to a set of rules quite unlike that of any other form of relating. Intimacy is presented as being of value *per se*, and this notion has to do with changing concepts of self in post-modernity where, as Taylor has argued, there is a general sense of loss of tradition and shared morality (Taylor, 1991). Yet is the counselling relationship really one of intimacy, and if so what is its value?

The Value of Intimacy within Counselling

As stated, intimacy is commonly assumed by various scholars of counselling as a *desirable* state (Berne, 1964; Dryden, 1989; Ehrenberg, 1992; Lerner, 1989; Rogers, 1951) and as offering fulfilment of the highest value. Dorothy Rowe, for example, claims that 'intimacy with other people [is] the greatest pleasure we can know' (1991: 244), while Eric Berne suggests it is the 'most perfect form of human living' (1964: 55).

Typically, where intimacy is presented as an explicit phenomenon, it is discussed with regard to relationships with partners, and various prerequisites for intimacy are suggested. Rowe (1991: 246), for example, invokes the need to be authentic. Dowrick (1992) suggests the need for a 'boundaried self', while Solomon allows for the temporary removal of boundaries when in counselling, to allow intimacy to occur 'when regressive needs can be met . . . reciprocally' (1989: 26).

Such conceptualizations lead to a perspective where people's success in relationships may be understood as proportional to their ability to achieve intimacy. Many clients in counselling and therapy are there because they want to be able to 'relate better', to achieve some norm of ability to have fulfilling relationships (Solomon, 1989). Thus it becomes taken for granted that the pursuit of intimacy is not only personally beneficial in our society, but also a legitimate therapeutic goal. What is more, the claim for intimacy as a fundamental prerequisite of counselling *per se* has permeated humanistic counselling discourse so deeply that it can become an assumed aim of the therapeutic relationship.

Never mind that there are grave questions about the value of intimacy *per se* as a social phenomenon, that it may in fact lead to excessive and destructive demands within relationships (Wynne and Wynne, 1986), or to a tyrannous demand on ways of relating within societal frameworks (Sennett, 1988). Instead, humanistic counsellors seem to make extraordinary demands to achieve intimacy within counselling practice. Take for example the learning of counselling. Now that the masters have experientially learned enough to define counselling as a teachable activity, intimacy is demanded amongst counselling students in learning environments (Egan, 1973; Rogers, 1983). It is common for trainees to contract into an open sharing atmosphere within the learning group, at the very least, and at Diploma level upwards it is now becoming mandatory on accredited courses to agree to 'do group', where intimate self-disclosure is seen as necessary to self-awareness and self-development, essential attributes for the good counsellor. Interestingly enough, it is not the student who assesses the success of their own displayed intimacies; 'student-centred' counselling training exists in a paradox noted by Dexter (1996), whereby the development of the student in personal terms is somewhat directively encouraged and evaluated by peers and tutors to an agreed (subjective) standard. Recruitment is influenced by the interviewees' perceived abilities to be open and intimate in a formal structured situation, and any failure to do so will be marked down and held in evidence against them (Dexter and Russell, 1998).

When the glorified and *assumed* value of intimacy is then transferred to the therapeutic relationship, we see some interesting claims. In humanistic counselling, intimacy is generally viewed as a *positive* concept in terms of making for successful counselling. One account of counsellors' 'successes' offers the observation that 'such caring, such willingness simply to be fully in each other's presence, always led to creative movement in the end' (Mearns in Mearns and Dryden, 1990).

If intimacy is experienced as threatening or difficult, then two different explanations tend to be offered. One is that the counsellor has overstepped the boundary to serve his or her own ends. This happens of course and is a complex phenomenon to tease out, with motives ranging from exploitation to a lack of experience or professionalism. The other possible explanation is that, actually, intimacy with some people at some times is simply not a positive move. This last is seen as largely unpalatable to many schools of counselling. A preferred justification is that the client is not yet 'ready', implying that one day, when more confident and self-actualized, then more and more intimacy within the counselling relationship will be possible.

This links to my second observation on the value ascribed to intimacy within the counselling relationship and the counselling movement – that intimacy is by nature a *positive* state or concept to be *replicated* within the counselling relationship. My research with counsellors into their understanding of relating and intimacy discovered that they saw themselves as 'modelling' an intimate relationship with their clients, often perhaps the first one that the clients had ever experienced. Where clients came with accounts of distressing and destructive intimate relationships, then counsellors concluded that this could not have been proper intimacy. Through such rationalization, the value of intimacy can remain unscathed and it may take its place in our world of positive and negative evaluation as high on the positive side – as long as it is done 'properly', the counselling setting being one context for such an experience. Where intimacy within the counselling relationship has been experienced by clients as damaging, then it is assumed that unethical or unprofessional conduct has taken place, or the wrong kind of therapy practised. Therapists or counsellors may be suspended and sent for therapy, to learn to become more 'appropriately' intimate with clients (Russell, 1993).

Take the following example, which may typify the kind of uncertainties that are produced through the insistence that the counselling relationship be one of (ultimately positive) intimate dimensions. A client is contracted to counselling to achieve some identifiable end, perhaps to 'complete' a grieving process, or to make decisions about the future of their marital relationship. At the end of the contracted period, the objective has been met. However, the client would like to continue the counselling because they enjoy it; they have established a 'positive' and intimate relationship with their counsellor, in which they feel listened to and valued, and regard this in itself as worthwhile.

The counsellor, then, is faced with a dilemma. Dare they be hard-line enough to suggest that the counselling is over, and that the relationship must end? Will they then attract the scorn of their more analytic colleagues who have a deeper and more mystical understanding of the value of the relationship *per se*, with its notions of transference, countertransference, stages of dependency and so on, as intrinsically worthwhile? If they continue the counselling, however, on the basis that the relationship itself is a worthwhile outcome of counselling, at what point have they entered the realms of surrogacy? What is the difference between this counsellor and the prostitute who claims that most of her regulars are not interested in the sex, more in the relationship which they have established whereby the client can feel understood and 'be themselves' for a paid hour a week (McCleod, 1982)?

In either case, intimacy itself has been ascribed a value which overrides all else. However, it may be useful to remember that accounts of intimacy within the counselling relationship which represent experiences which were conceptualized as inappropriately intimate (Russell, 1993, 1996; Rutter, 1990) suggest a *situational* aspect of intimacy, in a context where counselling may be seen as being a defined role (cf. Sennett, 1977: 33-6). Within this, there are expectations of particular behaviours, for example that there is an 'appropriate' level or type of self-disclosure for the counsellor to offer, and that there are specific 'boundaries' to how and where this might take place.

Because of the lack of clarity in definitions of counselling (Feltham, 1995), and because each counselling relationship may be claimed as distinctive, it is difficult to identify precisely what *is* significant within the therapeutic encounter. It is difficult to separate those effects which result from 'intentional' activities, and those which result from the 'healing' qualities and nuances of the specific interactions (Ehrenberg, 1992).

However, intentionality is concerned with deliberate techniques which are applied with some cognitive awareness, and which may then be repeated with any client, while other factors concerned with healing, or 'therapeutic action' (Ehrenberg, 1992: ix) may be more subtle, more complex, more unique to each encounter and less in awareness. It is the intentional factors, I would suggest, which make counselling a learnable activity and which should make us question whether the relationship we then form with our clients is really intimate in anything other than a professional sense. We might also bear in mind the possibility that not only is interpersonal intimacy not always useful in social situations, as Sennett (1977, 1988) has suggested, but that it may for some people, be intra-personally destructive or undesirable. Psychiatric literature is more concerned with the state of mind of an individual in the sense of recognizing that helping someone get in touch with their emotions can be the prelude to personal overload or disaster (Dexter and Wash, 1995). Such is the faith of the counsellors, that generally speaking, far less caution is to be found.

I am suggesting, then, that intimacy is accepted as desirable within humanistic counselling discourse. It is seen as being both intrinsically valuable, and as being instrumental within the counselling relationship. The modelling role of how counsellor relates to client is delightfully contradictory; counsellors fancy that they can model intimacy, but only within defined professional parameters. These are unique to the profession, and few people would conduct their private lives on the lines of contracted, timed meetings, where one person's perspective is seen as the key 'content' of any dialogue or encounter. So we might wonder what it is, actually, that we are modelling.

Two major questions are begged by this state of affairs. What socio-cultural factors need to be considered when counsellors and clients relate to one another, with what effect on the socio-cultural conceptualizations of personhood? And are ways of relating within counselling *necessarily*, or even really, of an intimate nature for both parties?

Socio-Culturally Specific Contexts of Relating Within Counselling

The notion of self on which counselling is based, with its accepted components of self-determination, self-esteem, self-awareness, self-actualization, has developed within western modernist culture. This carries with it a variety of values, specifically those of authenticity, autonomy and independence, and relies heavily on specific and limited philosophical postulates. While I will argue elsewhere that these values may have negative consequences to communities and society (Russell, 1999), within any stated theoretical framework, the current concept of the counselling relationship faces various challenges to do with gender, race and other cultural characteristics. It is generally deemed to be a positive move to work on a cross-cultural basis. The positive connotation is to do with the desire to be genuinely non-prejudicial, and to prove perhaps that difference is a negotiable boundary. However, there are various issues which arise from this perspective. On a micro-level, there is the challenge of transcending any barriers to do with cultural norms and mores, so that difference can produce a harmonious and constructive dialogue. Respect is invoked as an essential attitude to this task.

There is, however, a discernible trend which is related to the modernist, individualist notion of self which requires that openness demands a sharing of the client's emotional world with the counsellor, and indeed preferably to have that capability with everyone else (Heelas, 1992). Whether or not this is in fact a good thing in relation to the individual, the community and the society, within the counselling context it is little discussed. We develop as human beings in all sorts of ways, experiencing and being in the world within a multi-filtered crucible in which we create our reality; sensory filters, linguistic ones, layers of beliefs and values, and cultural filters. I have argued elsewhere that counselling discourse is largely developed from the work of white, western males. Their dominant cultural values and ideas may be challenged on a feminist basis, particularly if we consider the work of theorists such as Carol Gilligan (1988). It is pertinent to ask what other cultural permutations might affect how we relate in the counselling context, and what implications these have for counselling as a social practice.

I use culture to refer to the predominant culture in which we are raised, whether within a nation state, a country or region, and which may or may not be related to racial characteristics. Cultural norms and beliefs have a fundamental influence on who we are and how we relate. Counselling as a mainstream movement accepts in principle that it is possible to relate cross-culturally in a counselling context. While I also accept this fully, and while there is an increasing body of literature and bodies which purport to help us do this better, and enhance the quality of our cross-cultural ways of relating to make effective counselling, a more global issue is raised. While there is an argument that we must understand more sociological facets of people's cultural development (Dupont-Joshua, 1997), we need also to consider just how culture might affect the counselling relationship and vice versa. The concept of self espoused within counselling creates a reflective loop – once counselled according to certain self-concepts, we might reasonably expect the 'fully functioning' individual to have influence on the culture in which they live. It is possible then that, cross-culturally, counselling may become, through the very 'relationship', that is, way of relating, that it espouses, an agent of assimilation to dominant western culture. In other words, at a micro-level, counselling might ostensibly be respecting difference while imposing a dominant culture notion of self, and western ideals of how we *should* relate, simply because of the theories which inform it and the context in which it has developed.

Having counselled and trained in various cross-cultural contexts, whether in Birmingham, Kuwait, Poland, Brighton, the north-east of England, or in working with Bosnian Muslims, I am very aware that the concept of self to be related can vary considerably. Does counselling take account of this? I think not, not in any seriously challenging way. In orthodox Muslim cultures, for example, the principle of self-determination is necessarily at odds with the idea of divine guidance or will. Working with delegates from Hong Kong, I have become aware that the idea of empathizing with the emotional world may be seen as impertinent and invasive. Some Polish practitioners have voiced a reluctance to self-disclose arising from the experience of living in a closed culture where trust and secrecy have very different meanings from those ascribed within more imperialist western cultures. And in Kuwait, counselling was seen as very much a practice where the counselling relationship demanded no more of the self than that of psychiatric or general medicine.

None of these cultures is totally homogeneous, of course, yet the points raised are interesting ones. If we teach counselling according to the dominant values of the discourse which has produced it, and insist on a relationship within it which demands a particular and specific notion of engagement with self, what consequences might this have? Obviously, my own experience is limited, yet I suspect that I am currently in a situation where I am more likely to be invited into another culture to offer rather than receive counselling training with all its (inevitably middle-class) notions of what is necessary to the counselling relationship. No matter how flexible and responsive I might be, however much I learn from others, there is an inevitable discursive trend to the work that I might do.

Within training cultures, there is also an interesting dimension to cross-cultural work and the demands on relationship which it makes. Because of the move to promote cross-cultural difference and similarity as areas of work which are inherently useful, and even demand 'celebration', it is increasingly common to work with training groups based in Britain which have attracted a multi-national, multi-cultural recruitment. This move inevitably produces richness and perspectives which might enhance understanding and relationships. However, if counselling demands that the relationship between counsellor and client is of a particular type and quality, then it might also be seen as potentially problematic. For no matter what culture a person has come from, counselling training demands that one can demonstrate a type of selfhood and way of relating which may be quite different for the trainee, and all this through the medium of a second language. One trainer has even suggested to me that this is potentially abusive, given the reality that there is inevitably a conformist aspect of counselling training, particularly now that counselling is becoming so professionalized.

There are many aspects of culture, including age, race, physical abilities, gender, dress, sexual orientation, class and so on. As yet, despite best efforts on many people's part, and despite a growing dialogue and move to educate individuals regarding cultural knowledge and in challenging individual prejudices, there is little real multi-cultural integration of psychological theory into the demands of the counselling relationship. Major theorists to be found underlying most training remain those white males whose names recur again and again: Rogers, Freud, Yalom, Ellis, Perls, Egan, Erikson, and so on. Is it really enough to take their somewhat limited and dated principles of self and relationship as the fundamental guiding light of a multi-cultural perspective? I wonder.

The Myth of Mutual Self-Disclosure in Relation to the Above

From my own research and through existing literature, it is possible to discern that the counselling relationship is often posed as one which requires a sharing of our culturally specific self with the client, and notions of mutuality are invoked. Two areas of meaning may be identified within the concept of self-disclosure. One is in the content of what is disclosed: do counsellors actually reveal of themselves and their emotions as the client does? This would depend on the definition of self-disclosure as being the traditionally accepted version, that is, 'a communication process in which one person verbally provides personal information about his or her thoughts, needs, or feelings to another person' (Falk and Wagner, 1985: 558). This view, however, may be seen as narrow. Talk may define relationships, yet this might be indirectly through 'subtle signs of intimacy and distance', as well as through the words used (Duck and Pond, 1989: 26–7). The second perspective understands self-disclosure as the revelation of self through manner and surroundings. Both of these modes seem to be used to indicate intimacy, and indeed are sometimes used almost synonymously with it.

It is possible however to distinguish differences between the counsellor's and the client's levels of self-disclosure, in terms of type and of role. One way to do this is to make a distinction between self-presentation and self-disclosure. Strategies of self-presentation include dress, decoration of physical surroundings, and what manner may be engaged. All of these are deliberate and imply some form of rationale. In Goffman's terms, the furniture in the house and the pictures on the wall are part of the 'front' of self-presentation, as are the mode of 'performance' that the counsellor will offer to the client, the attitudes of respect and acceptance, and so on (1959: 33–40). Both are forms of 'expressive equipment', routinely offered, and will be designed to increase legitimacy for the particular setting. A counsellor who works from home will know that whatever picture s/he puts on the wall is open to public gaze, that his/her choice of clothes and hairstyle will present some aspect of self to others for their evaluation (Argyle, 1967: 44).

The counsellor's manner will reflect his/her motivation, personality and training in communication and social skills, all of which will be deliberately presented in a learned sequence (Trower et al., 1978: 29). The counsellor will be disclosing in a way which is both appropriate and purposeful to the role (Ingram, 1991: 408), and not be seeking a particular response in terms of her/his own self-esteem. This is quite unlike the rules of other developing relationships where reciprocity is part of the normal sequence of events (Duck, 1988: 44). Self may be disclosed, but, certainly initially, this is a controlled disclosure which does not entail high degrees of emotion, risk or trust, which have been identified as constituents of intimacy. Any client may come and see the pictures on the walls, all will be offered warmth and genuineness as these are part of the ethos, principles and skills of counselling, requiring no negotiation that is dependent on patterns of response usually required for developing relationships.

The type of disclosure will constitute part of the measure of intimacy. To declare that 'I like this picture and choose these clothes' is quite different from 'I have some severe fears about my personal relationships with considered others' (ibid.: 57). While self-disclosure may be necessary for intimacy to occur, self-disclosure on its own does not necessarily constitute intimacy. Responses which try to understand the perspective of another are seen as favourable to the development of intimacy (Falk and Wagner, 1985). No such response might be made to the kind of revelation of self being claimed by the counsellors. It may instead constitute a mode of presentation of self. In this sense there is no uniqueness offered to the client, a trait which Simmel (1950) has identified as essential to intimacy. It is merely one step in a procedure whose quality depends on the *response* to that self-disclosure. The majority of the counsellors in my research, however, argued that such disclosure was a part of the mutual intimacy of the relationship. This seemed to be highly related to modelling how one *should* be in relationship, which is very much connected both to the social construction of self, and the notion of the Therapist as ideal character in this process (MacIntyre, 1981).

Of course, self-presentation can change to become more intimate self-disclosure, and there might be some facets of the therapeutic relationship which might be challenging to the self of the counsellor. This is certainly suggested within some schools of therapy (Ehrenberg, 1992; Ingram, 1991), and I am well aware that in some counselling relationships, the counsellor may feel very involved and use their own responses, their own emotional world, as a medium of therapeutic change, and I would not devalue this possibility. Equally, there is the paradox that although the counsellor ostensibly fulfils the social ideal role of Therapist, all worked out and nowhere to go, in reality, it could also be suggested that many counsellors are drawn into counselling precisely *because* of their own needs and lack of intimacy in their own life (Guy, 1987). In this case, from a sociological point of view, using the counsellor as medium may be seen as in fact an extremely bizarre social activity.

It would seem, however, that whatever the 'depth' of relating, perhaps the counselling relationship might be seen as a product of two people developing intimacy with themselves, in the presence of each other. Since intimacy with self, or self-revelation, is (rightly or wrongly) seen as therapeutic, then this would present a different dimension to how counsellor and client relate. Some counsellors, at some times, might find their work intensely demanding of themselves, and the client might recognize and appreciate this dimension of the work. Other clients might value their counselling in a quite different way. One accurate response, delivered at the right time, might be all that is needed to effect desired change, and the client might have no strong feelings about the relationship which they have experienced. Such differences might well be related to the purpose of counselling; some clients wish to explore issues of meaning, identity and existence, while others might have a more tangible and specific purpose to their work which demands a different way of relating with their counsellor. It is quite simplistic to prescribe, therefore, an idealized version of a counselling relationship which is necessary to all situations. The only common thread which might really be suggested is that the counsellor needs to engender the kind of relationship which allows the client to develop the degree of self-knowledge which is necessary to their change process.

Concluding Comments

It seems to me that there are some large questions to be addressed regarding the counselling relationship. If the purpose of counselling is truly to respectfully help the client feel empowered to make whatever changes or leaps of understanding they wish, then the only possible demand of a counselling relationship is that it is ethical and effective. This leaves it wide open to a variety of methods, and it is possible within it to respect many versions of selfhood. If it is, however, constrained by demands of intimacy and pseudo-intimacy, then we may lose a richness of possibilities both for the individual and for the development of counselling as a social practice. Perhaps considering the following points might encourage counsellors to take a wider perspective:

■ What are the received philosophies which underlie most counselling theories? How do they relate to different cultures?
■ How many texts are central to my thinking and training which are *not* written by white males?
■ How do I see the discourse, that is, the practice, words and images of counselling theory, influencing social ideas of the self?
■ Do I see any problems here?

- Where does counselling come from?
- How might I relate in diverse ways to different clients?
- What differences do I experience in any of my counselling relationships? How do these enhance my work?

References

Argyle, M. (1967) *The Psychology of Interpersonal Behaviour.* Harmondsworth: Penguin.

Berne, E. (1964) *Games People Play: The Psychology of Human Relationships.* Harmondsworth: Penguin.

Dexter, G. (1996) 'Personal construct changes in students of counselling courses', PhD thesis, University of Durham.

Dexter, G. and Russell, J. (1998) *Challenging Blank Minds and Sticky Moments in Counselling.* York: Insight Press.

Dexter, G. and Wash, M. (1995) *Psychiatric Nursing Skills: A Patient-Centred Approach* (2nd edn). London: Chapman Hall.

Dowrick, S. (1992) *Intimacy and Solitude: Balancing Closeness and Independence.* London: Women's Press.

Dryden, W. (ed.) (1989) *Key Issues for Counselling in Action.* London: Sage.

Duck, S. (1988) *Relating to Others.* London: Sage.

Duck, S. and Pond, C. (1989) 'Rhetoric and reality', in C. Hendrick (ed.), *Close Relationships.* London: Sage.

Dupont-Joshua, A. (1997) 'Working with issues of race in counselling', *Counselling,* 8 (4): 282–5.

Egan, G. (1973) *Face to Face: The Small Group Experience and Interpersonal Growth.* Monterey: Brooks/Cole.

Ehrenberg, D.B. (1992) *The Intimate Edge: Extending the Reach of Psycho-analytic Interaction.* New York: W.W. Norton & Co.

Elias, N. (1978) *The Civilising Process: The History of Manners.* Oxford: Blackwell.

Falk, D. and Wagner, P.N. (1985) 'Intimacy of self-disclosure and response processes as factors affecting the development of interpersonal relationships', *Journal of Social Psychology,* 125 (5): 557–70.

Feltham, C. (1995) *What is Counselling?* London: Sage.

Giddens, A. (1991) *Modernity and Self-Identity.* Cambridge: Polity Press.

Giddens, A. (1992) *The Transformation of Intimacy: Sexuality, Love and Eroticism in Modern Societies.* Cambridge: Polity Press.

Gilligan, C. (1988) *Mapping the Moral Domain.* Cambridge, MA: Harvard University Press.

Goffman, E. (1959) *The Presentation of Self in Everyday Life.* Harmondsworth: Penguin.

Guy, J.D. (1987) *The Personal Life of the Psychotherapist.* New York: Wiley.

Heelas, P. (1992) 'The sacralization of the self and New Age capitalism', in N. Abercrombie and A. Warde, *Social Change in Contemporary Britain.* Cambridge: Polity Press.

Ingram, D.H. (1991) 'Intimacy in the psychoanalytic relationship: a preliminary sketch', *American Journal of Psychoanalysis*, 51 (4): 403–11.

Lasch, C. (1978) *The Culture of Narcissism*. New York: Norton.

Lerner, H.G. (1989) *The Dance of Intimacy*. London: Pandora Press.

MacIntyre, A. (1981) *After Virtue: A Study in Moral Theory*. London: Gerald Duckworth & Co.

McCleod, E. (1982) *Women Working: Prostitution Now*. London: Croom Helm.

Mearns, D. and Dryden, W. (eds) (1990) *Experiences of Counselling in Action*. London: Sage.

Rogers, C.R. (1951) *Client-Centered Therapy*. London: Constable.

Rogers, C.R. (1957) 'The necessary and sufficient conditions of therapeutic personality change', *Journal of Consulting Psychology*, 21 (2): 95–103.

Rogers, C.R. (1983) *Freedom to Learn in the 80s*. Columbus, OH: Charles E. Merrill Pub. Co.

Rowe, D. (1991) *Wanting Everything*. London: Fontana.

Russell, J. (1993) *Out of Bounds: Sexual Exploitation in Counselling and Therapy*. London: Sage.

Russell, J. (1996) 'Sexual exploitation in counselling', in R. Bayne (ed.), *New Directions in Counselling*. London: Chapman Hall.

Russell, J. (1997) 'Accomplishing intimacy: self and relationships in the counselling context', PhD thesis, University of Durham.

Russell, J. (1999) 'Counselling and the social construction of self', *British Journal of Guidance and Counselling*, 27(3).

Rutter, P. (1990) *Sex in the Forbidden Zone*. London: Mandala.

Sennett, R. (1977) *The Fall of Public Man*. Cambridge: Cambridge University Press.

Sennett, R. (1988) 'Destructive Gemeinschaft', in R. Bocock, P. Hamilton, K. Thompson and A. Waton (eds), *An Introduction to Sociology: A Reader*. Milton Keynes: Open University Press.

Simmel, G. (1950) *The Sociology of Georg Simmel* (ed. and trans. by Kurt Wolff). New York: Free Press.

Solomon, M. (1989) *Narcissism and Intimacy: Love and Marriage in an Age of Confusion*. London: Norton.

Stanton, M. (1990) *Sandor Ferenczi*. London: Free Association Books.

Taylor, C. (1991) *The Ethics of Authenticity*. Cambridge, MA: Harvard University Press.

Trower, P., Bryant, B. and Argyle, M. (1978) *Social Skills and Mental Health*. London: Methuen & Co.

Wynne, V. and Wynne, G. (1986) 'The quest for intimacy', *Journal of Marital and Family Therapy*, 12 (4): 383–94.

10 *Learning from Research into the Counselling Relationship*

Roxane Agnew-Davies

Introduction

Earlier chapters in this book have outlined foundational propositions and theories about therapeutic relationships. This chapter turns to examine some of the empirical work, and explores to what extent research can answer the following questions:

1. What is the role of the relationship in counselling?
2. How is the counselling relationship measured?
3. What can we learn from empirical measures?
4. What affects the formation and maintenance of a counselling relationship?
5. How does the counselling relationship alter over the course of counselling?
6. What are the implications of the research for clinical practice?

1. What is the Role of the Relationship in Counselling?

After more than 30 years of research, it is now clearly established that counselling is more helpful than no treatment (Howard et al., 1986; Lambert and Bergin, 1992; Smith et al., 1980). Once this finding was accepted, researchers began to examine the relative merits of different types of therapy, each with distinct technical and theoretical features. The results were interesting: despite demonstrations by process researchers that there *are* systematic differences in the methods and techniques used by therapists from different theoretical schools (DeRubeis et al., 1982; Greenwald et al., 1981; Jones and Pulos, 1993), reviews of counselling outcome research indicate little or no difference in their effectiveness (Bergin and Garfield, 1994; Elkin et al., 1989).

Stiles, Shapiro and Elliott (1986) and Lambert and Bergin (1994) discussed possible means of resolving this paradox of outcome equivalence and content non-equivalence. One possibility is that common or 'non-specific' factors of psychological change underlie (or override) different therapeutic techniques (referred to as 'specific' factors), and that it is these common factors which determine effectiveness (Horvath and Greenberg, 1989; Horvath and Luborsky, 1993). Of the potential range of common factors (Goldfried, 1980; Lambert and Bergin, 1994; O'Connell, 1983), the relationship has become regarded as one of the most important, and its maintenance as essential for the continuation of counselling, regardless of theoretical orientation (Hartley and Strupp, 1983).

This focus on the relationship as a significant determinant of counselling success is supported by empirical findings of positive associations between measures of the strength of the relationship and various indices of outcome (Gaston, 1990; Horvath and Greenberg, 1986; Kivlighan, 1990; Mallinckrodt, 1993; Orlinsky and Howard, 1986b). In a meta-analysis of 24 studies linking the therapeutic relationship and outcome, Horvath and Symonds (1991) found an overall effect size of .26. In other words, of all the factors that influence how people change (such as life events, client symptomatology, therapist skill and treatment characteristics) the therapeutic relationship will explain about 9 per cent. In another survey of 38 samples of counselling relationships, 31 were regarded as significantly predictive of outcome (Luborsky, 1994), with levels ranging from .20 to .45 (that is, accounting for from 4 per cent to 25 per cent of the variance in outcome, depending on the specific alliance scale and study design). While these figures may seem small (since 75 per cent of change is not explained by reference to the relationship) they nevertheless indicate a statistically and clinically significant association between the quality of the counselling relationship and the likely success of treatment.

The impact of the relationship on treatment outcome has been examined in behaviour therapy (Raue and Goldfried, 1994), cognitive therapy (Rounsaville et al., 1987), Gestalt therapy (Horvath and Greenberg, 1989; Watson and Greenberg, 1994) and psychodynamic therapy (Eaton et al., 1988). At least one meta-analysis (Luborsky, 1994) and several studies of alliance–outcome correlations have not found differences across treatment approaches (Alexander and Luborsky, 1986; Goldfried et al., 1990; Gomes-Schwartz, 1978; Henry and Strupp, 1994; Horvath and Luborsky, 1993; Horvath and Symonds, 1991), lending indirect support to the view of the relationship as a common factor which might transcend differences in therapeutic technique. Indeed, the positive association of the therapeutic relationship with outcome is the most consistent finding of process–outcome research to date (Goldfried et al., 1990; Orlinsky et al., 1994).

However, it could be argued that the relationship is just a by-product of therapeutic gains (Horvath, 1994a); that is, that the quality of the alliance is simply a consequence of improvement, rather than an active ingredient which determines outcome. Empirical findings reviewed by Horvath and Luborsky (1993) refute this position. Firstly, the development of the relationship does not track therapeutic progress in a linear way; positive outcome has been associated with an initially good alliance which decays and recovers through successful resolutions of ruptures in the relationship (Horvath and Marx, 1990; Safran et al., 1994). Secondly, the size of alliance–outcome relations does not follow therapeutic gains at a parallel rate. Early measures of the alliance have been more potent predictors of outcome than ratings at the midpoint of counselling (Horvath and Symonds, 1991); ratings of the alliance after the first session have predicted premature termination (Kokotovic and Tracey, 1990), and alliance ratings have obtained stronger associations with subsequent than current outcome (Horvath, 1994a). Thirdly, alliance ratings predicted 36–57 per cent of the variance in post-therapy outcome, beyond short-term improvements (Gaston et al., 1991).

What, then, is the role of the relationship in the success or failure of counselling? At least two possibilities are open (Gaston, 1990): the relationship may be therapeutic in and of itself, or the relationship may be a prerequisite for and/or interact with specifics (such as counsellor technique) to determine treatment outcome. As the archetype of the position that the relationship is therapeutic in and of itself, Rogers (1957; Rogers et al., 1967) proposed that the quality of the relationship may be not only necessary but also sufficient for treatment success. However, the potency and generalizability of the Rogerian therapeutic conditions are not as great as once thought (Gaston, 1990; Gelso and Carter, 1985; Lambert et al., 1978; Meltzoff and Kornreich, 1970; Mitchell et al., 1977; Parloff et al., 1978). More recently, Gaston and Marmar (1994) suggested that the role of the relationship as effective in and of itself would be supported by empirical findings that alliance improvements were associated with decreases in symptomatology. Increases in ratings of relationships have paralleled changes on various indices of symptoms (Eaton et al., 1988; Moras and Strupp, 1982; O'Malley et al., 1983; Tracey and Dundon, 1988), although further research on these associations is required (Luborsky, 1994).

Empirical findings that poor outcomes were almost always associated with poor alliances, while good outcomes occurred in cases with variations in the quality of alliances, led to suggestions that the relationship afforded 'a set of variables that are necessary but not sufficient for explaining counselling outcomes' (Hartley and Strupp, 1983: 34). In other words, although the relationship does not uniquely contribute to therapeutic benefit, it is a prerequisite for the client to work in treatment (Bordin, 1994) and mediates the efficacy of interventions by providing the context in which they can promote change (Bowlby, 1988; Gaston, 1990; Raue and Goldfried, 1994).

This view of the relationship and counsellor techniques as complementary change agents (Hartley and Strupp, 1983) is a move away from the over-simplistic 'either–or' question in the specificity debate. Rather than dichotomizing 'specific' and 'nonspecific' factors, the action of psychotherapeutic techniques is better understood as integrally related to and in the context of the interpersonal environment in which they occur (Butler and Strupp, 1986; Frank, 1982; Henry and Strupp, 1994; Parloff, 1986; Safran et al., 1990). The relationship can be seen both as a gauge of therapeutic progress and of the efficacy of therapeutic strategies, and as an enabling process factor, the quality of which might determine success or failure in outcome (Frieswyk et al., 1986).

In summary, the counselling relationship has at least three roles: as a means to resolve the equivalence paradox, as a factor which accounts for counselling success, and as a prerequisite for, or complementary adjunct to, counsellor techniques in determining outcome. All three point to the significance of the counselling relationship, although all construe the counselling relationship at too high a level of abstraction; that is, in global terms as a uni-dimensional entity, with little differentiation of its multiple aspects. Previous chapters have documented historical developments and progressive articulation of the relationship within different theoretical perspectives. An overview of some of the conceptual contributions made by different schools and disciplines to under-standing the counselling relationship and inherent dimensions is to be found in Chapter 1. This chapter turns to examine how these theoretical models of counselling relationships and com-ponents therein have been measured in practice.

2. How is the Counselling Relationship Measured?

Within the psychodynamic tradition, the main body of research has concentrated on the working alliance, only one component of a broad relationship (Luborsky, 1994). Five clusters of related measures of the working alliance have been applied in the majority of investigations (Horvath, 1994b; Horvath and Symonds, 1991):

a)   the Working Alliance Inventory (WAI; Horvath, 1981)
b)   the Vanderbilt Therapeutic Alliance Scale (VTAS; Hartley and Strupp, 1983)
c)   the Therapeutic Alliance Scale (TAS/TARS; Marziali, 1984a)
d)   the California Psychotherapy Alliance Scales (CALPAS; Gaston and Ring, 1992)
e)   the Penn Helping Alliance Scales (HAq, HAcs, HAr; Alexander and Luborsky, 1986)

The Working Alliance Inventory (WAI)
The Working Alliance Inventory (WAI; Horvath, 1981, 1994a; Horvath and Greenberg, 1986, 1989) was devised to measure the three components of the working alliance proposed by Bordin (1979): collaboration between participants on tasks, collaboration on goals, and the affective bond between counsellor and client. Measuring development entailed successive rating procedures

until consensual agreements were achieved that specific items represented theoretical parameters (Horvath and Greenberg, 1989).

The Vanderbilt Therapeutic Alliance Scale (VTAS)
The Vanderbilt Therapeutic Alliance Scale (VTAS; Hartley and Strupp, 1983; Moras and Strupp, 1982) drew on the Vanderbilt Psychotherapy Process Scale (VPPS; Gomes-Schwartz, 1978; Suh et al., 1986) and the work of Bordin (1979), Greenson (1965), Langs (1976) and Luborsky (1976). Three sub-scales proposed on an *a priori* basis to reflect counsellor contributions, client contributions and the interaction were not supported by empirical findings (Hartley and Strupp, 1983), which factored items into six dimensions: Positive Climate, Patient Resistance, Therapist Intrusiveness, Patient Motivation, Patient Responsibility and Patient Anxiety.

The Therapeutic Alliance Rating System (TARS)
The Therapeutic Alliance Rating System (TARS; Marmar et al., 1986; Marziali, 1984a,b; Marziali et al., 1981) drew on the theoretical work of Freud (1913), Greenson (1965) and Zetzel (1956). Construction aimed to emphasize attitudinal and affective, rather than technical, aspects of the alliance, along with client self-observation and self-reflection (Gendlin, 1962; Klein et al., 1986). TARS was developed through consensus of four expert clinicians to comprise four sub-scales assessing clients' and counsellors' positive and negative contributions.

The California Psychotherapy Alliance Scales (CALPAS)
Extending Marziali's work on the TARS through successive empirical refinements (Marmar et al., 1989a) and theoretical considerations (Marmar and Gaston, 1989; Marmar et al., 1989b) led to CALPAS (Gaston and Marmar, 1994), comprising four alliance dimensions: Patient Commitment (reflecting affective aspects of the therapeutic alliance), Patient Working Capacity (skilful aspects of the working alliance), Therapist Understanding and Involvement, and Working Strategy Consensus (congruence on goals and tasks).

The Penn Helping Alliance Scales (HAq, HAcs, HAr)
The Penn Helping Alliance Scales include the Penn Helping
Alliance Counting Signs Method (HAcs; Luborsky, 1976; Luborsky
et al., 1983); the Helping Alliance Rating Method (HAr; Morgan
et al., 1982); and the Helping Alliance Questionnaire Method
(HAq; Luborsky, 1984; Luborsky et al., 1985). Across measures,
the helping alliance was defined as the client's experience of
treatment or therapist (Alexander and Luborsky, 1986), tapping
both the cooperative aspects of transference (Curtis, 1979; Greenspan and Cullander, 1975), and affective aspects (Freud, 1913;
Luborsky, 1976). Helping Alliance Type 1 was operationalized as
the client's experience of therapist helpfulness or capacity to provide help, and Helping Alliance Type 2 as the client's experience
of the treatment as a process of working together or collaborating
with the therapist toward the goals of treatment.

Turning now to research generated in the client-centred tradition, measures have been derived primarily through attempts to
operationalize the facilitative conditions. The **Barrett-Lennard
Relationship Inventory** (BLRI; Barrett-Lennard, 1962, 1986), a
64-item measure of the four conditions of empathic understanding, congruence, level of regard and unconditionality of regard,
has been widely used in this respect. There are now at least 10
variants of this instrument (Barrett-Lennard, 1986), inhibiting
direct comparisons across studies.
   Within the cognitive-behavioural school, researchers have sometimes turned to scales developed outside the field, such as the
Relationship Inventory, and adapted it for their purposes (Emmelkamp and Hout, 1983; Keijsers et al., 1990). Several research
groups have developed specific measurement systems applicable
to cognitive behavioural treatments. For instance, the **Therapist
Client Rating Scale** (TCRS: Bennun et al., 1986) categorizes
therapists' relationship skills under three major dimensions –
positive regard/interest, competency/experience and activity/
direct guidance – and client behaviours into positive regard,
self-disclosure/engagement and cooperation/goal/orientation. The
Counselor Rating Form (CRF; Barak and LaCrosse, 1975, 1977)
was designed to measure Strong's (1968) social influence conceptualization of the relationship by operationalizing therapist
expertness, attractiveness, and trustworthiness.
   In an attempt to bridge different theoretical schools (and

measurement systems therein) Orlinsky and Howard (1975, 1987) developed their generic model of therapy and designed the 'Therapy Session Report'. By drawing on dynamic and inter-personal theory, they sought to define the relationship in terms of the style rather than content of participants' activity. The **Therapeutic Bond Scale** (TBS) was developed on a consensual basis by Saunders et al. (1989) from client-rated Therapy Session Reports and subsequently subjected to psychometric revision. Three factors were proposed: Working Alliance, Empathic Reson-ance and Mutual Affirmation. The Global Bond scale was a com-posite of the three sub-scales.

3. What Can we Learn from Empirical Measures?

The diversity in operationalized constructs of the counselling relationship (apparent from the list above) has created both some confusion and redundancy within the research arena, and the body of empirical findings. This section addresses three questions about measures of counselling relationships:

■ What do the measures, or factors therein, tell us about the critical dimensions of counselling relationships?
■ Which dimension(s) of the counselling relationship predicts outcome?
■ Who should assess the counselling relationship?

Which Dimension(s) of the Counselling Relationship are Critical?

Despite some commonalities, disagreement about the internal structure of the counselling relationship is rife (Gelso and Carter, 1985; Hatcher, 1990; Horvath and Symonds, 1991). Two main approaches can be adopted to clarify core elements underpinning the large array of proposed dimensions (Horvath, 1994b; Horvath and Greenberg, 1989): theoretical analysis (as represented by earlier chapters) and empirical investigations of the co-variance across measures and their component sub-scales.

A number of studies have compared two or more different instruments, by calculating global scores (offering a crude and general index of the quality of the relationship) and sub-scale scores (each measuring a more specific aspect of the relation-ship). On the whole, correlational analyses have indicated that the measures tapped a similar global construct, but there was a wide range of overlap at the level of sub-scales, depending on the specific scales examined and the perspective of the rater (Bachelor, 1991; Hatcher et al., 1992; Safran and Wallner, 1991; Salvio et al., 1992; Tichenor and Hill, 1989). In other words, the substantial associations between global ratings of working alliance measures indicate commonalities at the most coarse level of analysis, and support our theoretical understanding of the basic structure or essential core of the relationship (Horvath and Luborsky, 1993). Large variations in the size of correlations obtained between sub-scale scores of various instruments could mean that while some sub-scales assess similar specific dimensions of the alliance (such as the extent to which client and counsellor agree on the goals of therapy), others measure distinct and separate components of the alliance, not captured by alternative sub-scales. For instance, both the HA scales and the CRF appear to capture different theoretical aspects of the relationship than the majority of alliance measures, (Horvath, 1994a; Horvath and Greenberg, 1989; Sabourin et al., 1990; Tichenor and Hill, 1989).

Partly because of methodological issues, no one instrument can be ratified as the best index of the therapeutic relationship, nor can any one scale be clearly excluded from the field. Progress in measuring the counselling relationship has been constrained by redundancy in the defining characteristics of any one component and confusion about the inter-relationships between them, and within measures by the following:

1 Items within scales sometimes reflect the technical work of the therapist, or the success of therapy, rather than the relationsh p *per se*. For instance, empirical examination of the HAq has shown the second factor, with items such as 'I have been feeling better recently', to be confounded with outcome (Crits-Christoph and Beebe, 1988).

2 Measures tend to focus on the contributions or characteristics of the client or counsellor, rather than the interactional nature of the counselling relationship (Horvath and Greenberg, 1994; Martin et al., 1986; Orlinsky and Howard, 1986b).

3 Most instruments measure some, but not all, aspects of the relationship.

4 Development work has struggled to differentiate adequately between distinct components of the relationship. For example, the independence of the dimensions assessing congruence on

goals and tasks has not gained empirical support (Marmar and Gaston, 1989; Tracey and Kokotovic, 1989), while the therapeutic conditions, as assessed by the BLRI, have been described as neither conceptually nor empirically orthogonal (Horvath and Greenberg, 1994; Hayes and Tinsley, 1989).

In an attempt to establish which scales within any one measure may be regarded as independent or distinct, correlations between sub-scales have also been examined (Gaston and Ring, 1992; Horvath and Luborsky, 1993). Sub-scale correlations tend to be higher for theoretically derived measures, such as the WAI (Horvath and Luborsky, 1993; Horvath and Greenberg, 1994), and lower for empirically derived scales, such as CALPAS (Gaston and Ring, 1992; Horvath and Symonds, 1991). Indeed, reviews (Gaston et al., 1991; Gaston and Marmar, 1994) indicate some advantage to CALPAS over other instruments in obtaining separate dimensions of the relationship. In general, however, inter-scale correlations are high (Al-Darmaki and Kivlighan, 1993; Horvath and Greenberg, 1989; Mallinckrodt and Nelson, 1991), so that empirical findings have not always obtained support for conceptual distinctions between different components of the alliance (Bachelor, 1991; Gaston, 1990; Luborsky et al., 1983).

That correlations between sub-scales are often high raises an interesting conundrum: either the relationship is a unitary phenomenon (and this is reflected in the empirical work), or the relationship is indeed multidimensional, in which case the empirical measures are flawed, in so far as they have failed to discriminate between different dimensions. The latter view is supported by two categories of empirical findings: first, on the basis of step-wise multiple regression analyses, different sub-scales have predicted a significant incremental proportion of outcome (Horvath and Greenberg, 1989) and second, greater differentiation among scales has been achieved for more heterogeneous client populations (Gaston and Marmar, 1994). Further developments are required before a comprehensive yet succinct measure of the significant aspects within counselling relationships is obtained.

Which Dimension(s) of the Counselling Relationship Predict Outcome?

In general, associations between ratings of the counselling relationship and change scores on various measures of outcome have been obtained across a variety of modalities, populations and rating sources (Horvath and Symonds, 1991), even when studies have controlled for pre-therapy symptomatology (Gaston, 1990; Gaston and Marmar, 1994; Raue and Goldfried, 1994).

Though the vast majority of studies have investigated single instruments, a small number have examined several relationship measures within the same study. For instance, Bachelor (1991) compared ratings of HA, VPPS (Vanderbilt Psychotherapy Process Scale, from which the VTAS was derived) and TARS from three perspectives. She found client-rated HA (Type 1) scores to be the strongest predictor of improvement, accounting for 48 per cent of client-rated change. In other words, nearly half of the improvements reported by clients could be explained by their perception of the quality of their relationship with their therapist (although it is worth noting again that items within these alliance scales may be confused with outcome). Of the VPPS, two aspects obtained the strongest associations with outcome: Therapist Exploration and Therapist Warmth and Friendliness scales, which predicted from 24–35 per cent of supervisor-rated improvement. From the counsellors' perspective, the strongest predictor was the VPPS Patient Participation scale, explaining from 13–21 per cent of the variance on different outcome measures. Of the three instruments compared in this study, therefore, specific dimensions within the VPPS and HA appeared more associated with client change than TARS scales or other sub-scales, depending on the perspective reported.

Turning to those studies which have focused on a single relationship measure, in a meta-analysis of eight studies of WAI-outcome associations, Horvath (1994a) reported a reasonably robust effect size of .33 for client-based measures. Although most studies have failed to link VTAS scores and outcome (Hartley and Strupp, 1983), in a review of the Vanderbilt Scales, Henry and Strupp (1994) found the VPPS Patient Involvement (PI) scale the best predictor of outcome. With respect to the TARS, Marziali (1984a) found that scores accounted for 9–14 per cent of the variance in client improvement. A number of studies have been conducted on associations between different versions of CALPAS, and changes on various outcome measures, after controlling for initial symptomatology. For instance, Gaston (1991) obtained significant correlations between clients' ratings of all CALPAS dimensions and their satisfaction with counselling, although CALPAS scores were not significantly related to changes on the Beck Depression Inventory at termination (Gaston and Marmar, 1994).

In the Penn Psychotherapy Project, the helping alliance score was the strongest during-treatment predictor of outcome (Luborsky et al., 1983; Luborsky and Auerbach, 1985). While associations might reflect an overlap between these scales and outcome measures, in another sample Alexander and Luborsky (1986) argued that benefits measured by the HAq at the end of the third session were minimal in contrast to outcome criteria after six months of treatment. The Rogerian therapeutic conditions have obtained moderate associations with outcome, the strongest associations being obtained for client-perceived empathy (Jones et al., 1986; Lambert et al., 1978; Orlinsky and Howard, 1986b) and for clients' perception of (rather than actual) counsellor behaviour (Horvath and Luborsky, 1993). Associations reported between CRF sub-scale ratings and measures of therapeutic outcome have been modest and fluctuated across modalities (Greenberg and Adler, 1989; Kokotovic and Tracey, 1987). In a study of TSR ratings, Kolden (1991) found that Therapeutic Bond scores accounted for significant proportions of the variance in short-term outcome, while Saunders et al. (1989) reported significant correlations between the TSB (Global) scores and outcome.

However, no one instrument has clearly emerged from the field as the 'best predictor of counselling outcome' (Horvath, 1994b). It is difficult to draw firm conclusions about specific instruments, since the size of associations obtained between the alliance and outcome have fluctuated across rating source (that is, clients, counsellors or external observers; the subject of the next section); the specific outcome measure applied (Horvath and Symonds, 1991; Marmar et al., 1986; Raue and Goldfried, 1994) and the modality of treatment investigated (Mitchell et al., 1977; Orlinsky and Howard, 1986b). In general, an effect size of .26 (Horvath and Symonds, 1991) between ratings of alliance measures and outcome has been obtained, but there are variations in the degree to which component sub-scales within instruments account for variance in outcome (Bachelor, 1991; Gaston et al., 1991; Safran and Wallner, 1991). For example, it would appear that the Task dimension within the WAI (Greenberg and Adler, 1989; Horvath and Greenberg, 1986, 1989), the Patient Involvement scale in the VPPS (Gomes-Schwartz, 1978; Henry and Strupp, 1994), the Patient Working Capacity scale within CALPAS (Marmar and Gaston,

1989a,b), the Empathy scale within the RI and the Global Bond Scale within the TBS are superior to other dimensions in accounting for variance in outcome scores. On these grounds, counsellors seeking to gain clinical insights into their relationships with clients may consider selecting specific dimensions from several different instruments, and consider the long-term impact(s) anticipated by the goals of therapy (since the quality of their relationship may differentially affect change scores on instruments designed to measure specific problems, such as depression, or more global measures of outcome, or client satisfaction ratings).

Do Clients and Counsellors Agree about their Relationship?

With limited exceptions (Mallinckrodt, 1991; Marziali, 1984b; Tryon and Kane, 1990) empirical findings have converged inasmuch as they have consistently demonstrated a lack of agreement between clients', counsellors' and external judges' assessments of the therapeutic encounter (Al-Darmaki and Kivlighan, 1993; Horvath, 1994b; Mallinckrodt, 1993; Marmar et al., 1989b; Tichenor and Hill, 1989). For instance, correlation coefficients between clients' and counsellors' ratings of the WAI ranged from .0 to .4 (Horvath and Greenberg, 1994) and in a review of 13 studies of the RI, Gurman (1977) reported correlations between clients' and counsellors' ratings ranging from .02 to .46.

Clinicians and researchers attempting to account for these differences have examined potential clinical and methodological factors within each perspective. Some investigators (e.g. Gelso and Carter, 1994; Marziali, 1984b) argued that clients can not assess the quality of the relationship accurately because their patient status is inherently inclined towards distorted perceptions of the interaction. (However, others, such as Greenberg (1994), Beutler and Sandowicz (1994) and Patton (1994) pointed out the conceptual dilemma of attempting to distinguish between perception and reality.) Alternatively, clients may experience cognitive dissonance and find it difficult to deprecate a source of help, or their own sense of hope, and/or be unaware of their own negativity (Marmar et al., 1986) with consequent ceiling effects in their ratings (Heppner et al., 1992). In addition, clients manage the counselling session without the formal and explicit parameters available to counsellors and clinically trained observers (Mintz et al., 1973). Clients will typically have experience of only their current therapeutic relationship, while counsellors may express a professional judgement of the quality of a given therapeutic relationship as it compares with others they have experienced (and hence counsellors' ratings may be more prone to a central tendency effect).

In other words, counsellors may have a relatively articulated understanding of the desirable features of a counselling relationship (Horvath and Greenberg, 1989; Tryon and Kane, 1993), although this may be coloured by their specific theoretical perspective. Congruence between client and counsellor ratings of the alliance may also vary with counsellor experience and/or competence (Mallinckrodt, 1993), such that inexperienced counsellors may in some way 'protect' themselves by lower ratings (LaCrosse, 1977; Xenakis et al., 1983). Alternatively (or conjointly), it has been argued that systematic misjudgements by counsellors may occur as a function of countertransference (Marmar et al., 1986) or the counsellors' own early object-relations (Henry and Strupp, 1994) and/or as a function of their investment in the counselling process (Beutler and Sandowicz, 1994). For instance, 'over-optimistic' counsellors may mistake clients' over-compliant behaviour for genuine collaboration (Horvath and Symonds, 1991).

Differences across perspectives have also been attributed to methodological issues in the design of relationship measures. Since counsellor scales tend to be parallel forms derived from instruments intended for clients, rather than generated through an attempt to collate the salient features of counsellors' perceptions of the alliance, counsellors are often required to evaluate clients' inner experience (infer their beliefs or feelings), while clients report only on their direct and immediate experience (Horvath, 1994b; Horvath and Luborsky, 1993). Similarly, clinical raters lack direct access to participants' subjective intentionality, affective or cognitive experience, or non-verbal cues in the session (Hill and Corbett, 1993; Horvath and Greenberg, 1986).

In summary, rather than one 'truth', there are multiple realities depending on the perspective of the rater (Hill, 1994; Hill and Gronsky, 1984; Hinde, 1979; Mintz et al., 1973). While no one vantage point is infallible, each perception offers potentially important information (Kokotovic and Tracey, 1990; Buckley et al., 1984; Hadley and Strupp, 1976). The clinician might bear in mind that their own, their client's and their supervisor's views of the quality of their relationship are likely to differ, each shedding light from different aspects on the therapeutic process (rather than any one being more accurate than the other).

The chapter now turns to examine variables which might affect the development and maintenance of a counselling relationship, and in doing so, raises the issue of fluctuations in the quality of the relationship over the course of the counselling process.

4. What Affects the Formation and Maintenance of a Counselling Relationship?

This question is posed to explore the extent to which empirical findings can help the counsellor select clients for treatment, decide on the length of treatment contract, and recognize that particular attention to the therapeutic alliance is required.

Variables within the literature which might facilitate or hinder the development of the therapeutic relationship have been categorized as client characteristics, counsellor characteristics and treatment factors (Al-Darmaki and Kivlighan, 1993). To facilitate the interpretation of a broad spectrum of client variables, three further sub-categories have been differentiated, as suggested by Horvath and Luborsky (1993) and Horvath (1994b): interpersonal capacities or skills, intrapersonal variables and diagnostic features.

Interpersonal Capacities of the Client
Empirical findings have tended to suggest that the quality of clients' interpersonal relationships prior to counselling is prognostic of their ability to form a counselling relationship (Kokotovic and Tracey, 1990; Mallinckrodt, 1991, 1992; Moras and Strupp, 1982). Clients who have difficulty maintaining social relationships (Gaston 1991; Kivlighan, 1990; Marmar et al., 1989a) or who have poor family relationships (Kokotovic and Tracey, 1990) have tended to develop weaker alliances. Past rather than current levels of interpersonal functioning seem more strongly related to the quality of the counselling relationship; for instance, Piper et al. (1991) obtained significant associations between the quality of object relations and alliance ratings, but not between current interpersonal functioning and the alliance. Mallinckrodt (1992, 1993)

found that the client's current level of social support accounted for more of the variance (5 per cent) in clients' ratings of the WAI than parental bonds (1 per cent), although the quality of early parental bonds explained 13 per cent of the variance in counsellors' ratings of the WAI.

Of course, this association is not necessarily always held, and is open to counsellor intervention. Clients judged to have sound interpersonal relationships may relatively consistently form strong therapeutic relationships, but clinical judgements of moderately to severely impaired extra-counselling relationships are less reliable predictors of subsequent therapeutic alliances (Hartley and Strupp, 1983; Moras and Strupp, 1982). In simple terms, the attention counsellors pay to the therapeutic alliance when working with clients who have, or have a history of, poor relationships with others may be critical for the outcome of therapy.

Intrapersonal Variables

This category includes demographic variables (e.g. Al-Darmaki and Kivlighan, 1993) and indices of client attitudes (e.g. Kokotovic and Tracey, 1990). Findings on gender, age and expectations have been inconsistent. Although age has not been significantly related to WAI ratings (Al-Darmaki and Kivlighan, 1993; Horvath, 1994a; Kivlighan, 1990; Kivlighan and Schmitz, 1992), associations between age and CALPAS scores have been reported (Marmar et al., 1986), such that observers rated older clients as making stronger positive contributions to the alliance. Similarly, although no main effects of gender were found on ratings of the WAI (Al-Darmaki and Kivlighan, 1993; Horvath, 1994a; Kivlighan, 1990; Kivlighan and Schmitz, 1992), studies which examined the interaction effects of counsellor–client gender *matches* in large samples have obtained complex and multifaceted results (see for example, Jones and Zoppel, 1982).

Associations have been obtained between clients' expectations of the relationship and ratings of the relationship during counselling (Al-Darmaki and Kivlighan, 1993), and people with little (self-reported) hope for success have been predisposed to develop weak alliances (Ryan and Cicchetti, 1985). Other studies have not found main effects, but have suggested that the quality of the relationship may be influenced by the extent to which the counsellor matches client expectations prior to counselling (Morgan et al., 1982) or by the degree of congruence in clients' and counsellors' expectations (Al-Darmaki and Kivlighan, 1993). While further work is required, this body of findings highlights the importance of exploring the clients' expectations of therapy and the counselling relationship at an early stage.

Diagnostic Features

In general, severity and type of symptomatology appear to have relatively little impact on the development of positive counselling relationships (Burns and Nolen-Hoeksema, 1992; Horvath and Luborsky, 1993; Mallinckrodt and Nelson, 1991; Marmar et al., 1986; Moras and Strupp, 1982). However, Marmar et al. (1989a) reported that ratings of Patient Working Capacity (but not other CALPAS sub-scales) showed a moderate negative association with pre-counselling general symptomatology, indicating that the formation of at least some aspects of the therapeutic relationship might be impeded by the level of distress experienced by the client.

Kokotovic and Tracey (1990) found associations between level of adjustment and counsellors' (but not clients') WAI ratings, although elsewhere, scores on the three WAI dimensions have seemed independent of clients' state of anxiety and self-concept ratings (Horvath and Greenberg, 1986). Clients' somatic problems correlated negatively with subsequent ratings of HA measures (Luborsky et al., 1983; Alexander and Luborsky, 1986). Measures of the clients' psychological Health–Sickness were inconsistently correlated with their alliance scores, depending on the alliance measure applied (HAcs or HAr; Luborsky et al., 1980; Luborsky et al., 1983; Luborsky, 1994). The magnitude of associations between pre-counselling symptomatology and ratings of therapeutic relationships may also alter according to type of treatment. The WAI ratings of more symptomatic clients (with higher pre-treatment SCL–90 scores) were less positive than those of clients with lower levels of distress in psychodynamic-interpersonal, but not cognitive-behavioural, therapies (Raue et al., 1993).

Overall, reviewers (e.g. Horvath, 1994b; Horvath and Luborsky, 1993) conclude that both intrapersonal and interpersonal client variables have similar and significant effects on the subsequent relationship in counselling (with coefficients of .30 and .32 respectively), but that diagnostic features have little impact on the formation of the counselling relationship.

Counsellor Characteristics

Despite long-standing arguments that the counsellor should be regarded as an active human participant in a reciprocal interaction rather than a neutral, impersonal conveyor of techniques (Davanloo, 1978), research on the role and possible impact of counsellor personality characteristics and willingness to enter a counselling relationship is still in its infancy (Horvath, 1994b; Horvath and Luborsky, 1993).

As yet, the findings have suggested that socio-demographic characteristics (gender or age) of counsellors are unrelated to ratings of the counselling relationship, as measured by CALPAS (Gaston et al., 1988) or WAI (Al-Darmaki and Kivlighan, 1993; Kivlighan, 1990; Kivlighan and Schmitz, 1992). Although Bachelor (1991, 1994) suggested that the bulk of research has not found a significant association between length of counsellor experience and alliance ratings, several studies have indicated that more experienced counsellors tend to form stronger alliances with their clients (Cummings et al., 1993; Henry and Strupp, 1994; Luborsky et al., 1983; Mallinckrodt and Nelson, 1991).

In summary of the main empirical findings of the Vanderbilt studies, Henry and Strupp (1994) concluded that counsellors are vulnerable to countertransference reactions, can have difficulty forming productive alliances (Strupp, 1980a, b, c, d) and exhibit very different interpersonal processes (despite remaining consistent in their technical strategies) across good and poor outcome cases (Henry et al., 1986). However, research on the role of counsellor characteristics on the formation of the relationship is limited not only in extent but in the clarity of findings. Counsellors interested in examining their contribution to the therapeutic relationship might try self-assessment on several different measurement systems, a selection of which is to be found in Horvath and Greenberg (1994) *The Working Alliance: Theory, Research and Practice*.

Treatment Characteristics

Relatively few studies have explored counsellors' technical contribution to the alliance (Horvath, 1994b; Luborsky et al., 1985; Windholz and Silberschatz, 1988). Despite marked differences in technical activity across modalities, ratings of therapeutic relationships have not generally differed as a function of treatment length or mode, either in terms of clients' or counsellors' ratings of

CALPAS (Gaston, 1991; Gaston et al., 1991, 1994; Marmar and Gaston, 1989; Marmar et al., 1989b), or the RI or WAI (Salvio et al., 1992).

Some variations in this context of a general equivalence have been reported (e.g. Hentschel et al., 1992). While levels of rapport or empathy offered by psychoanalytic, behavioural and Gestalt therapists were not qualitatively different, behaviourists offered more supportive communications, such as reassurance, praise and sympathy (Brunink and Schroeder, 1979). Observers' ratings of the WAI across cognitive-behavioural (CB) and psychodynamic-interpersonal (PI) therapies (Raue et al., 1993) indicated more positive alliances in CB therapies, with greater variability in PI treatments. The authors suggested that greater emphasis on structure and collaboration within CB therapies might enhance clients' understanding of tasks and goals, while the lower and more variable ratings within PI therapies might be attributable to a focus on negative aspects of, and to ruptures within, the relationship, respectively.

There is increasing research interest in the ways that counsellors might improve the quality of therapeutic relationships. With respect to the ruptures, or strains, in the therapeutic relationship, Safran et al. (1994) identified process markers of ruptures (using a six-item modification of the WAI) consequent on the client's dysfunctional interpersonal schema and explored the counsellor's role in retarding or facilitating their amendment. In another study, Safran and Segal (1990) identified seven rupture types, broadly categorized into confrontation or withdrawal types (Harper, 1989a,b). Task analyses indicated that successful resolutions of withdrawal ruptures entailed attending to the rupture marker, focusing on immediate experience, and exploring the rupture experience (including the client's expression of negative feelings and counsellor expression of empathy and acceptance of responsibility for their contribution) in conjunction with an exploration of client fears and avoidance.

In summary, the contribution of technical activity to the formation and maintenance of the therapeutic relationship has been difficult to ascertain, partly because of variations in therapist behaviour across modalities. Despite these variations, however, the strength of the relationship has not appeared to differ significantly as a function of therapeutic orientation (consistent with the possible role of the relationship as a common factor).

5. Does the Counselling Relationship Alter over the Course of Counselling?

The preceding section focused on variables which might precede or need particular attention at the beginning of the counselling, but counselling is best understood as a dynamic process, responsive to the changing demands of different phases, rather than as a static entity (Sexton and Whiston, 1994). This section focuses on what can be learned from research about the dynamics, or time course, of the therapeutic relationship.

The broad categorization of the course of the relationship into three distinct phases (Horvath and Luborsky, 1993), suggested by a number of theoretical models (Gelso and Carter, 1994; Greenson, 1967; Langs, 1973; Mann, 1973), has as yet gained only weak and indirect empirical support (Golden and Robbins, 1990; Miller et al., 1983; Sexton, 1993).

In the first phase of counselling, Mann (1973) proposed that client feelings toward the counsellor would be positive and steadily improve, motivated by an unrealistic view of the counsellor as one who will compensate for past relationship failures. Empirical work has suggested that the development of the alliance over the first five sessions (peaking at session three; Saltzman et al., 1976) entails the development of collaboration (Gelso and Carter, 1994; Horvath and Greenberg, 1994) and/or client involvement (Hartley and Strupp, 1983; O'Malley et al., 1983). Initially, there may be difficulties in establishing a supportive relationship or agreement about therapeutic tasks (Horvath and Luborsky, 1993). There is evidence that failure to develop good alliances at the initial stages can lead to drop-out or impede a good outcome (Frank and Gunderson, 1990; Kokotovic and Tracey, 1990; Saunders et al., 1989). Theoretical and empirical work has converged to suggest that the alliance either fails to form over the first three sessions, or is sufficiently well-formed to act as a substrate for the second phase (Bordin, 1994; Gelso and Carter, 1985; Hartley and Strupp, 1983; Henry and Strupp, 1994).

Mann (1973) characterized the second phase of counselling as one of heightened client ambivalence, in which the client struggles to accept that their initial fantasies will not be gratified. Along similar lines, Horvath and Luborsky (1993) proposed that as the counsellor becomes more challenging, the client may perceive a loss of support and a reactivation of dysfunctional relationship schema, which threaten the alliance. These propositions are congruent with theoretical models of ruptures in counselling relationships (Bordin, 1994; Gelso and Carter, 1994; Luborsky et al., 1985; Safran et al., 1990; Strupp and Binder, 1984), such that the earlier strength of the alliance may diminish as the strain emerges, and increase again as the rupture is resolved. A small body of empirical findings (e.g. Safran et al., 1990; Safran et al., 1994) has lent weak support for models of rupture–repair cycles in successful therapy, by finding a decline in client-rated working alliance during the second phase. For instance, the results of two intensive case studies (Golden and Robbins, 1990; Horvath and Marx, 1990) indicated that alliance ratings at the mid-points of treatment were lower than at the beginning or end.

If there is to be a third phase, the relationship must be repaired for a successful outcome (Gelso and Carter, 1994; Horvath and Luborsky, 1993). Mann (1973) argued that the success of the counselling rested on a resolution of termination issues in the final phase. Cummings et al. (1993) suggested that the therapeutic relationship regains prominence in the last session, when clients and counsellors face ending. There is some empirical support for these expectations of a recovery in scores (Golden and Robbins, 1990).

However, many empirical findings do not easily map on to theoretical models and/or have been equivocal. Fluctuations in the strength of various aspects of the relationship over time have been reported (Barkham and Shapiro, 1986; Eaton et al., 1988; Hartley and Strupp, 1983; Hentschel et al., 1992; Horvath and Luborsky, 1993; Horvath and Marx, 1990; Marziali, 1984a). However, other findings appear to contravene the above by reporting stability in relationship ratings over time (Gaston et al., 1991; Gaston and Ring, 1992; Gaston et al., 1994; Gomes-Schwartz, 1978; Klee et al., 1990; Luborsky et al., 1983; Marmar et al., 1989b; Morgan et al., 1982; Tichenor and Hill, 1989). The equivocal nature of these findings may be attributable to at least three sources: differences across (or within) alliance measures and constructs therein, variation across dyads in outcome and methodological differences.

Cummings et al. (1993) reported that counsellors' ratings of the Bond scale increased over the course of counselling, but changes were not obtained in client ratings. Marziali (1984a) and Marmar et al. (1986) found a significant increase in client and counsellor positive (but not negative) contributions from the first and third sessions to the last session of treatment. Together, these studies indicate that the meaning or salience of particular components of the relationship may fluctuate across time, and across perspective; for instance, it has been suggested that as counselling progresses, clients attend less to the different aspects of counsellor behaviour, and make more global evaluations (Heesacker and Heppner, 1983).

Of course, global generalities about patterns within counselling relationships are limited; for example, Kivlighan and Schmitz (1992) identified an increase in alliance scores over time in some dyads but not others. At least some of these variations might depend on type and length of treatment, and/or levels of client symptomatology. For instance, while successful therapies are typified by increases in the strength of the alliance across time, this pattern is not apparent in unsuccessful cases. Klee et al. (1990) found that the positive contributions of clients with a successful outcome (but not those with a less successful outcome) increased significantly from early to late in treatment. Hartley and Strupp (1983) found that more successful clients showed a pattern of increasing alliance strength over the early course of counselling (peaking after about 25 per cent of the sessions) and tailing off in later sessions. In contrast, scores of less successful clients fell from initial equality with the other group, before rising again at mid-point in counselling (although they never achieved the level of the peak in the successful group). Successful dyads have tended to show a curvilinear (high–low–high) pattern of satisfaction about the session over the course of counselling, while an underlying steadily increasing trend in counsellor satisfaction has been detected (Tracey, 1989). A curvilinear pattern in the same direction has been found in successful dyads for topic-following complementarity (Tracey and Ray, 1984) and session smoothness and positivity (e.g. Mallinckrodt, 1993).

Although no significant differences were obtained between HA ratings early and late in counselling (Luborsky et al., 1983; Morgan et al., 1982), successful clients showed non-significant increases in Type 2 scores (Luborsky, 1976; Morgan et al., 1982), and positive HAcs signs, while negative signs remained stable (Alexander and Luborsky, 1986; Luborsky et al., 1983). By contrast, negative signs increased over time in the less improved group, with little change in the positive signs (Luborsky et al., 1983). Gelso, Kivlighan, Wine and Jones (1993) found counsellor ratings of transference begin at low levels, rise in the middle phase of counselling (perhaps as core issues emerged) and continue to rise in unsuccessful cases, but decrease again in successful cases. The results of this study coincide with those above if transference is understood as a distorted aspect of the relationship, operating in reverse to the real relationship or working alliance. Only one study does not accord with the general pattern of steadier increases in positivity about relationships in successful cases. Successful cases were characterized by a decline in alliance scores (as measured by the VTAS sub-scales) whereas the scores of premature terminators increased (Hartley and Strupp, 1983; Henry and Strupp, 1994), perhaps because counsellors 'try harder' in unsuccessful cases.

In summary, there appears to be a general pattern in the findings that some (positive) aspects of the alliance increase in strength at least over the early stages of counselling; in contrast, less successful outcomes may not demonstrate this pattern, and/ or show increases in negative or distorted aspects of the relationship. Within the second phase of counselling, it appears that decreases in alliance scores might have clinical significance (for the early recognition of cases at risk, and potential interventions to counteract ruptures in the relationship). As in previous sections, however, variations in methodological procedures have masked potentially significant clinical phenomena.

Research Paradigms

In closing this chapter, it is worth noting that the research findings presented have almost all been extracted from studies within the extensive analysis research paradigm, which has typified investigations of counselling relationships, despite increasing concern about the adequacy of such an approach (Barlow and Hersen, 1984; Jones and Pulos, 1993; McCullough, 1984a,b; Persons, 1991; Rice and Greenberg, 1984). It is only relatively recently that researchers have begun to augment conventional reliance on these methods. Intensive analysis paradigm studies (Safran et al., 1988; Strupp and Binder, 1984) have moved from the application of general process scales applied at random points in time to focus on clinically significant change events (Greenberg, 1986; Silberschatz et al., 1986; Windholz and Silberschatz, 1988). Task analysis (Rice and Greenberg, 1984; Safran et al., 1988) is based on a case-specific approach that informs clinical practice at a molecular level. These approaches not only permit a microscopic examination of the moment-to-moment process (Rice and Greenberg, 1984), but capture fluctuations within individual dyads (Horvath and Marx, 1990) and may discover effects obscured by the collapsing of data in large-group comparison designs (Horwitz et al., 1991). However, while the counselling relationship serves different purposes for different dyads (or for the same dyad at different times), it is also useful to consider the common functions that the relationship might have across clients and therapies (Kolden et al., 1994). Although each dyad is unique, there may be features of the relationship that will be valid for a range of dyads. Kolden et al. (1994) argued that research which searches for general principles can support clinicians' struggles to bridge the gap between individual clients' reality, and their own socialization into general theories. In other words, while appreciating the reality of the client, the clinician must employ their theoretical and therapeutic knowledge in any individual relationship.

What Are the Implications of the Research for Clinical Practice?

In reviewing research on the counselling relationship, it is apparent that the empirical literature suffers from an 'embarrassment of riches' (Carson, 1969), with a wide array of measures and a large body of findings, but the field lacks coherent direction and integration. While there is general agreement on a global relationship dimension, different sub-scales within instruments capture different specific components. It is not possible to specify precisely which dimensions are most valuable, since strengths and limitations can be identified in all. There are surprisingly few attempts as yet to integrate divergent operationalizations, so that research on counselling relationships has progressed in a non-synergistic manner.

Nevertheless, there are several implications which can be drawn for counsellors in their clinical practice:

■ Whatever the mode of counselling adopted, the quality of the counselling relationship is an important factor which may facilitate or impede successful outcome. Although the relationship does not uniquely determine therapeutic benefit, it is a prerequisite for work in treatment and it both mediates and is mediated by the efficacy of interventions.

■ Empirical measures have concurred on the importance of client and counsellor agreement on tasks and goals of treatment. When there are discrepancies (for instance, if the client expects to discuss medication and the counsellor to explore past relationships, or the client expects the outcome to be a decision to leave a relationship, while the counsellor is anticipating changes in the inner child), it may be important for the counsellor to address these differences and re-negotiate with the client.

■ The research on dimensions of empirical measures of the counselling relationship also indicates that the outcome of treatment may be influenced by the 'real relationship', calling upon the counsellor to offer therapeutic conditions (including understanding and level of regard) of high quality. The counsellor might also usefully examine the degree to which each participant takes responsibility for the work in treatment and the clients' degree of participation and/or their capacity to work in the counselling process.

■ The counselling relationship is a dynamic rather than a static phenomenon. Particular attention might be paid to the development of the relationship over the first three to five sessions. A change for the worse in the perceived quality of the relationship may have clinical significance for early recognition of cases at risk of drop-out and/or the occurrence of a rupture in the relationship which should be addressed (as outlined in the section on how the counselling relationship might alter over time). Attention to the resolution of ruptures and of termination issues may enhance outcome.

■ Particular attention to the formation and maintenance of the counselling relationship may be appropriate if the client has had impoverished relationships in the past. It is worth exploring client expectations of the counselling relationship at an early stage.

■ Clients and counsellors may well perceive the counselling relationship in different ways. For instance, clients may have a more global view of the relationship, while the counsellor may be able to guide them toward, and enhance the counselling process through, a more differentiated understanding of the various dimensions within their relationship. For example, the counsellor might explicitly address the responsibility that each partner takes for working together, or invite the client to explore their confidence in the counsellor. Moreover, the counsellor who is willing to articulate relationship issues is in a position to resolve a rupture in the therapeutic relationship that otherwise might lead to client withdrawal or even premature termination.

Acknowledgement

This chapter is based on the introductory sections of a PhD, which was guided and supported from inception to completion by Bryn Davies and Michael Barkham.

References

Al-Darmaki, F. and Kivlighan, D.M. (1993) 'Congruence in client–counselor expectations for relationship and the working alliance', *Journal of Counseling Psychology*, 40 (4): 379–84.

Alexander, L.B. and Luborsky, L. (1986) 'The Penn Helping Alliance Scales', in L.S. Greenberg and W.M. Pinsof (eds), *The Psychotherapeutic Process: A Research Handbook*. New York: Guilford Press, pp. 325–66.

Bachelor, A. (1991) 'Comparison and relationship to outcome of diverse dimensions of the helping alliance as seen by client and therapist', *Psychotherapy: Theory, Research and Practice*, 28: 534–9.

Bachelor, A. (1994) 'Effects of therapist level of experience on dimensions of the therapeutic alliance'. Paper presented at the Society for Psychotherapy Research Annual Meeting, York.

Barak, A. and LaCrosse, M.B. (1975) 'Multidimensional perception of counselor behavior', *Journal of Counseling Psychology*, 22: 471–6.

Barak, A. and LaCrosse, M.B. (1977) 'Comparative perceptions of practicum counselor behavior: a process and methodological investigation', *Counselor Education and Supervision*, 16: 202–8.

Barkham, M. and Shapiro, D.A. (1986) 'Counselor verbal response modes and experienced empathy', *Journal of Counseling Psychology*, 33: 3–10.

Barlow, D.H. and Hersen, M. (1984) *Single Case Experimental Designs: Strategies For Studying Behavior Change*. New York: Pergamon.

Barrett-Lennard, G.T. (1962) 'Dimensions of therapist response as causal factors in therapeutic personality change', *Psychological Monographs*, 76 (43, Whole No. 562).

Barrett-Lennard, G.T. (1986) 'The Relationship Inventory now: issues and advances in theory, method and use', in L.S. Greenberg and W.M. Pinsof (eds), *The Psychotherapeutic Process: A Research Handbook*. New York: Guilford Press, pp. 439–75.

Bennun, I., Hahlweg, U., Schindler, L. and Langlotz, M. (1986) 'Therapist's and client's perceptions in behavior therapy: the development and cross-cultural analysis of an assessment instrument', *British Journal of Clinical Psychology*, 25: 275–83.

Bergin, A.E. and Garfield, S.L. (1994) 'Overview, trends and future issues', in A.E. Bergin and S.L. Garfield (eds), *Handbook of Psychotherapy and Behavior Change* (4th edn). New York: Wiley, pp. 821–30.

Beutler, L.E. and Sandowicz, M. (1994) 'The counseling relationship: what is it?' *The Counseling Psychologist*, 22 (1): 98–103.

Bordin, E.S. (1979) 'The generalizability of the psychoanalytic concept of the working alliance', *Psychotherapy: Theory, Research and Practice*, 16 (3): 252–60.

Bordin, E.S. (1994) 'Theory and research on the therapeutic working alliance: new directions', in A.O. Horvath and L.S. Greenberg (eds), *The Working Alliance: Theory, Research and Practice*. New York: Wiley, pp. 13–37.

Bowlby, J. (1988) *A Secure Base: Clinical Applications of Attachment Theory*. London: Routledge & Kegan Paul.

Brunink, S.A. and Schroeder, H.E. (1979) 'Verbal therapeutic behavior of expert psychoanalytically-oriented, Gestalt and behavior therapists', *Journal of Consulting and Clinical Psychology*, 47: 567–74.

Buckley, P., Hope, R.C., Plutchik, R., Wild, K.V. and Karasu, T.B. (1984) 'Psychodynamic variables as predictors of psychotherapy outcome', *American Journal of Psychiatry*, 141 (6): 742–8.

Burns, D.D. and Nolen-Hoeksema, S. (1992) 'Therapeutic empathy and recovery from depression in cognitive-behavioral therapy: a structural equation model', *Journal of Consulting and Clinical Psychology*, 60 (3): 441–9.

Butler, S.F. and Strupp, H.H. (1986) 'Specific and nonspecific factors in psychotherapy: a problematic paradigm for psychotherapy research', *Psychotherapy*, 23 (1): 30–40.

Carson, R.C. (1969) *Interaction Concepts of Personality*. London: Allen & Unwin.

Crits-Christoph, P. and Beebe, K. (1988) 'The role of the helping alliance and other process variables in cognitive therapy'. Panel presentation, Society for Psychotherapy Research Annual Meeting, Santa Fe, New Mexico.

Cummings, A.L., Slemon, A.G. and Hallberg, E.T. (1993) 'Session evaluation and recall of important events as a function of counselor experience', *Journal of Counseling Psychology*, 40 (2): 156–65.

Curtis, C. (1979) 'The concept of the therapeutic alliance: implications for the "widening scope"', *Journal of the American Psychoanalytic Association*, 27: 159–92.

Davanloo, H. (1978) 'Evaluation criteria for selection of patients for short-term dynamic psychotherapy: a meta-psychological approach', in H. Davanloo (ed.), *Basic Principles and Techniques in Short-Term Dynamic Psychotherapy*. New York: Spectrum Publications, pp. 1–34.

DeRubeis, R.J. and Feeley, M. (1991) 'Determinants of change in cognitive therapy for depression', *Cognitive Therapy and Research*, 14 (5): 469–82.

DeRubeis, R., Hollon, S., Evans, M. and Bemis, K. (1982) 'Can psychotherapies for depression be discriminated? A systematic investigation of cognitive therapy and interpersonal therapy', *Journal of Consulting and Clinical Psychology*, 50: 744-56.

Eaton, T.T., Abeles, N. and Gutfreund, M.J. (1988) 'Therapeutic alliance and outcome: impact of treatment length and pretreatment symptomatology', *Psychotherapy: Theory, Research and Practice*, 25: 536-42.

Elkin, I., Shea, T., Watkins, J., Imber, S., Sotsky, S., Collins, J., Glass, D., Pilkonis, P., Leber, W., Docherty, J., Fiester, S. and Parloff, M. (1989) 'National Institute of Mental Health treatment of depression. Collaborative research program: general effectiveness of treatments', *Archives of General Psychiatry*, 46: 971-82.

Emmelkamp, P.M.G. and Hout, A. van der (1983) 'Failures in treating agoraphobia', in E.B. Foa and P.M.G. Emmelkamp (eds), *Failures in Behavior Therapy*. New York: Wiley, pp. 58-81.

Frank, A.F. and Gunderson, J.G. (1990) 'The role of the therapeutic alliance in the treatment of schizophrenia', *Archives of General Psychiatry*, 47: 228-36.

Frank, J.D. (1982) 'Therapeutic components shared by all psychotherapies', in J.H. Harvey and M.M. Parks (eds), *The Master Lecture Series*: vol. 1, *Psychotherapy Research and Behavior Change*. Washington, DC: American Psychological Association, pp. 5-37.

Freud, S. (1913/1958) 'On the beginning of treatment: further recommendations on the technique of psychoanalysis', in J. Strachey (ed.), *The Standard Edition of the Complete Psychological Works of Sigmund Freud*. London: Hogarth Press and Institute of Psychoanalysis, vol. 12, pp. 122-44.

Frieswyk, S.H., Allen, J.G., Colson, D.B., Coyne, L., Gabbard, G.O., Horwitz, L. and Newsom, G. (1986) 'The therapeutic alliance: its place as a process and outcome variable in dynamic psychotherapy research', *Journal of Consulting and Clinical Psychology*, 54 (1): 32-8.

Gaston, L. (1990) 'The concept of the alliance and its role in psychotherapy: theoretical and empirical considerations', *Psychotherapy*, 27 (2): 143-53.

Gaston, L. (1991) 'Reliability and criterion-related validity of the California Psychotherapy Alliance Scales', *Psychological Assessment*, 3: 68-74.

Gaston, L. and Marmar, C.R. (1994) 'The California Psychotherapy Alliance Scales', in A.O. Horvath and L.S. Greenberg (eds), *The Working Alliance: Theory, Research and Practice*. New York: Wiley, pp. 85-108.

Gaston, L. and Ring, J.M. (1992) 'Preliminary results on the Inventory of Therapeutic Strategies', *Journal of Psychotherapy Research and Practice*, 1: 1-13.

Gaston, L., Marmar, C.R., Gallagher, D. and Thompson, L.W. (1991) 'Alliance prediction of outcome beyond in-treatment symptomatic change as psychotherapy processes', *Psychotherapy Research*, 1 (2): 104-13.

Gaston, L., Marmar, C.R., Thompson, L.W. and Gallagher, D. (1988) 'Relation of patient pretreatment characteristics to the therapeutic alliance in diverse psychotherapies', *Journal of Consulting and Clinical Psychology*, 56 (4): 483-9.

Gaston, L., Piper, W.E., Debbane, E.G., Bienvenu, J. and Garant, J. (1994) 'Alliance and technique for predicting outcome in short- and long-term analytic psychotherapy', *Psychotherapy Research*, 4 (2): 121-35.

Gelso, C.J. and Carter, J.A. (1985) 'The relationship in counseling and psychotherapy: components, consequences, and theoretical antecedents', *The Counseling Psychologist*, 13 (2): 155–244.

Gelso, C.J. and Carter, J.A. (1994) 'Components of the psychotherapy relationship: their interaction and unfolding during treatment', *Journal of Counseling Psychology*, 41 (3): 296–306.

Gelso, C.J., Kivlighan, D.M., Wine, B. and Jones, A. (1993) 'Transference, insight, and working alliance across the course of more and less successful therapy'. Unpublished manuscript, University of Maryland. Cited in Gelso and Carter (1994).

Gendlin, E.T. (1962) *Experiencing and the Creation of Meaning*. New York: Free Press of Glencoe.

Golden, B.R. and Robbins, S.B. (1990) 'The working alliance within time-limited therapy: a case analysis', *Professional Psychology: Research and Practice*, 21: 476–81.

Goldfried, M.R. (1980) 'Toward the delineation of therapeutic change principles', *American Psychologist*, 35: 991–9.

Goldfried, M.R., Greenberg, L.S. and Marmar, C. (1990) 'Individual psychotherapy: process and outcome', *Annual Review of Psychology*, 41: 659–88.

Gomes-Schwartz, B. (1978) 'Effective ingredients in psychotherapy: prediction of outcome from process variables', *Journal of Consulting and Clinical Psychology*, 46 (5): 1023–35.

Greenberg, L.S. (1986) 'Change process research', *Journal of Consulting and Clinical Psychology*, 54: 4–9.

Greenberg, L.S. (1994) 'What is "real" in the relationship? Comment on Gelso and Carter (1994)', *Journal of Counseling Psychology*, 41 (3): 307–9.

Greenberg, L.S. and Adler, J. (1989) 'The working alliance and outcome: a client report study'. Paper presented at the 20th Annual Meeting of the Society for Psychotherapy Research, Toronto, Canada.

Greenson, R.R. (1965) 'The working alliance and the transference neuroses', *Psychoanalytic Quarterly*, 34: 155–81.

Greenson, R.R. (1967) *The Technique and Practice of Psychoanalysis*. New York: International Universities Press.

Greenspan, S. and Cullander, C. (1975) 'A systematic metapsychological assessment of the course of an analysis', *Journal of the American Psychoanalytic Association*, 23: 107–38.

Greenwald, D.P., Kornblith, S.J., Hersen, M., Bellack, A.S. and Himmelhoch, J.M. (1981) 'Differences between social skills therapists and psychotherapists in treating depression', *Journal of Consulting and Clinical Psychology*, 49 (5): 757–9.

Gurman, A.S. (1977) 'The patient's perception of the therapeutic relationship', in A.S. Gurman and A.M. Razin (eds), *Effective Psychotherapy: A Handbook of Research*. New York: Pergamon Press, pp. 503–43.

Hadley, S.W. and Strupp, H.H. (1976) 'Contemporary views of negative effects in psychotherapy', *Archives of General Psychiatry*, 33: 1291–1303.

Harper, H. (1989a) 'Coding guide I: identification of confrontation challenges in explanatory therapy'. Unpublished manuscript, University of Sheffield.

Harper, H. (1989b) 'Coding guide II: identification and classification of therapist markers and withdrawal challenges'. Unpublished manuscript, University of Sheffield.

Hartley, D.E. and Strupp, H.H. (1983) 'The therapeutic alliance: its relationship to outcome in brief psychotherapy', in J. Masling (ed.), *Empirical Studies of Psychoanalytic Theories*. Hillsdale, NJ: Analytic Press, vol. 1, pp. 1–37.

Hatcher, R. (1990) 'Transference and the therapeutic alliance'. Paper presented at the Society for Psychotherapy Research Annual Meeting, Wintergreen, VA.

Hatcher, R., Barends, A., Hansell, J. and Gutfreund, M.J. (1992) 'Therapeutic alliance as a dyadic phenomenon. Theoretical, methodological and empirical considerations'. Unpublished manuscript, University of Michigan Psychological Clinic.

Hayes, T.J. and Tinsley, H.E.A. (1989) 'Identification of the latent dimensions of instruments that measure perceptions of and expectations about counseling', *Journal of Counseling Psychology*, 36 (4): 294–7.

Heesacker, M. and Heppner, P.P. (1983) 'Using real client perceptions to examine psychometric properties of the Counselor Rating Form', *Journal of Counseling Psychology*, 30: 180–7.

Henry, W.P. and Strupp, H.H. (1994) 'The therapeutic alliance as interpersonal process', in A.O. Horvath and L.S. Greenberg (eds), *The Working Alliance: Theory, Research and Practice*. New York: Wiley, pp. 51–84.

Henry, W.P., Schacht, T.E. and Strupp, H.H. (1986) 'Structural analysis of social behavior: application to a study of interpersonal process in differential psychotherapeutic outcome', *Journal of Consulting and Clinical Psychology*, 54 (1): 27–31.

Hentschel, U., Kiessling, M., Heck, M. and Willoweit, I. (1992) 'Therapeutic alliance: what can be learned from case studies?' *Psychotherapy Research*, 2 (3): 204–23.

Heppner, P.P. and Dixon, D.N. (1981) 'A review of the interpersonal influence process in counseling', *Personnel and Guidance Journal*, 49: 542–50.

Heppner, P.P., Rosenberg, J.I. and Hedgespeth, J. (1992) 'Three methods in measuring the therapeutic process: clients' and counselors' constructions of the therapeutic process versus actual therapeutic events', *Journal of Counseling Psychology*, 39 (1): 20–31.

Hill, C.E. (1994) 'What is the therapeutic relationship? A reaction to Sexton and Whiston', *The Counseling Psychologist*, 22 (1): 90–7.

Hill, C.E. and Corbett, M.M. (1993) 'A perspective on the history of process and outcome research in counseling psychology', *Journal of Counseling Psychology*, 40 (1): 3–24.

Hill, C.E. and Gronsky, B. (1984) 'Research: why and how?' in J.M. Whiteley, N. Kagan, L.W. Harmon, B.R. Fretz and F. Tanney (eds), *The Coming Decade in Counseling Psychology*. New York: Character Research Press, pp. 149–59.

Hinde, R.A. (1971) 'Some problems in the study of the development of social behaviour', in E. Tobach, L.R. Aronson and E. Shaw (eds), *The Psychobiology of Development*. New York: Academic Press.

Hinde, R.A. (1979) *Towards Understanding Relationships*. London: Academic Press.

Horvath, A.O. (1981) 'An exploratory study of the concept of the therapeutic alliance and its measurement'. Unpublished doctoral dissertation, University of British Columbia, Vancouver, Canada.

Horvath, A.O. (1994a) 'Empirical validation of Bordin's pantheoretical model of the alliance: the Working Alliance Inventory perspective', in A.O. Horvath and L.S. Greenberg (eds), *The Working Alliance: Theory, Research and Practice*. New York: Wiley, pp. 109-28.

Horvath, A.O. (1994b) 'Empirical research on the alliance', in A.O. Horvath and L.S. Greenberg (eds), *The Working Alliance: Theory, Research and Practice*. New York: Wiley, pp. 259-86.

Horvath, A.O. and Greenberg, L.S. (1986) 'The development of the Working Alliance Inventory', in L.S. Greenberg and W.M. Pinsof (eds), *The Psychotherapeutic Process: A Research Handbook*. New York: Guilford Press, pp. 529-56.

Horvath, A.O. and Greenberg, L.S. (1989) 'Development and validation of the Working Alliance Inventory', *Journal of Counseling Psychology*, 36 (2): 223-33.

Horvath, A.O. and Greenberg, L.S. (1994) 'Introduction', in A.O. Horvath and L.S. Greenberg (eds), *The Working Alliance: Theory, Research and Practice*. New York: Wiley, pp. 1-9.

Horvath, A.O. and Luborsky, L. (1993) 'The role of the therapeutic alliance in psychotherapy', *Journal of Consulting and Clinical Psychology*, 61 (4): 561-73.

Horvath, A.O. and Marx, R.W. (1990) 'The development and decay of the working alliance during time-limited counseling', *Canadian Journal of Counseling*, 24: 240-59.

Horvath, A.O. and Symonds, B.D. (1991) 'Relation between working alliance and outcome in psychotherapy: a meta-analysis', *Journal of Counseling Psychology*, 38 (2): 139-49.

Horwitz, L., Allen, J.G., Colson, D.B., Frieswyk, S.H., Gabbard, G.O., Coyne, L. and Newsom, G.E. (1991) 'Psychotherapy of borderline patients at the Menninger Foundation: expressive compared with supportive interventions and the therapeutic alliance', in L.E. Beutler and M. Crago (eds), *Psychotherapy Research: An International Review of Programmatic Studies*. Washington, DC: American Psychological Association, pp. 48-55.

Howard, K.I., Kopta, S.M., Krause, M.S. and Orlinsky, D.E. (1986) 'The dose-effect relationship in psychotherapy', *American Psychologist*, 41: 159-64.

Jones, E.E. and Pulos, S.M. (1993) 'Comparing the process in psychodynamic and cognitive-behavioral psychotherapies', *Journal of Consulting and Clinical Psychology*, 61 (2): 306-16.

Jones, E.E. and Zoppel, C.L. (1982) 'Impact of client and therapist gender on psychotherapy process and outcome', *Journal of Consulting and Clinical Psychology*, 50 (2): 259-72.

Jones, E.E., Wynne, M.F. and Watson, D.D. (1986) 'Client perception of treatment in crisis intervention and longer-term psychotherapies', *Psychotherapy*, 23: 120-32.

Keijsers, G., Hoogduin, C.A.L. and Schaap, C. (1990) 'Therapeutic relationship enhancement procedures and the social power model', in H.G. Zapotoczky and

T. Wenzel (eds), *The Scientific Dialogue: From Basic Research to Clinical Interventions*. Amsterdam: Swets & Zeitlinger, pp. 305-13.

Kivlighan, D.M. (1990) 'Relation between counselors' use of intentions and clients' perception of working alliance', *Journal of Counseling Psychology*, 37 (1): 27-32.

Kivlighan, D.M. and Schmitz, P.J. (1992) 'Counselor technical activity in cases with improving working alliances and continuing-poor working alliances', *Journal of Counseling Psychology*, 39 (1): 32-8.

Klee, M.R., Abeles, N. and Muller, R.T. (1990) 'Therapeutic alliance: early indicators, course and outcome', *Psychotherapy*, 27 (2): 166-74.

Klein, M.F., Mathieu-Coughlan, P. and Kiesler, D.J. (1986) 'The experiencing scale', in L.S. Greenberg and W. Pinsof (eds), *The Psychotherapeutic Process: A Research Handbook*. New York: Guilford Press, pp. 21-72.

Kokotovic, A.M. and Tracey, T.J. (1987) 'Premature termination at a university counseling center', *Journal of Counseling Psychology*, 34: 223-32.

Kokotovic, A.M. and Tracey, T.J. (1990) 'Working alliance in the early phase of counseling', *Journal of Counseling Psychology*, 37 (1): 16-21.

Kolden, G.G. (1991) 'The generic model of psychotherapy: an empirical investigation of patterns of process and outcome relationships', *Psychotherapy Research*, 1 (1): 62-73.

Kolden, G.G., Howard, K.I. and Maling, M.S. (1994) 'The counseling relationship and treatment process and outcome', *The Counseling Psychologist*, 22 (1): 82-9.

LaCrosse, M.B. (1977) 'Comparative perceptions of counselor behavior: a replication and extension', *Journal of Counseling Psychology*, 24 (6): 464-71.

Lambert, M.J. and Bergin, A.E. (1992) 'Achievements and limitations of psychotherapy research', in D.K. Freedheim (ed.), *History of Psychotherapy: A Century of Change*. Washington, DC: American Psychological Association, pp. 360-90.

Lambert, M.J. and Bergin, A.E. (1994) 'The effectiveness of psychotherapy', in A.E. Bergin and S.L. Garfield (eds), *Handbook of Psychotherapy and Behavior Change* (4th edn). New York: Wiley, pp. 143-89.

Lambert, M.J., DeJulio, S.S. and Stein, D.M. (1978) 'Therapist interpersonal skills: process, outcome, methodological considerations, and recommendations for future research', *Psychological Bulletin*, 85 (3): 467-89.

Langs, R. (1973) *The Technique of Psychoanalytic Psychotherapy*, vol. 1. New York: Jason Aronson.

Langs, R. (1976) *The Therapeutic Interaction*, vol. 2. New York: Jason Aronson.

Luborsky, L. (1976) 'Helping alliances in psychotherapy: the groundwork for a study of their relationship to its outcome', in J.L. Cleghorn (ed.), *Successful Psychotherapy*. New York: Bruner/Mazel, pp. 92-116.

Luborsky, L. (1984) *Principles of Psychoanalytic Psychotherapy: A Manual for Supportive-Expressive Treatment*. New York: Basic Books.

Luborsky, L. (1994) 'Therapeutic alliances as predictors of psychotherapy outcomes: factors explaining predictive success', in A.O. Horvath and L.S. Greenberg (eds), *The Working Alliance: Theory, Research and Practice*. New York: Wiley, pp. 38-50.

Luborsky, L. and Auerbach, A. (1985) 'The therapeutic relationship in psycho-dynamic psychotherapy: the research evidence and its meaning for practice', in R. Hales and A. Frances (eds), *Psychiatry Update Annual Review*. Washington, DC: American Psychiatric Association, vol. 4, pp. 550-61.

Luborsky, L., Crits-Christoph, P., Alexander, L., Margolis, M. and Cohen, M. (1983) 'Two helping alliance methods for predicting outcomes of psychotherapy: a counting signs vs. a global rating method', *Journal of Nervous and Mental Disease*, 171: 480-91.

Luborsky, L., McLellan, A.T., Woody, G.E., O'Brien, C.P. and Auerbach, A. (1985) 'Therapist success and its determinants', *Archives of General Psychiatry*, 42: 602-11.

Luborsky, L., Mintz, J., Auerbach, A., Crits-Christoph, P., Bachrach, H., Todd, T., Johnson, M., Cohen, M. and O'Brien, C.P. (1980) 'Predicting the outcomes of psychotherapy: findings of the Penn Psychotherapy Project', *Archives of General Psychiatry*, 37: 471-81.

Mallinckrodt, B. (1991) 'Clients' representations of childhood emotional bonds with parents, social support, and formation of the working alliance', *Journal of Counseling Psychology*, 38: 401-9.

Mallinckrodt, B. (1992) 'Childhood emotional bonds with parents, development of adult social competencies and availability of social support', *Journal of Counseling Psychology*, 39: 453-61.

Mallinckrodt, B. (1993) 'Session impact, working alliance and treatment outcome in brief counseling', *Journal of Counseling Psychology*, 40 (1): 25-32.

Mallinckrodt, B. and Nelson, M.L. (1991) 'Counselor training level and the formation of the psychotherapeutic working alliance', *Journal of Counseling Psychology*, 38 (2): 133-8.

Mann, J. (1973) *Time-Limited Psychotherapy*. Cambridge, MA: Harvard University Press.

Marmar, C.R. and Gaston, L. (1989) 'Manual for the California Psychotherapy Alliance Scales (CALPAS)'. Unpublished manuscript. San Francisco: University of California.

Marmar, C.R., Weiss, D.S. and Gaston, L. (1989a) 'Towards the validation of the California Therapeutic Alliance Rating System', *Psychological Assessment*, 1: 46-52.

Marmar, C.R., Gaston, L., Thompson, L.W. and Gallagher, D. (1989b) 'Alliance and outcome in late-life depression', *Journal of Nervous and Mental Disease*, 177: 464-72.

Marmar, C.R., Horowitz, M.J., Weiss, D.S. and Marziali, E. (1986) 'The development of the therapeutic alliance rating system', in L.S. Greenberg and W.M. Pinsof (eds), *The Psychotherapeutic Process: A Research Handbook*. New York: Guilford Press, pp. 367-90.

Martin, J., Martin, M., Meyer, M. and Slemon, A. (1986) 'Empirical investigations of the cognitive mediational paradigm for research on counseling', *Journal of Counseling Psychology*, 33 (2): 115-23.

Marziali, E. (1984a) 'Prediction of outcome of brief psychotherapy from therapist interpretive interventions', *Archives of General Psychiatry*, 41: 301-5.

Marziali, E. (1984b) 'Three viewpoints on the therapeutic alliance: similarities, differences and associations with psychotherapy outcome', *Journal of Nervous and Mental Disease*, 172 (7): 417–23.

Marziali, E., Marmar, C. and Krupnick, J. (1981) 'Therapeutic alliance scales: development and relationship to psychotherapy outcome', *American Journal of Psychiatry*, 138 (3): 361–4.

McCullough, J.P. (1984a) 'Single case investigative research and its relevance for the nonoperant clinician', *Psychotherapy*, 21: 382–8.

McCullough, J.P. (1984b) 'The need for new single-case design structure in applied cognitive psychology', *Psychotherapy*, 21: 389–400.

Meltzoff, J. and Kornreich, M. (1970) *Research in Psychotherapy*. New York: Atherton Press.

Miller, J.M., Courtois, C.A., Pelham, J.P., Riddle, P.E., Spiegel, S.B., Gelso, C.J. and Johnson, D.H. (1983) 'The process of time-limited therapy', in C. Gelso and D.H. Johnson (eds), *Explorations in Time-Limited Counseling and Psychotherapy*. New York: Teachers College Press, pp. 175–84.

Mintz, J., Auerbach, A.H., Luborsky, L. and Johnson, M. (1973) 'Patients', therapists' and observers' views of psychotherapy: a "Rashomon" experience or a reasonable consensus?' *British Journal of Medical Psychology*, 46: 83–9.

Mitchell, K.M., Bozarth, J.D. and Krauft, C.C. (1977) 'A reappraisal of the therapeutic effectiveness of accurate empathy, non-possessive warmth and genuineness', in A.S. Gurman and A.M. Razin (eds), *Effective Psychotherapy: A Handbook of Research*. New York: Pergamon Press, pp. 482–502.

Moras, K. and Strupp, H.H. (1982) 'Pretherapy interpersonal relations, patients' alliance, and outcome in brief therapy', *Archives of General Psychiatry*, 39: 405–9.

Morgan, R., Luborsky, L., Crits-Christoph, P., Curtis, H. and Solomon, J. (1982) 'Predicting the outcomes of psychotherapy by the Penn Helping Alliance Rating Method', *Archives of General Psychiatry*, 39: 397–402.

O'Connell, S. (1983) 'The placebo effect and psychotherapy', *Psychotherapy: Theory, Research and Practice*, 20 (3): 337–45.

O'Malley, S.S., Suh, C.S. and Strupp, H.H. (1983) 'The Vanderbilt Psychotherapy Process Scale: a report on the scale development and a process-outcome study', *Journal of Consulting and Clinical Psychology*, 51 (4): 581–6.

Orlinsky, D.E. (1994) 'Time frames and temporal sequences'. Paper presented at the Society for Psychotherapy Research Annual International Meeting, York.

Orlinsky, D.E. and Howard, K.I. (1975) *Varieties of Psychotherapeutic Experience*. New York: Teachers College Press.

Orlinsky, D.E. and Howard, K.I. (1986a) 'The psychological interior of psychotherapy: explorations with the therapy session reports', in L.S. Greenberg and W.M. Pinsof (eds), *The Psychotherapeutic Process: A Research Handbook*. New York: Guilford Press, pp. 477–501.

Orlinsky, D.E. and Howard, K.I. (1986b) 'The relation of process to outcome in psychotherapy', in S.L. Garfield and A.E. Bergin (eds), *Handbook of Psychotherapy and Behavior Change* (3rd edn). New York: Wiley, pp. 311–84.

Orlinsky, D.E. and Howard, K.I. (1987) 'A generic model of psychotherapy', *Journal of Integrative and Eclectic Psychotherapy*, 6: 6–27.

Orlinsky, D.E., Grawe, K. and Parks, B.K. (1994) 'Process and outcome in psychotherapy – noch einmal', in A.E. Bergin and S.L. Garfield (eds), *Handbook of Psychotherapy and Behavior Change* (4th edn). New York: Wiley, pp. 270–376.

Parloff, M.B. (1986) 'Placebo controls in psychotherapy research: a sine qua non or a placebo for research problems?' *Journal of Consulting and Clinical Psychology*, 54 (1): 79–87.

Parloff, M.B., Waskow, I.E. and Wolfe, B.E. (1978) 'Research on therapist variables in relation to process and outcome', in S.L. Garfield and A.E. Bergin (eds), *Handbook of Psychotherapy and Behavior Change* (2nd edn). New York: Wiley, pp. 233–83.

Patton, M.J. (1994) 'Components of the counseling relationship – an evolving model: comment on Gelso and Carter (1994)', *Journal of Counseling Psychology*, 41 (3): 310–12.

Persons, J.B. (1991) 'Psychotherapy outcome studies do not accurately represent current models of psychotherapy: a proposed remedy', *American Psychologist*, 46: 99–106.

Piper, W.E., Azim, H.F.A., Joyce, A.S., McCallum, M., Nixon, G.W.H. and Segal, P.S. (1991) 'Quality of object relations vs. interpersonal functioning as predictor of therapeutic alliance and psychotherapy outcome', *Journal of Nervous and Mental Disease*, 179: 432–8.

Raue, P.J. and Goldfried, M.R. (1994) 'The therapeutic alliance in cognitive-behavior therapy', in A.O. Horvath and L.S. Greenberg (eds), *The Working Alliance: Theory, Research and Practice*. New York: Wiley, pp. 131–52.

Raue, P.J., Castonguay, L.G. and Goldfried, M.R. (1993) 'The working alliance: a comparison of two therapies', *Psychotherapy Research*, 3: 197–207.

Rice, L.N. and Greenberg, L.S. (1984) *Patterns of Change: Intensive Analysis of Psychotherapy Process*. New York: Guilford Press.

Rogers, C.R. (1957) 'The necessary and sufficient conditions of therapeutic personality change', *Journal of Consulting and Clinical Psychology*, 21: 95–103.

Rogers, C.R., Gendlin, E.T., Kiesler, D.J. and Truax, C.B. (1967) *The Therapeutic Relationship and its Impact: A Study of Psychotherapy with Schizophrenics*. Madison: University of Wisconsin Press.

Rounsaville, B.J., Chevron, E.S., Prusoff, B.A., Elkin, I., Imber, S., Sotsky, S. and Watkins, J. (1987) 'The relation between specific and general dimensions of the psychotherapy process in interpersonal psychotherapy of depression', *Journal of Consulting and Clinical Psychology*, 55: 379–84.

Ryan, E.R. and Cicchetti, D.V. (1985) 'Predicting quality of alliance in the initial psychotherapy interview', *Journal of Nervous and Mental Disease*, 173: 717–25.

Sabourin, S., Gaston, L., Caollier, J.C. and Drouin, M.S. (1990) 'Therapeutic alliance and perceptions of social influence in counselling: independent concepts or syncretic realities?' Paper presented at the Society for Psychotherapy Research Annual Meeting, Wintergreen, Virginia.

Safran, J.D. and Segal, Z.V. (1990) *Interpersonal Process in Cognitive Therapy*. New York: Basic Books.

Safran, J.D. and Wallner, L.K. (1991) 'The relative predictive validity of two therapeutic alliance measures in cognitive therapy', *Psychological Assessment: A Journal of Consulting and Clinical Psychology*, 3 (2): 188-95.

Safran, J.D., Greenberg, L.S. and Rice, L.N. (1988) 'Integrating psychotherapy research and practice: modeling the change process', *Psychotherapy*, 25 (1): 1-17.

Safran, J.D., Muran, J.C. and Wallner Samstag, L. (1994) 'Resolving therapeutic alliance ruptures: a task analytic investigation', in A.O. Horvath and L.S. Greenberg (eds), *The Working Alliance: Theory, Research and Practice*. New York: Wiley, pp. 225-55.

Safran, J.D., Crocker, P., McMain, S. and Murray, P. (1990) 'The therapeutic alliance rupture as a therapy event for empirical investigation', *Psychotherapy*, 27 (2): 154-65.

Saltzman, C., Leutgert, M.J., Roth, C.H., Creaser, J. and Howard, L. (1976) 'Formation of a therapeutic relationship: experiences during the initial phase of psychotherapy as predictors of treatment duration and outcome', *Journal of Consulting and Clinical Psychology*, 44 (4): 546-55.

Salvio, M.A., Beutler, L.E., Wood, J.M. and Engle, D. (1992) 'The strength of the therapeutic alliance in three treatments for depression', *Psychotherapy Research*, 2: 31-6.

Saunders, S.M., Howard, K.I. and Orlinsky, D.E. (1989) 'The therapeutic bond scales: psychometric characteristics and relationship to treatment effectiveness', *Psychological Assessment: A Journal of Consulting and Clinical Psychology*, 1 (4): 323-30.

Sexton, H. (1993) 'Exploring a psychotherapeutic change sequence: relating process to intersessional and posttreatment outcome', *Journal of Consulting and Clinical Psychology*, 61 (1): 128-36.

Sexton, T.L. and Whiston, S.C. (1994) 'The status of the counseling relationship: an empirical review, theoretical implications, and research directions', *The Counseling Psychologist*, 22 (1): 6-78.

Silberschatz, G., Fretter, P.B. and Curtis, J.T. (1986) 'How do interpretations influence the process of psychotherapy?' *Journal of Consulting and Clinical Psychology*, 54: 646-52.

Smith, M.L., Glass, G.V. and Miller, T.I. (1980) *The Benefits of Psychotherapy*. Baltimore, MD: Johns Hopkins University Press.

Stiles, W.B., Shapiro, D.A. and Elliott, R.K. (1986) 'Are all psychotherapies equivalent?' *American Psychologist*, 41 (2): 165-80.

Strong, S.R. (1968) 'Counseling: an interpersonal influence process', *Journal of Counseling Psychology*, 15: 215-24.

Strupp, H.H. (1980a) 'Success and failure in time-limited psychotherapy: a systematic comparison of two cases: Comparison 1', *Archives of General Psychiatry*, 37: 595-603.

Strupp, H.H. (1980b) 'Success and failure in time-limited psychotherapy: a systematic comparison of two cases: Comparison 2', *Archives of General Psychiatry*, 37: 708-16.

Strupp, H.H. (1980c) 'Success and failure in time-limited psychotherapy: a systematic comparison of two cases: with special reference to the performance of a lay counselor', *Archives of General Psychiatry*, 37: 831–41.

Strupp, H.H. (1980d) 'Success and failure in time-limited psychotherapy: a systematic comparison of two cases: further evidence (Comparison 4)', *Archives of General Psychiatry*, 37: 947–54.

Strupp, H.H. and Binder, J.L. (1984) *Psychotherapy in a New Key: A Guide to Time-Limited Dynamic Psychotherapy*. New York: Basic Books.

Suh, C.S., Strupp, H.H. and O'Malley, S.S. (1986) 'The Vanderbilt Process Measures: the Psychotherapy Process Scale (VPPS) and the Negative Indicators Scale (VNIS)', in L.S. Greenberg and W.M. Pinsof (eds), *The Psychotherapeutic Process: A Research Handbook*. New York: Guilford Press, pp. 285–323.

Tichenor, V. and Hill, C.E. (1989) 'A comparison of six measures of working alliance', *Psychotherapy*, 26 (2): 195–9.

Tracey, T.J. (1989) 'Client and therapist satisfaction over the course of psychotherapy', *Psychotherapy*, 26: 177–82.

Tracey, T.J. and Dundon, M. (1988) 'Role anticipations and preferences over the course of counseling', *Journal of Counseling Psychology*, 35: 3–14.

Tracey, T.J. and Kokotovic, A.M. (1989) 'Factor structure of the Working Alliance Inventory', *Psychological Assessment: A Journal of Consulting and Clinical Psychology*, 1 (3): 207–10.

Tracey, T.J. and Ray, P.B. (1984) 'Stages of successful time-limited counseling: an interactional examination', *Journal of Counseling Psychology*, 31: 13–27.

Truax, C.B. and Mitchell, K.M. (1971) 'Research on certain therapist interpersonal skills in relation to process and outcome', in A.E. Bergin and S.L. Garfield (eds), *Handbook of Psychotherapy and Behavior Change*. New York: Wiley, pp. 299–344.

Tryon, G.S. and Kane, A.S. (1990) 'The helping alliance and premature termination', *Counseling Psychology Quarterly*, 3: 233–8.

Tryon, G.S. and Kane, A.S. (1993) 'Relationship of working alliance to mutual and unilateral termination', *Journal of Counseling Psychology*, 40 (1): 33–6.

Watson, J.C. and Greenberg, L.S. (1994) 'The alliance in experiential therapy: enacting the relationship conditions', in A.O. Horvath and L.S. Greenberg (eds), *The Working Alliance: Theory, Research and Practice*. New York: Wiley, pp. 153–72.

Windholz, M.J. and Silberschatz, G. (1988) 'Vanderbilt Psychotherapy Process Scale: a replication with adult outpatients', *Journal of Consulting and Clinical Psychology*, 56 (1): 56–60.

Xenakis, S.N., Hoyt, M.F., Marmar, C.R. and Horowitz, M.J. (1983) 'Reliability of self-reports by therapists using the therapist action scale', *Psychotherapy: Theory, Research and Practice*, 20 (3): 314–20.

Zetzel, E.R. (1956) 'Current concepts of transference', *International Journal of Psycho-Analysis*, 37: 369–76.